☆

PROFITS
and
PRINCIPLES

Profits and Principles

GLOBAL CAPITALISM AND HUMAN RIGHTS IN CHINA

Michael A. Santoro

CORNELL UNIVERSITY PRESS

ITHACA AND LONDON

Copyright © 2000 by Cornell University

All rights reserved. Except for brief quotations in a review, this book, or parts thereof, must not be reproduced in any form without permission in writing from the publisher. For information, address Cornell University Press, Sage House, 512 East State Street, Ithaca, New York 14850.

First published 2000 by Cornell University Press

Printed in the United States of America

Library of Congress Cataloging-in-Publication Data

Librarians: A CIP catalog record for this book is available from the Library of Congress.

Cornell University Press strives to use environmentally responsible suppliers and materials to the fullest extent possible in the publishing of its books. Such materials include vegetable-based, low-VOC inks and acid-free papers that are recycled, totally chlorine-free, or partly composed of nonwood fibers.Books that bear the logo of the FSC (Forest Stewardship Council) use paper taken from forests that have been inspected and certified as meeting the highest standards for environmental and social responsibility. For further information, visit our website at www.cornellpress.cornell.edu.

Cloth printing   10   9   8   7   6   5   4   3   2   1

★

For Patty

CONTENTS

PREFACE

This book is about the human rights responsibilities of multinational corporations operating in China. It also describes how multinational corporations are making a positive contribution to democratization and human rights in China. Because trade and foreign investment play a central role in foreign policy toward China, the findings and conclusions expressed in this book also have significant implications for U.S.-Sino relations in general, as well as for specific issues such as the debate over China's entry into the World Trade Organization.

This is principally a theoretical book concerned with fundamental moral questions arising when businesses operate in countries where human rights violations are serious and pervasive. However, it is also factual, drawing on published sources and personal interviews conducted during several research trips to China.

The methodology of the book is interdisciplinary and highly practical. It, therefore, risks offending purists in a variety of fields, including moral philosophers, economists, Sinologists, political scientists, sociologists, business journalists, and human rights lawyers, to name the first that come to mind. Others who might regard this work as an intellectual impertinence include foreign affairs specialists, management scholars, and experts on cross-cultural interactions. The offense is not intentional. The subject is very complex, and, therefore, I was required to draw from a wide array of intellectual fields. I am in some measure beholden to all of these disciplines. It is impossible to do good interdisciplinary work unless one can rely on good disciplinary work.

This book is intended for several nonacademic audiences. First and foremost, it is meant to serve as a moral compass for business executives of multinational firms with operations in developing nations. Although the book draws primarily on the Chinese context, much of what it has to say is of use to executives throughout Southeast Asia and other developing regions. The aim is to equip such managers to make the difficult decisions they inevitably encounter about matters involving human rights. The book offers a framework for managers to understand the extent and limits of corporate moral responsibility for human rights. This framework enables managers to distinguish those situations requiring the sacrifice of profit on account of principle from those in which they can pursue profits without worrying that they are sacrificing principles.

Because of my background and network of contacts, this book primarily, but by no means exclusively, discusses U.S. foreign policy, U.S. firms, U.S. managers, and U.S. consumers. With apologies to Mexicans, Canadians, and South Americans, I sometimes use *America* and *American* when I am referring to the United States. Moreover, I am cognizant that there are many differences in moral outlooks and business practices in America and Europe and many differences *within* these areas as well. Although the scope of this book does not allow for these differences to be described in detail, I hope that the empirical observations and moral analysis will also resonate with Europeans and others. The text often refers to "Western" business practices, by which I mean to suggest that I am describing phenomena that apply with roughly equal validity to the United States and Europe. I do so despite the fact that some readers will very likely (with some justification) regard many of the premises and goals of the book as peculiarly American in character.

This book offers practical advice about how to honor human rights responsibilities and run a successful business at the same time. Indeed, two of the primary assumptions are that good ethics have a very strong (although not perfect) overlap with business success and that the better managers are at understanding and deciding ethical questions, the more successful they will be in achieving their financial goals. In this respect, a sound grasp of ethics is an essential management skill. My expectation is that businesspeople who pick up this book might do so out of some sense of moral duty. As they read it, I hope they see that it can also help them to run a successful business in China.

This book also is intended for policymakers who want to understand the various ways that multinational corporations can influence human rights and how this power might most effectively be harnessed to promote human rights. There is no shortage of opinions about the proper human rights role of the multinational corporation. However, most of these opinions are based on hardened rhetorical positions, cynicism, or just plain ignorance about either the realities of business or the dictates of morality. This book sets forth a well-defined and limited human rights role for the multinational corporation. It does so based on a sustained analysis of the purposes and powers of the multinational corporation, and of the various sorts of moral duties human rights create for a diversity of actors in the international system—including international institutions, national governments, nongovernmental organizations, the press, and individuals. The analysis draws some sharp lines between what it is and is not reasonable to expect corporations to do about human rights. These distinctions are meant to inform those policymakers and nongovernmental organizations who are advocating that multinational corporations adopt various human rights policies and codes of conduct.

The book is also intended to inform the debate over China's accession into the World Trade Organization. Trade and investment offer the West a tremendous opportunity to influence the development of human rights conditions in China. Much of this influence is extremely positive, but some can be quite negative. Understanding both the positive and negative power of trade is essential for an informed decision about whether and under what terms the West should trade with China. This understanding is also essential to determining whether it is appropriate for the World Trade Organization to serve as a mechanism for enforcing workers' rights, an issue that caused considerable controversy and upheaval at the World Trade Organization meeting in Seattle in November 1999.

Human rights advocates are yet another audience for this book. Because of their single-minded focus and idealistic temperament, human rights advocates are sometimes professionally disinclined to listen sincerely to the concerns and perspectives of businesspeople. As a result, human rights advocates often have been unable to forge useful links with the business community. By offering a broad perspective on moral responsibility for human rights and by offering insight into how corporate executives view the human rights demands made of them, this book can aid these advocates to devise successful strategies for engaging the business community and thereby be more effective in harnessing the power of multinational corporations to promote human rights.

This book has been written with an appreciation for the social contribution made by those who run a profitable business lawfully and with integrity, and for the practical limitations faced by multinational corporations in China and other developing markets. Therefore, it will disappoint those who regard the multinational corporation as an all-powerful and unavoidably evil institution that brings only harm to developing nations. Also disappointed, however, will be those who think that the sole responsibility of a corporate executive is to make profits for the shareholders of the corporation. Often, the moral duties created by human rights complements the goal of profit maximization, but sometimes they conflict quite dramatically. This book sometimes challenges corporate executives to uphold human rights principles even at the risk of losing profits.

Because of its conspicuous power and wealth, many social activists look to the multinational corporation to solve a myriad of social problems. Among other things, multinational firms are being asked to assume a broad and extensive role in promoting and protecting human rights. For multinational executives, the suggestion that they should assume responsibility for one of the world's most controversial and complex social issues is a source of deep consternation. After all, business executives are trained to think about marketing, capital finance, accounting, market share, profits, and return on capital. They have little expertise in or understanding about human rights. It thus should come as no surprise that the most common reaction of businesspeople to the idea that they need to think about human rights in China is complete denial. The comments one is most likely to hear in response to such a suggestion resemble the following: "Why do I have to think about these things? This isn't my job. It's the government's job to do something about these issues. My job is just to focus on making profits for my shareholders." In China, particularly, this understandable tendency to avoid a confusing and unfamiliar subject is exacerbated by a sobering thought: confronting the government by taking a strong stand on human rights might very well mean the loss of significant commercial prospects because the government invariably holds the key to permits, contracts, and the like. Indeed, in their zeal to avoid taking a commercially risky stand on human rights, some multinational executives go too far and wind up becoming unwitting cheerleaders for government repression.

At the same time that multinational corporations attempt to sidestep the subject of human rights, they are being pressured to do more about them. Government officials and nongovernmental organizations increasingly are demanding that they tackle an issue that for decades has defied resolution in the international community. Indeed, human rights advocates have shifted the spotlight to private corporations at least in part because they have been unable to forge a consensus at an intergovernmental level.

Since the adoption of the Universal Declaration of Human Rights on December 10, 1948, human rights advocates have struggled to transform its powerful vision into reality. These hopes increasingly have focused on multinational corporations. Instead of cooperation, however, tension is growing between corporations and human rights advocates. This tension is part of a broader trend described in a Notre Dame–Price Waterhouse study, which found that 41% of nongovernmental organizations concerned with international social issues regarded their relationship with multinational firms as "antagonistic," and another 47% said it was "ambivalent."* One also senses from conversations with corporate executives that, as far as multinational corporations are concerned, those feelings are mutual.

How do we bridge this gap between what is being demanded of the multinational corporation and what is possible? What should the world reasonably expect multinational firms to do about human rights? How can the West trade with China without sacrificing principles? These are the central practical and moral questions addressed in this book. A guiding tenet in the analysis that follows is that both extremes are wrong when answering these questions. Clearly, it cannot be the case that corporations have no responsibility for human rights. After all, corporations reap great rewards from the flow of trade and capital across national borders. With these rewards comes the moral responsibility to act in a manner benefiting the societies that enable them to accumulate such wealth. Moreover, multinational corporations have the potential to serve as powerful agents of progress in democracy and human rights. They possess great resources, and they have the capacity in China and

*Georges Enderle and Glen Peters, *A Strange Affair? The Emerging Relationship between NGOs and Transnational Companies* (1998), available at http://www.pw.com/uk/ngoreview.htm.

elsewhere to effect social change through their employees, their customers, and others with whom they come into contact.

Although multinational firms have an important role to play in human rights, it is unrealistic to think that corporations can do the work of all of the other actors in the international community. The multinational corporation is but one actor among many in the international system who have human rights responsibilities. What we can reasonably expect of the multinational corporation in China and elsewhere is that it do its "fair share." This book charts a human rights role for the multinational corporation that is both morally responsible and practically attainable. The ultimate aim is to help the world inch closer to achieving the noble vision of humanity expressed in the 1948 Universal Declaration of Human Rights.

As should be apparent already, another central premise of this book is that the idea of human rights, despite its intellectual origins in Western culture, has moral power even in the context of Chinese culture and society. I am not, in other words, a moral relativist when it comes to human rights. Neither, however, do I wish to be a cultural imperialist. At various points this moral premise is explicated and defended, but the book does not begin with this defense. It launches full sail for the goal of understanding the moral duties created for multinational corporations by human rights. Too many discussions about human rights remain essentially at port while long and terribly interesting discussions take place about whether it is worth taking the journey and what the destination should be. I respectfully ask all readers to begin the journey with me. Along the way, the validity of this objective will be justified. For some, this justification is unnecessary. For others, it will never be adequate. It is my hope that all will find the journey itself interesting.

This book should also be of interest to those who are concerned about the meaning and social consequences of globalization. Although globalization encompasses a much broader array of topics than is addressed here, the human rights impact of multinational corporations in China offers an illuminating perspective on the positive and negative forces unleashed by the free flow of capital and goods across borders that characterizes the present-day global economy. The multinational corporation is in many respects the most important conduit of globalization. My hope is that understanding the effects of multinational corporations on human rights can help us to understand the broader social effects of globalization and the moral responsibilities of the multinational corporation to channel these effects in a way that enhances global welfare.

As part of my research, I have spoken with hundreds of multinational business executives, diplomats, government officials, and Chinese workers. For the most part, these conversations have been off the record and informal. They nonetheless constitute an important "deep background" source for the development of the ideas presented here. As the concept of human rights "spin-off" became clear in my own mind, however, I began to realize that it would be useful to conduct additional interviews of a more formal nature; thus, I conducted several dozen formal interviews, which principally form the basis for Chapter 4. In all cases involving Chinese citizens, I have avoided using real names. These interviews were conducted on the premise of anonymity, and in any event, I would not wish to expose them to potential retaliation from their government. Many businesspersons, diplomats, and others also have requested anonymity, and I have honored those requests.

When I first began to investigate the idea of human rights spin-off, I was quite skeptical. I was surprised when, in my interviews, I began to see that it was a very real phenomenon. I would have liked to interview additional Chinese workers in a more systematic way and thereby have produced more "data." However, a number of factors constrained my ability to do so, not the least of which was the fact that I felt it necessary to keep a relatively low profile in asking pointed questions about human rights conditions in China.

The argument in this book is meant to be considered as a whole. Therefore, it is worth setting out the plan of the book at the outset and describing how each chapter relates to the book as a whole. Chapter 1 describes an American company, an American manager, and several Chinese workers in foreign-owned enterprises. These portraits are very different from the typical images one encounters in the West and are meant to serve as a visceral introduction to some of the themes of the book.

Chapter 2 introduces the two main themes of the book—how multinational corporations sometimes can create positive "human rights spin-off" simply by following their self-interest, and how self-interest sometimes can lead multinational corporations to abuse human rights. The rest of the book is organized roughly around these two opposing forces of globalization, seeking in essence to figure out how to unleash the positive human rights forces set in motion by globalization and how also to control the negative forces. In nearly every chapter and in every broad theme addressed, moral reasoning and empirical observation are mixed with public policy analysis and management issues.

Chapters 3 and 4 are devoted, respectively, to theoretical and empirical analyses of human rights spin-off. Chapter 5 assesses the implications of human rights spin-off for foreign policy toward China.

Chapter 6 turns back to the negative forces of globalization and sets forth the ways that profit-making activities conflict with human rights in the Chinese context. As a prelude to understanding the moral duties of multinational corporations when profits conflict with principles, Chapter 7 provides some historical perspective on human rights. In particular, it assesses the extent to which the world has achieved a consensus about the meaning and universality of human rights.

Chapter 8 sets forth a broad "fair share" theory of human rights that attempts to provide a basis for understanding of when multinational corporations have a moral obligation to sacrifice profits for human rights principles. Chapter 9 applies the fair share theory to the issue of labor rights and explicates the responsibilities of multinational corporations for conditions in factories operated by their subcontractors and other business partners. Chapter 10 applies the fair share theory to the issue of corporate responsibility for the Chinese government's repression of political and religious dissidents.

ACKNOWLEDGMENTS

I am grateful to my colleagues in the Department of International Business and Business Environment at Rutgers Business School for providing a congenial atmosphere and encouraging my work on this book. Edwin M. Hartman read and wrote detailed and insightful comments on the entire manuscript. His wise counsel, generosity of time, and friendship have been invaluable to my development as a scholar. My debt to him is of the magnitude and sort that can only be repaid as part of an unbroken chain to scholars who follow me at the beginning of their own careers. Wayne Eastman also read and commented on the entire manuscript. James T. Gathii read a number of chapters as well and generously shared with me his knowledge of human rights law. I have profited greatly from many conversations with Wayne and James on several subjects discussed in this book.

Other colleagues at Rutgers also have contributed to this book. In particular, Chao C. Chen helped me to appreciate some of the subtleties of the academic research on cross-cultural studies. Marybeth Schmutz shared her considerable knowledge of the human rights issues involved in collegiate apparel licensing. Jerry Rosenberg, Rosa Oppenheim, Farok Contractor, Don McCabe, Richard Romano, Robert Werner, dt ogilvie, Barbara Stern, Yangru Wu, Helen Paxton, Judith Mayo, Dave Muha, and Jacintha Geborde, among others, provided encouragement and support.

I am very grateful for the careful reading and very useful comments of two anonymous reviewers. They made many penetrating criticisms that convinced me to fortify and rewrite several areas of the manuscript, although perhaps not as much as they would have liked.

I owe a continuing debt to my dissertation advisors at Harvard—Lisa L. Martin, Lynn Sharp Paine, and Frederick Schauer—who by their example taught me many unwritten lessons about scholarship, including intellectual honesty, dedication, and commitment to excellence. I must add a special note of thanks to Lynn, a woman of awe-inspiring intellect and integrity, whom I am blessed to have as a mentor and a friend.

I am fortunate to have as a good friend Kermit Hummel, a publisher to the bone. Kermit read numerous early drafts, engaged the project on an intellectual level, and assured me quite usefully at various moments of self-doubt that, in his professional opinion, what I was writing would eventually become a book.

John Kamm, Brewer Stone, Pamela Yatzko, and David Youtz read and commented on some or all of the manuscript. I am very grateful to them for patiently sharing their deep understanding and appreciation of China. Sylvia Sansoni, Laurel Baig, Carter Daniel, and Prakash Sethi also read parts of the manuscript and contributed helpful comments.

An earlier version of the fair share theory was presented at a meeting of the Society for Business Ethics, and a number of colleagues there made useful suggestions.

The French politician and diplomat Georges Clemenceau famously said that war was too important to be left solely to the generals. The same can be said, with all due respect, of China and the Sinologists. There are in the West very few true China "experts." Yet there is so much about China that we need to understand. If, therefore, we are ever to learn how best to interact with its people, more non-Sinologists must venture bravely and write about this daunting subject. For my own intrepid foray, I must thank Lynn White of Princeton University. I hope Professor White does not regret his innocent encouragement to me that it was acceptable—indeed useful—for a non-Sinologist to write about China. I am also grateful to Mrs. Sally Stewart, then of the University of Hong Kong, who generously introduced me to Professor White and others at a critical stage in my research.

A Fulbright Fellowship enabled me to conduct research in Hong Kong and China during the 1993–1994 academic year. Patrick Corcoran of the United States Information Service offered gracious hospitality and invaluable introductions during my Fulbright year. The Institute for the Study of World Politics, the Harvard Graduate School of Arts and Sciences, and the John F. Kennedy School of Government provided financial support during my time as a graduate student. More recently, Rutgers Business School provided a summer travel grant that was critical to the completion of this manuscript.

I have been traveling to China every year for almost a decade. In that time, I have discussed the matters in this book with hundreds of Western and Chinese businesspeople, lawyers, diplomats, human rights advocates, workers, government officials, and others who gave generously of their time and insights. Although I cannot name all of them (nor, incidentally, would most of them wish to be named), I want to note my appreciation for the contributions they have made to this work.

I gratefully acknowledge the able research assistance of Changsu Kim. Also contributing to the book were Andrew Dubuque and one other person who wishes to remain anonymous because of the potential effect on future work in China.

Aimée Hamel patiently, professionally, and cheerfully typed and retyped the many versions of the manuscript. Over the years, she has become a partner in the work, offering many useful suggestions.

Many good friends provided all manner of support and encouragement throughout the writing of this book. Among them are Skip and Pam Cutrell, Andrea Silber and Phil Dickey, Howard and Jane Barnet, Mitchell Dolin, Joe Ruggiero, Tony James, Romana Vysatova, Eric Ingersoll, Marc and Manon Roudebush, Jagjit Dillon, Lisa Hull, Gretchen Worth, Mary Child, Desiree Green, Barbara Moses, Karen Li, and Camille LeBlanc. I am also indebted to my brother, Salvatore Santoro, and sister-in-law, Diane Santoro, and to her whole Iacobacci clan.

I express a special note of gratitude to Fran Benson of Cornell University Press. Fran's vision and her unwavering faith in a first-time author were a great and guiding light.

Toward the latter stages of writing this book I met and married my wife Patty Cateura Santoro. A gifted painter, Patty understands the importance of time and dedication to creative pursuits. She also understands the importance of inspiration. I am in this respect twice-blessed. I not only have a muse, I fell in love with and married her.

★

**PROFITS
and
PRINCIPLES**

CHAPTER ONE

★

From the Sweatshop to the Office Suite: Changing Perceptions of Western Business in China

There are things which ten hundred brushstrokes cannot depict but which can be captured by a few simple strokes if they are right.

The Mustard Seed Garden Manual of Chinese Painting (1679–1701)

The predominant image of the multinational corporation doing business in China is not an attractive one. Ask most people in the United States, or for that matter most members of the U.S. Congress, to describe a typical Western business in China, and the word "sweatshop" immediately comes to mind. The imagined setting may be Asian, but the atmosphere is a Dickensian cliché. They typically picture a dark, dirty, and overcrowded factory— perhaps with bars on the windows. It is a dangerous place in which a limb can easily be severed or a fire might break out and kill everyone inside. The work is numbingly boring and arduous. The hours are long and the pay barely enough to subsist. At night, the workers are herded off to crowded and unpleasant dormitories, fed a meager meal, and sent to bed exhausted.

The image of the typical American manager is also an ugly one. Who is this loathsome creature who has traveled to a distant land to take advantage of the unfortunate Chinese workers? He is a pure breed of the global capitalist pig. He is culturally insensitive—disdainful of and completely ignorant about the language, customs, and mores of his workers. He is domineering and happily takes advantage of his superior economic position. He enjoys being in a country where he can bark orders to docile workers. He doesn't care about his employees or their families. His principal management objective is to manufacture a cheap product for as little cost as possible, regardless of the negative impact on workers, the environment, or the broader Chinese society.

The image of the typical Chinese worker is similarly bleak. He has migrated from a rural province and has little education. He is illiterate and in poor health. He is desperate and willing to work for a couple of dollars a day. In the worst-case scenarios, he is perhaps a child, a twelve-year-old who has dropped out of school to work in a dangerous environment making toys for rich American children. Some Americans might even think that the typical Chinese worker is a prisoner of conscience forced to assemble cheap housewares in between beatings and indoctrination sessions. Each image of the working experience conjured is one of exploitation and abuse.

Images possess enormous power to shape public opinion and policy. Inaccurate images can lead to misinformed opinions and faulty policies. There can be no doubt that the unattractive images of the multinational corporation in China have a profound effect on American thinking. They color the moral judgments of press pundits, nongovernmental organizations, members of Congress, and the general public. Because of such images, some go so far as to say that it is immoral for multinational corporations to do business in China at all. At best, say critics, these corporations are helping to support a corrupt and repressive regime. At worst, they are participating in and profiting from repression. Others argue that the China operations of multinational corporations need to be legally controlled. As a result, Congress has considered various bills that attempt to mandate a minimum standard of behavior for American corporations operating in China.[1] Underlying all such moral judgments and policy proposals are the dreadful stereotypical images of American business in China.

These negative images also threaten to undermine America's foreign policy of "comprehensive engagement" with China. Combined with reports of the Chinese government's increased repression of dissidents, these images contribute to the perception that engagement sacrifices human rights principles at the altar of economic expediency. These negative images also fuel the opposition to China's entry into the World Trade Organization (WTO). Horrid images of sweatshop labor are sometimes invoked to discredit the very idea of free trade and a global economy. If free trade and foreign investment have such morally repugnant consequences for the human rights of workers, then perhaps we should rethink the expansion of economic openness and interdependence.

In short, significant foreign policy decisions depend in large measure on the images we hold about multinational corporations in China. For the *New York Times* columnist A. M. Rosenthal, no less than "our national soul" is at stake when we ponder our policy toward China. Rosenthal himself is quite self-assured about the disgraceful moral consequences of engagement with China. He writes:

> The sardonic promise . . . that this engagement would improve Chinese human rights . . . is a nasty joke by now to everybody but the U.S.-China business lobbies and their groupies in the U.S. Government and press.
>
> The engagers besmirch the American nation. By using their money and influence to strengthen Chinese Communist power, they brand the U.S. unfaithful to the freedoms that sustain America itself.
>
> Western money . . . helps the Politburo dispose of dissidents, condemn millions to forced labor and give Christians the choice between worshipping in Government-controlled churches and going to jail for praying underground.[2]

Many other intelligent, well-meaning people in the West who also are genuinely concerned about human rights conditions in China share Mr. Rosenthal's outraged assessment of the moral bankruptcy of economic engagement with China. However well-meaning those who share Mr. Rosenthal's view might be, however, such negative moral judgments are based on an unbalanced, indeed distorted, view of actual conditions in China. The challenge for these well-meaning people is, therefore, to readjust their moral judgments in light of the facts. It is difficult for someone who has come to adopt a definitive and serious moral position to revise that position, but a good way to begin that process is to probe the factual predicates of that moral position. What if the negative images are misleading? What if the actual activities of Western corporations in China are as not morally repugnant as some may imagine? What if Western businesses are making a positive contribution to Chinese society? What if they are part of the solution rather than part of the problem? What consequences should this have for our moral judgments and our policies?

For those inclined to believe the worst about the greed and venality of multinational corporations, many real examples of labor abuses can be found that correspond to the predominant negative images.[3] However, for anyone who actually has traveled to China, visited the operations of Western companies, and spoken with Western managers and Chinese workers, it is abundantly obvious that these images do not justly represent the complete story of Western business in China. In fact, one who visits China and takes the time to observe conditions there will come to realize that Western firms are dramatically improving the lives of a great many Chinese citizens. The changes are not, moreover, solely material. Western companies also are imparting radically new ideas and values to their workers that are helping to foster democracy and human rights in China. Before this complex phenomenon can be understood and appreciated, however, the distorted snapshots of Western business in China that dominate public perception must be replaced with images that conform more closely to reality. These more benign images confound simplistic thinking about the effects of multinational corporations on human rights and challenge us to form a more balanced moral view of economic engagement with China.

MOTOROLA: HIGH-TECH VALUES

Motorola's operations in China rest on the same two key beliefs that guide our operations worldwide—respect for the integrity of the individual and uncompromising integrity in everything we do. These beliefs help create an environment of empowerment for all in a culture of participation. . . . Motorola's commitment to teamwork and continuous learning is also key in developing the company's operations in China and its partnership with the Chinese people.

Motorola in China (company document, 1998)

Anyone who thinks that all Western corporations exploit and degrade the Chinese people should visit the Motorola complex in the northern industrial city of Tianjin. It is a new and gleaming world-class facility that would be considered state-of-the-art if it were located in Cambridge, Massachusetts, or Austin, Texas. The Tianjin facility employs about ten thousand workers. In one building, pagers and cellular phones are assembled. Another building contains one of the largest semiconductor factories in the world, producing 10 million high-quality integrated circuits each week.

Walking through the Tianjin facility, one cannot help but be impressed. It is spacious, clean, and well lit. The hallways are wide. Like most high-tech facilities concerned about competitive intelligence, there are very few windows, but the air conditioning and bright lighting make the atmosphere pleasant. Sophisticated machinery and computers abound and whir. Many areas utilize robotics. Indeed, the technology is so advanced that President Clinton, during his 1998 trip to China, was rumored to have cancelled a scheduled visit to the facility, for fear of highlighting the overwhelming display of valuable technology being transferred to China by American companies doing business there.

Although the physical layout of Tianjin is impressive, even more remarkable are the people working there and the ambience of the place. Walking around the facility for a few hours, one can view hundreds if not thousands of workers. None of them appear to be in the least bit haggard or oppressed. Nearly all are in their twenties or early thirties. They are casually but cleanly and often smartly dressed. Most are university graduates happy to have challenging engineering jobs. Others have had good secondary school educations and are working as technicians. Motorola is known among young workers as one of the best foreign employers, and its employees are among the best and the brightest technical graduates China has to offer. Many of them are being promoted rapidly through the managerial ranks.

The Tianjin facility is radically different from the sweatshop images that occupy public consciousness in the United States. It is also a far cry from what these young people would experience outside the plant. On my tour, I could not help thinking what a haven it was from some of the normal, not-so-pleasant aspects of everyday life in China. The morning I set out to visit Tianjin, I rose early in my modest hotel in a traditional Beijing *hutong*, or walled community. I passed the local public bathroom, noting its stench, passed the food stalls, already crowded, and fought my way into a crowded bus, which then honked its way through the chaotic and pollution-infested streets of Beijing. It was a scene that could be replayed in any other Chinese city, from Shanghai and Guangzhou to Chengdu and Wuhan. Within the walls of the Motorola factory, however, was another world—a clean and orderly world. In the 1950s, Chairman Mao's ill-fated Great Leap Forward promised the Chinese people that by sheer dint of will China could be transformed from a feudal rural economy to an industrial nation. The result was disastrous; an estimated 30 million people died of famine when agricultural production fell short of politically correct forecasts. Here in Tianjin, however, thanks to Motorola, a few thousand Chinese workers were truly experiencing a Great Leap Forward into a postindustrial age that would have been unimaginable in China even as late as the 1980s.

In the company cafeteria, workers queue up politely for a variety of free and nutritious meals. One area is set aside for a pregnancy well-care program. A booth is open at which appointments can be made with the company medical staff. There is a bank branch dedicated to employee needs. It is a scene that one might expect in a Fortune 500 corporate campus in the United States. The overwhelming sense is of a pleasant, orderly place in which people are fulfilled in their work. It is a place that a young graduate of Purdue, North Carolina State, or Cal Tech would find congenial.

There is, however, more of interest to the Motorola plant than its pleasantness and cleanliness. These workers are learning many ideas and values on the job. Each year, Motorola provides its employees in China with an average of seventy hours of training. Even more impressive is the informal learning that takes place. In the hallways are posters in Chinese script encouraging workers to speak out if there is a dangerous condition or some process at the plant that can be improved. Other posters announce an award for interfunctional team projects that improve productivity. Workers at the plant are presented with a booklet describing the company's "I Recommend" program. The booklet, which is translated into Chinese, describes the purpose of the program as follows:

> The employees often find that something can be improved in the daily work, some of them affect our work, and some bring us inconvenience, so they think and get the solutions via the [I recommend] channel. The management can get the good suggestions and ideas; the employees have the chance to take part in the management, help the manager to improve the factory system, and improve the business performance.[4]

Motorola is investing a lot of money and time in developing its corporate culture in China and elsewhere in the world. As Glenn Gienko, Motorola's executive vice-president and director of human resources, trumpets, "Motorola's facilities in China are world-class in all aspects and demonstrate what is possible when you apply Motorola's global values of 'Constant Respect for People and Uncompromising Integrity' with the talents of our Chinese associates."[5] The human resources objectives and corporate values that underpin this corporate culture are as state-of-the-art as the high-tech machinery in Tianjin. The company is trying to create a first-class corporate workforce of Chinese workers. It wants its line personnel and managers to take initiative, exert leadership, assume responsibility, manage rapid change, and work in teams. These kinds of behaviors (and the values that underpin them) are typical of successful organizations in the United States and Europe. In many respects, however, they are antithetical to the values and behaviors a Chinese worker would typically learn by working in a state-owned enterprise and living in Chinese society. The motivations of Motorola and other Western companies that train their technical and white-collar Chinese employees in such state-of-the-art management skills are far from political. Mostly, these companies are interested in building market share, profitability, and sustainable businesses. They know that to do so they must nurture local managerial talent. Nonetheless, one cannot help but think that profound long-term social and political change will ensue from this learning. At the very least, it is clear that the simplistic image of the inhumane sweatshop does not tell the whole story about the multinational corporation in China.

THE BEST AND THE BRIGHTEST WESTERN MANAGERS

It's important for people to understand that China is a work in progress. There is a saying here among foreign workers, TIC—This Is China, referring to the fact that so many things are different here. Well, I like to say AIP, Anything Is Possible.

—Diane Long, U.S. business executive

Diane Long is the general manager of the Shanghai office of an American branded apparel company.[6] A California native and Stanford University graduate, Diane has a low-key, easygoing manner. Growing up in a working-class family in a small, provincial Northern California town, Diane recalls that her favorite subject was geography. From a young age, she was "very aware of the fact that I was Swedish and from a different place."

After graduating from Stanford, Diane worked for five years at an international trading company in San Francisco. Shrewdly recognizing the growing commercial importance of China, she set about learning Mandarin. One of her first important lessons in understanding China came from her language course. "*Ni chi le ma*—have you eaten yet?—is a common Chinese greeting," says Diane. "I'm a product of the 1960s America, where life is prosperous, and at first I couldn't understand what this emphasis on eating was about. In fact, the greeting typified a preoccupation with the many famines that had ravaged China. After studying the language, I began to intuit many things like this."

Deciding that she wanted to travel to China, Diane applied for and was accepted to Stanford's "Volunteers in Asia" program. The Stanford program has counterparts at other schools, such as Oberlin's Shansi Program, the Yale-China Association, and Princeton-in-Asia. Michigan, Johns Hopkins, and Harvard, among others, have similar educational exchange programs, in which a significant number of the American managers in China have learned the Chinese language and developed an appreciation for the distinctive history and culture of China. As does the Stanford program, the Oberlin and Yale programs require a two-year commitment to live and teach in smaller Chinese cities. David Youtz, former Hong Kong director of the Yale-China Association, explained that this requirement is intended to help participants to "unlearn" many American preconceptions about China:

> By the end of two years you have learned enough language and experienced enough of China to be humbled by the concepts of "understanding" and "changing" this society. Without question, however, you have also made profound impressions in these two years on hundreds of Chinese students, friends, and colleagues and inadvertently opened a window onto Americans and the outside world, which I have to think is positive and subversive.[7]

As part of the Stanford program, Diane lived in a remote village in Anhui Province. Explaining her decision to teach English in the countryside rather than a big city like Beijing, Diane comments, "I didn't just want to be with a foreign clique. I really wanted an opportunity to be responsible in the system that I was participating in." Years later, Diane's sense of social responsibility in China is evident as she reflects on her current job as a Western manager: "Business is not a charity, but we don't have to mistreat anyone to be successful. We take our community responsibility quite seriously."

Diane admits that her initial efforts at getting on in China weren't all that successful. "At first I was like a bull in a China shop. (No pun intended.) I was completely *gung ho* on America. I look back on it, not with embarrassment mind you, but just laughing uproariously at myself." One lesson Diane learned early was the seemingly ineluctable penchant of foreigners to criticize Chinese practices. Sitting in her sleek, modern office in Shanghai, surrounded by her Chinese coworkers, Diane is careful to distance herself from such attitudes. Diane recounts that even when "Chinese people say 'please tell us how to improve,' they don't really mean 'criticize me.' They really mean 'Will you please tell us how wonderful we are?' When I first visited China I didn't understand that comment. I'm sure I caused all kinds of consternation. Of course, from an American point of view, we are not just criticizing for the sake of criticizing but with the hopes of improving. That missionary zeal is so inbred in us."

Diane is married to a Chinese man, and they have a son. She obviously relishes her life in Shanghai. "As mundane as it sounds, I'm just living a life. We have a home, a life, and friends. On a personal level, however, it's very, very exciting. I feel I'm developing levels of sensitivity, maturity, and awareness of the universality of people on a greater level by living here than staying in the United States."

On a professional level, Diane believes she is contributing to the development of her employees: "I'm trying to open the doors to a wider experience for them. They are very smart, naturally gifted, hard-working people. But they lack exposure and experience. Their expectations in life are much faster, much higher than their experience. They don't even know what they don't know. Part of it is being young," she says laughing, "we all were the same."

Despite her aversion to cultural imperialism, Diane freely admits that part of her job as a manager is to overcome some deep-rooted cultural patterns of behavior among her Chinese staff. She explains:

I think we challenge people here. We challenge them to question their beliefs—their ways of doing things. We expect accountability. The goal of our training is self-sufficiency. Taking responsibility. Taking the initiative. We want them to think "I want to take the initiative and I will take responsibility if I fail or am successful." The education system and the culture don't teach this. You can't expect 21-year-olds who have had a lifetime of education where they have been told "don't put your head above the crowd or it gets shot off," to suddenly accept this. We are asking them to do that. That's one hundred percent different than what they are taught. Another change is that we are giving them the right to express opinions. It takes a long, long time before they build that trust and speak out. . . . In the long run, you have to ask if it is a good thing to teach people to speak out. I think it's a good thing.

Diane does not think that Western corporations should attempt to apply pressure on the Chinese government to directly influence social and political conditions. Nonetheless, she sees business as playing a subtle, indirect role in transforming Chinese social and political culture: "I believe that in our everyday actions we will teach more about what democracy means than if we stand on a soapbox. If I have a meeting with ten people and I ask 'What is your opinion about this?', or if I put out an idea to vote, I will be making a point. It works better in a country like this when you just show it by action."

When it comes to human rights, Diane shares with other American businesspeople in China the desire to avoid speaking about an unfamiliar and uncomfortable subject. "As soon as I hear that now my first reaction is, What do you mean? What is a human right? It is a relative concept—based on how you define it and the value you put on it." Even when it comes to workers' rights, she prefers to refer to them as "labor abuses" rather than "human rights" violations.

Although Diane's story is in some ways unique, in most respects it is typical of many foreign managers working in China. These committed managers are not there by accident. They arrive with a sense of adventure and historic mission in helping to open the Chinese economy, and a genuine affection for the Chinese people. They are excited about living and working in China, eager to help their employees and coworkers navigate the ways of western capitalism. Anyone who meets Diane Long and the many other foreign managers like her would have a hard time reconciling that encounter with negative images of Western business executives in China.

China's New White Collar and Technological Elite

Multinational corporations provide a variety of job opportunities for Chinese workers. At one end of the spectrum are low-wage factory jobs. Western media attention has focused on the appalling conditions in some factories where labor-intensive goods are manufactured for export to Western countries. However, multinational corporations are also creating other, higher paying and more desirable opportunities. For young college graduates, white collar and technical jobs in Western corporations are among the most coveted positions in China. It should come as no surprise that the Chinese workers found in managerial and technical positions at these corporations are highly intelligent and self-confident. They represent an entirely different social stratum than do the poor and illiterate workers toiling in sweatshops. Moreover, these mostly young men and women are learning ideas and values at work that are quite radical in the context of Chinese society.

One such young Chinese worker, referred to here as "Tom" to protect his identity, is an engineer by training, but he has risen rapidly through the managerial ranks of his American corporate employer. Dressed in his neatly pressed white shirt and tie, Tom is the very model of a rising corporate executive. On introducing himself, Tom is careful to note that his Ph.D. in theoretical physics from a prestigious university was earned with honors. At first, Tom comes across as a bit of a braggart as he recounts his various academic accomplishments and swift rise through the managerial ranks. It soon becomes apparent, however, that the reason he touts his credentials is that he is proud of achieving his position on the basis of his talents rather than through personal connections. Tom is very careful to contrast his own career with that of his father, who was, according to Tom, a "number one boss" at a factory in Hebei province. Tom's father rose to his position largely as a reward for being a People's Liberation Army soldier at the time of the founding of the People's Republic of China in 1949. Tom, however, is eager to be judged by his technical and business acumen.[8]

Tom is quick to point out differences between his managerial style and his father's: "Facts, data . . . we use them at every stage of decision making here. My father's firm never used data." Tom also noted that his father's idea of a meeting was to call a bunch of people into a room and yell. Tom is very conscious of acting as a "mentor" to those who work under him, admitting that one of the most challenging aspects of his job was figuring out how to get the most out of those whom he supervised.

"Ling," a woman in her mid-thirties, works as a business strategist for an American company. She is originally from Northwest China but went to college in Shanghai. Before joining her American employer, she spent several unhappy years working at a state-owned enterprise (SOE). When she moved to her current job, she increased her income fourfold over her previous job. Ling is immaculately dressed in a pastel blue suit. With her stylish glasses and poised demeanor, she exudes great confidence. Her English is flawless, and she is careful and thoughtful in responding to questions. She would not seem out of place at a top Western investment bank or consulting firm even though she has never traveled outside of China.

Ling also stresses generational issues when she compares working for an SOE with her current job. Ling calls her current working environment "more suitable for young people." She reports that in the SOE there were "lots of idle people" and that her current job is more challenging. She contrasts her new employer with her old one: "As long as you perform, you will get promoted. SOEs are large and old. You are behind a lot of people for a promotion."[9]

Although it is true that millions of low-skilled and semi-skilled laborers are working in foreign-owned factories in China, a new white-collar and technical middle class, working in foreign-owned companies, is rapidly emerging. Tom and Ling are typical of this new "meritocracy" class of workers who are learning radically new ideas and cultural values in their corporate settings. Anyone who wants to fairly assess the impact of Western corporations in China must take into account the emergence of this new meritocratic class.

TOWARD A BALANCED VIEW OF WESTERN BUSINESS IN CHINA

The negative images of the sweatshop, the abusive manager, and the child laborer do not accurately represent the full story about Western business in China. To be sure, these exist in China, but so do good companies such as Motorola, caring managers such as Diane Long, and empowered workers such as Tom and Ling. These polar opposite images rise out of two very different business models for exploiting the vast and diverse economic potential existing in China. Each of these two business models represents not only a different approach to doing business in China, but also a distinctive strategic response to the powerful forces of economic globalization. These two faces of globalization raise distinctive moral and public policy considerations that are analyzed in the remaining chapters of this book.

CHAPTER TWO

☆

The Two Faces of Globalization: How the Strategic Imperatives of Global Capitalism Unleash Both Positive and Negative Forces

Since the late "paramount leader" Deng Xiaoping famously declared that "to get rich is glorious" and began to privatize China's economy in the late 1970s, China has attracted billions of dollars in foreign investment (Figure 2.1). In the 1990s, China became a red-hot target for multinational corporations. The World Bank estimates that China soaks up more than one-fourth of foreign direct investment in all developing nations.[1] According to the U.S.-China Business Council, foreign investors poured $222 billion into China between 1979 and 1997, more than one-half of which came in the last three years of that period.[2]

Accompanying all of this investment activity has been considerable speculation about whether China already is an economic and political superpower; when, if ever, it will become one; and what China's emergence will mean for the Asia-Pacific region and the rest of the world. Amidst this speculation, it has become clear that the massive influx of foreign capital is helping to turn China's emergence as an economic superpower into a self-fulfilling prophecy. The steady flow of large sums of foreign capital is fueling not only China's economic growth, but also its case for being taken seriously as a geopolitical superpower. Lest one get carried away by the hype, however, it should be pointed out that China's economic and geopolitical ascendancy is far from inevitable. The country faces innumerable social, political, and economic challenges, any one of which could potentially derail its progress.

Given China's large population and rapid economic development, it is not surprising that the most serious limits to growth are ecological and environmental. The World Bank estimates that 178,000 people in major cities suffer premature deaths each year because of pollution. In rural

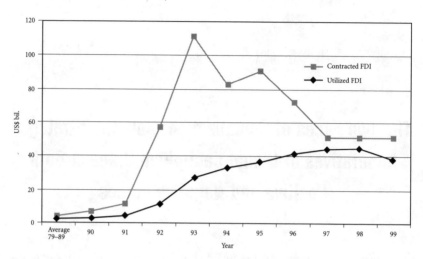

Figure 2.1 Foreign direct investment (FDI) in China, 1979–99. Value for 1999 is author's projection based on 1999 data for January through March. (Data from U.S.-China Business Council; Ministry of Foreign Trade and Economic Cooperation.)

areas, an estimated 110,000 people die each year from indoor air pollution resulting from burning coal and biomass for cooking and heating. In 1995, the total damage to human health from air and water pollution was at least US$54 billion, or 8 percent of gross domestic product. Anyone who has spent more than a few days in a major Chinese city will attest to the reality behind these statistics. Green park space is rare in urban areas. In cities such as Beijing, Shanghai, and Guangzhou, the sky is visibly darkened by pollution, and the sight of citizens wearing surgical masks to protect their lungs is common on the streets. The government's response to the environmental problem has been slow and inadequate, as exemplified by the fact that China's Environmental Protection Agency did not achieve ministerial status until 1998. Although strong environmental laws and regulations are now in effect, implementation continues to be extremely lax, particularly for small firms and geographical areas outside of the major economic regions.[3]

Another major impediment to growth is the potential for volatile social unrest. The threat emanates from a variety of sources. For example, economic inequality is increasing, especially between urban and rural areas, and between the relatively wealthy coastal regions and the interior provinces. Another source of unrest is a "floating population"

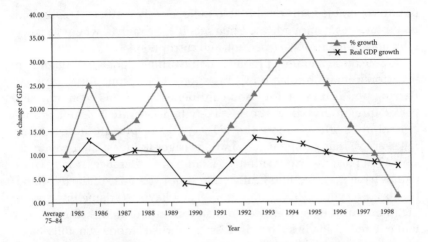

Figure 2.2 Gross domestic product (GDP) growth of China, 1975–98. Percentage of growth = [(current year – preceding year) / (preceding year)] × 100. Real GDP growth is purchasing power parity–weighted GDP. (Data from *China Statistical Yearbook*, China Statistical Bureau 1998; Ministry of Foreign Trade and Economic Cooperation; World Economic Outlook, Wahington, DC: International Monetary Fund, various issues.)

of tens and possibly hundreds of millions of unemployed workers who have become redundant in the agricultural sector or who are being let loose from formerly secure "iron rice bowl" jobs in SOEs. Finally, ethnic and religious-based independence movements in Tibet and Xinjiang present additional threats to stability and the control of the central government.

During the late 1990s, the flow of capital investment into China abated somewhat. This leveling-off resulted from a number of factors, including fears about spillover from the Asian financial crisis of 1997 and the high-profile bankruptcy in 1999 of the Guangdong International Trust and Investment Corporation, the government's "flagship" foreign investment conduit for Southern China. Investors also were worried about the downturn in China's growth rate from its historic highs (Figure 2.2). Chinese consumers, concerned about what privatization means for the future of their pensions, health care, and housing benefits, are saving more—an average of 40 percent of their income—and spending less. Exacerbating all this are serious problems in the banking sector, which has been squandering a good portion of those hard-earned personal savings. It has been estimated that 40 percent of a total loan portfolio of US$1 trillion consists of unrecoverable loans attributable to hopelessly inefficient SOEs; bad real estate deals in overheated markets like Shanghai, where vacancy rates are approximately 70 percent; and corruption.[4]

Despite these daunting problems and warning signals, many foreign investors remain bullish on China's long-term economic prospects. Barring political instability or a confluence of serious economic setbacks, foreign investment seems likely to accelerate if China is successful in its efforts to join the WTO. Why, despite all these serious risks, are so many foreign corporations eager to invest their capital in China? In part, the explanation is "irrational exuberance." Many companies have marched into China quite simply because of the hype and because everyone else was doing it—They have no compelling strategic plan, but they still expect to reap immediate riches. Companies that entered China in such a clueless "gold rush" mode generally have lost a lot of money. Beyond the hype, however, China does offer two distinct and very real commercial opportunities, both of which, not surprisingly, stem from the country's sheer size. With 1.3 billion people, China holds one-fifth of the world's population. This means that China has one-fifth of the world's labor pool and one-fifth of the world's consumers. However, these compelling factors offer no guarantee of success. Any company seeking to successfully exploit these opportunities must develop a sound China entry strategy that complements its overall global strategy. It must also learn how to operate effectively within the country's unique business environment and rapidly changing market conditions.

To understand why, despite the risks, it is so attractive to foreign investors, the opportunities China presents must be placed within the broader context of economic globalization. According to the International Monetary Fund, "globalization refers to the growing interdependencies of countries worldwide through the increasing volume and variety of cross-border transactions in goods and services, and of international capital flows; and also through the rapid and widespread diffusion of all kinds of technology."[5] In a competitive environment in which goods and capital flow freely and swiftly across national borders, China offers multinational corporations two distinct kinds of strategic opportunities. Some multinational corporations view China as an opportunity to execute what might be termed a *cost-minimization strategy* (i.e., the country provides a place to conduct large-scale, low-tech, low-cost production of labor-intensive goods that can be exported to and sold in existing markets around the globe). A second and wholly distinct opportunity is the potential to create new markets for existing products within China. Companies pursuing what might be called a *market-building strategy* view China primarily as a rapidly growing, potentially vast consumer and business market.

Each of these two business strategies—cost minimization and market building—represent firm-level strategic efforts to survive and prosper in the global economy. Each has different investment objectives, different time frames for success, and different operational requirements. Each strategy also results in very different interactions between multinational corporations and Chinese society. As a consequence, each strategy raises distinct moral and public policy questions.

Cost Minimization as a Global Business Strategy

Multinational corporations following a cost-minimization strategy search out the globe for places to manufacture large quantities of labor-intensive, low-tech goods as cheaply as possible. For companies whose competitive situations require them to minimize costs to survive, China has a powerful economic allure. It has hundreds of millions of non-farm laborers, the vast majority of whom are ready, willing, and able to work in unskilled and semiskilled jobs for wages that are a fraction of those paid in developed countries and competitive with wages in other developing countries.

The minimum wage in China is US$35 to $45 per month, depending on the locality. This wage structure compares favorably with other low-wage nations. As of 1997, the average daily wage in Shanghai was US$0.90, as compared to $1.80 in Jakarta, $4.60 in Kuala Lumpur, and $3.00 in Bangkok. The currency devaluations following the 1997 Asian financial crisis have reduced the wage gaps somewhat, but the labor cost advantages of manufacturing in China remain significant. Combined with the sheer operational scale that is possible in China because of the seemingly limitless labor pool, the low-wage structure makes it a very attractive manufacturing base for companies that must minimize production costs to compete in the global trading markets. To put it simply, in many industries, greater volume can be manufactured more cheaply in China than anywhere else in the world. As a result, in labor-intensive, low-tech industries such as textiles, garments, and household products, China takes away foreign direct investment and export share from Thailand, Indonesia, Malaysia, and the Philippines.[6]

China's emergence as an export manufacturing base can be appreciated more fully in historical perspective. Nicholas Lardy has observed that although China's export strategy began in the early 1980s with an emphasis on coal and petroleum, by the 1990s exports were predominantly composed of labor-intensive manufactured products. China, in other words, started exporting the kinds of goods in which it had a comparative advantage (i.e., goods that required a ready supply of cheap, low-skilled labor). By 1990, textiles, apparel, footwear, toys, and sporting goods alone accounted for 40 percent of total exports. Electrical equipment—such as telephones, television sets, and videocassette recorders—made up another 10 percent. However, as Lardy writes, even these products "which might appear to be more capital intensive, are based overwhelmingly on processing and assembly-type activity. Thus they too are labor intensive since imported components account for four-fifths of the value of exports."[7]

This shift toward the export of labor-intensive manufactured goods has been accompanied by another trend Lardy notes. By 1993, more than one-fourth of China's exports were tied to foreign investment.[8] What all this boils down to is that, in the 1990s, many foreign investors discovered that China was the optimal place to manufacture and assemble low-tech goods requiring abundant quantities of cheap labor. Cost-minimizing firms thus naturally regard China as an important place to invest and conduct operations.

Foreign Temporary Indirect Investments: How the Subcontracting System Diffuses Moral Responsibility for Labor Abuses

Companies following a cost-minimization strategy sometimes invest capital directly into China. They build their own manufacturing facilities (alone or in a joint venture with a local partner), and the goods produced are shipped out of China to be sold in the United States, Europe, Japan, and other markets. More often, however, cost-minimizing companies subcontract manufacturing work to factories owned by local provincial governments, Chinese investors, or "overseas Chinese" (i.e., ethnically Chinese) investors from Taiwan, Hong Kong, Singapore, and other Asian countries.

The subcontracting process typically involves many layers of complex supply relationships. Before China emerged as a favored manufacturing site, the "Asian Tigers"—especially Hong Kong and Taiwan—were leading hubs for the labor-intensive manufacture of products—such as textiles, garments, plastics, and electronics—requiring simple technologies and basic labor skills. At the bottom of the subcontracting chain were homeworkers. Teresa Shuk-ching Poon has described the subcontracting network as follows:

> The subcontracting network . . . is initiated by the foreign buyers or the sourcing agents of the multinational trading groups interested in buying finished consumer goods from local manufacturers. They bring with them the design of the products to be manufactured, and the local producers are responsible only for the actual production. The local trading companies usually try to find appropriate producers who, if they successfully win the contract, will become the first-line contractors. . . . The subcontracting network . . . begins with the local large factories, through the small and medium sized firms (or even smaller factories and workshops), and ends with the homeworkers.[9]

At each successive level of subcontracting, pressure is applied to reduce costs, because each entity in the subcontracting chain can make money only by obtaining cheap production from below. In the well-established manufacturing environment found in Southeast Asia, the system as a whole functions in a highly efficient and flexible manner, providing low-cost goods to the United States, Europe, and Japan. But the system also has unfortunate consequences for workers, particularly those at the bottom of the chain. As Teresa Shuk-ching Poon writes,

> the operation of the subcontracting network seems to be based entirely on downward exploitation along the subcontracting chain. Usually, the lower down the chain a unit is, the more the unit has to survive cumulative pressure from above. . . . The ultimate losers in the subcontracting network may be the homeworkers who do not have anybody further down the subcontracting chain to squeeze.[10]

With the emergence of China as a manufacturing base, the scale of the subcontracting network relationships has grown dramatically. Poon estimates that almost 80 percent of the manufacturers in Hong Kong have transferred production to approximately twenty-five thousand factories in the Pearl River delta in Southern China. Hong Kong–controlled manufacturing firms alone employ between 3 and 4 million workers in Southern China. One effect of this quick ramping up of production in

China has been unemployment for workers in other parts of Southeast Asia. Americans and Europeans are used to thinking that only their workers experience job losses as a result of free trade and the resulting competition from cheap foreign labor. However, Poon reports, hundreds of thousands of unskilled and semiskilled workers in Hong Kong have lost their jobs due to the labor competition from China. As a result, she observes, overall Hong Kong unemployment in 1995 was at its highest level in a decade.[11] One of the agonizing ironies of globalization is that Chinese workers have replaced Hong Kong workers at the bottom of the subcontracting chain, and now it is Chinese workers who suffer exploitation and Hong Kong workers who, as do their counterparts in the West, suffer unemployment.

The movement of manufacturing from places like Hong Kong and Taiwan to China involves more than simply a change in location and an increase in scale. After globalization pushed the subcontracting system into China, the pressure to minimize costs persisted, as did the downward exploitation of workers. Now, however, at the bottom of this chain of exploitation are millions of desperate, mostly illiterate workers who have migrated from the Chinese countryside. Poon reports that in the smaller-scale networks of production in Hong Kong and Taiwan connections of community and kinship exist between workers and bosses.[12] Without such ties, which can act as a natural check against abuse, the possibilities for exploitation in the subcontracting system are magnified. The often abysmal state of labor conditions in the low-tech Chinese factories that manufacture textiles, apparel, electronics, and plastic goods is the abusive endgame of globalization. Chinese workers form a seemingly limitless, faceless mass of unskilled and semiskilled labor willing to work at rock-bottom wages in miserable conditions. As a result of this labor "resource," the capital and manufacturing operations of firms following cost-minimization strategies find their way ineluctably into China.

The subcontracting system of manufacturing also serves to diffuse and obscure moral responsibility for labor abuses. Often, cost-minimizing Western companies are doing business in China only in the loosest sense of the phrase. They are separated from the workers who manufacture their products by layers of subcontractors and suppliers. As a result, they can disavow knowledge and responsibility for working conditions in the factories that produce for them. Moreover, since cost-minimizing firms rely so heavily on subcontractors, they tend to conduct minimal shell operations in China. They might open a representative office in a manufacturing region to oversee contracts with local suppliers. For the larger companies, a few dozen domestic workers might staff such a representative office. In many cases, however, cost-minimizing firms may not even have a permanent presence within China. After all, the main point of the subcontracting arrangement is to keep costs down. The smaller the operation in China, the lower the overall costs of producing there. The company's physical presence and ties to the community are minimal or nonexistent, and so too are the bonds of social responsibility and trust between Western companies and the workers who manufacture products for export to Western markets.

Cost-minimizing firms also have a very short time horizon within which they measure the success of their operations in China. From their perspective, the crucial factors are that this year's product be manufactured on time, that quality is acceptable, and that cost is minimized. If local subcontractors can satisfy these criteria consistently, then cost-minimizing firms might be interested in making long-term contractual commitments. In general, however, the level of commitment to China is very low. If the supply costs become more favorable somewhere else, the costs of moving operations to another country are small. In such a case, cost-minimizing firms would quickly abandon China and move operations to the lower-cost alternative supplier.

The ability to shift operations quickly is one of the key factors imposing downward exploitation pressure in the subcontracting system. Indeed, the ability to shift investments and contractual relationships swiftly and with little cost is precisely what allows cost-minimizing firms to succeed. Subcontractors in China know that if they do not offer good prices, their customers might easily be persuaded to relocate production to another part of China, or even to factories in Indonesia or the Philippines. The ease and speed with which manufacturing arrangements can shift also puts pressure on governments. Local, provincial, and national governments in China and elsewhere are all eager to attract investors, employ workers, and generate hard currency through exports. The mobility of capital and manufacturing arrangements thus creates perverse incentives for lax enforcement of local and national labor laws governing, among other things, wage levels, overtime, and safety conditions.

*How the Global Economy Forces Multinational Corporations
to Choose between Economic Survival and Moral Principle*

It is tempting to condemn the moral character of the mostly Asian subcontractors who perform the dirty work of cost minimization. One even hears whispers among American and European business executives that the worst instances of human rights abuses of workers occur by Asians against other Asians, a sad fact that is confirmed by some Chinese labor activists.[13] Before succumbing to feelings of moral superiority, however, it is important that Westerners try to understand the global economic forces that drive companies to pursue a cost-minimization strategy, and to accept our own role in facilitating these human rights abuses.

A fact of life in an efficient global economy is that manufacturing profit margins will be squeezed. This is good for consumers, who enjoy lower prices as a result. For manufacturers, however, it is a mixed blessing. To be sure, open markets mean more customers, but they also mean more competitors. The competitive pressure to minimize costs is accentuated by the free movement of capital and goods across borders. Global competition in many industries has become so intense that companies cannot hope to compete and remain profitable unless they pursue a global cost-minimization strategy. This means finding the lowest production costs—after taking into account shipping and other expenses—in the world. Companies manufacturing athletic shoes, consumer electronics, toys, and apparel, among other products, simply cannot stay in business unless they reduce manufacturing costs to meet global competition. (It should be noted that, according to strategy guru Michael Porter, firms that slavishly try to compete in the global economy by producing at the lowest possible cost are destined to be low performers. Porter does not regard cost minimization as a "strategy" at all, because it provides no hope for sustaining a highly profitable competitive advantage.[14])

Because of consumer price expectations, the global marketplace pits cost-minimizing companies in a virtual zero-sum game against workers. Human rights claims (e.g., the right to be paid a "living wage" and the right to a safe and environmentally healthy workplace) impose on multinational corporations numerous duties that are owed to workers. Honoring these duties in most instances creates additional manufacturing costs. In this particular context, therefore, free trade and global capital markets pose a threat to human rights. Moreover, the multinational corporation stands precariously on a tightrope stretched in the middle of this threat. At one end, the multinational corporation is threatened with extinction if it does not follow the global imperative of cost minimization. At the other end, the multinational corporation remains morally responsible for human rights violations that are the consequence of pure cost-minimization strategies.

Corporate casualties are found at both ends of this economic and moral tightrope. Faced with such conflicting and in many respects irreconcilable demands, many corporations are tempted to sacrifice their moral principles in the name of profits. In the 1990s, a number of well-known companies suffered tarnished reputations when press reports presented evidence that their goods were produced in factories abusing the human rights of workers. In most cases, however, apart from embarrassment, these companies did not experience a significant financial penalty. They continued to be successful despite the bad publicity. On the other end of the spectrum, however, it is a sad fact of the global economy that many companies which attempt to balance principles with profits often are unable to survive. Some companies have gone out of business because they could not successfully minimize production costs to meet competition. Few of these stories make it into the newspaper because such failure is a mundane fact of life in the harsh world of business competition. It is, nonetheless, worth pondering an example of this process. After the breakup of AT&T, its consumer products division spent nearly a decade attempting unsuccessfully to build a profitable telephone answering machine business. First, it built a state-of-the-art factory in Louisiana. However, labor costs were too high to meet competition. Reluctantly accepting the realities of global competition, AT&T began opening manufacturing plants abroad—first in Singapore, then Thailand, and finally in Mexico. In each case, AT&T paid prevailing wages but incurred significant extra costs to establish environmental and safety practices that were consistent with its corporate values. AT&T, however, was never able to simultaneously sustain economic viability and meet its human rights moral duties as it saw them. Eventually, it had to exit from the business.[15]

Economic and Moral Connections: How Western
Consumers Contribute to Labor Abuses in China

What economic and moral roles do Western consumers play in the exploitation of laborers in China? Frankly, we have learned to like our cheap clothes and shoes. Rising consumer expectations are creating a feedback effect and helping to further fuel the frenzy of global competition. Consumers in the United States and Europe have come to expect cheap, high-quality manufactured goods. The extent of such expectations became startling to me when I opened my mail one night and saw an advertisement for a cotton polo shirt in a well-known catalog. The ad announced that the very same polo shirts that were being sold last year for $21 were being sold this year for $3 less! I wondered how this was possible. What enabled this cost reduction? Clearly, the cost savings could not be attributed to a heroic Schumpeterian technological innovation. Perhaps leftover inventory was the explanation. It was also possible, however, that this company had found a cheaper place to make shirts. Perhaps the company switched production from Hong Kong to Southern China. Or maybe it found a middleman who beat his competitor's contract price. What was remarkable to me was the fact that this well-known company felt that it needed to sell its "high-quality" shirt for $3 less than it did last year to retain customers. It is because of such consumer-driven economic compulsions that companies compelled to follow a cost-minimization strategy are drawn to China as a manufacturing base, and that downward pressure is created to exploit workers in the subcontracting system. Before we condemn the morals of those who manufacture and sell these products, we should consider our own shopping priorities and take a clear-eyed look in our own closets and drawers.

Companies such as Levi Strauss, Liz Claiborne, and Nike have discovered the hard way that even a strong brand name does not exempt apparel manufacturers from pursuing cost-minimization strategies. People are willing to pay a little more for a good brand name, but they still want a competitive price. Global competition puts companies that have strong brand names in a difficult moral position. As do companies selling nonbranded apparel, they must achieve cost minimization. However, because so much goodwill is bound up in a brand name, the consumer holds the company with a strong brand name accountable for the human rights conditions in its factories. Indeed, human rights advocates target branded apparel companies precisely because of the attention that is drawn to companies that conduct mass media marketing campaigns.

Consumers have, for example, strong preferences for branded athletic wear. They pay more for a pair of shoes or a shirt because their hero dunks a basketball or hits a home run while wearing the same logo. If consumers find out, however, that those products were manufactured in factories that violate the human rights of workers, then some of them become shocked and outraged. There is, I think, a certain amount of hypocrisy involved in this outrage. Although some consumers are willing to pay more for goods manufactured in factories that honor the human rights of employees, many other consumers expect both low costs and moral integrity. And most consumers simply don't care. A notable exception to this moral complacency can be found in the consumer activism of students at Rutgers, Princeton, Duke, North Carolina, Brown, Oberlin, Notre Dame, and other prestigious universities. Students at these schools have organized and joined with concerned administrators from their collegiate licensing departments to take responsibility for human rights conditions at the factories manufacturing apparel that bears the name of the school. These students and college officials, it seems to me, perfectly well understand that we as consumers profit materially from human rights abuses in Chinese factories.[16]

The foregoing discussion about consumer responsibility is not meant to absolve marketers and manufacturers of moral responsibility for human rights abuses. However, when it comes to human rights, it is important to understand that we all have moral duties because we are all economically linked, as consumers or in some other fashion, to the workers who make the products we hold dear.

MARKET BUILDING AS A GLOBAL BUSINESS STRATEGY

Whereas the exigencies of the global economy pit the interests of multi-national corporations following a cost-minimization strategy against the human rights of workers, a completely different dynamic prevails in the case of companies following a market-building strategy. Market-building firms have very different investment objectives, time frames for success, labor relations, and operational requirements. As a result, they have a vastly different and more positive impact on the societies in which they do business. The powerful economic forces unleashed by globalization propel market builders to operate in a way that enhances the welfare of Chinese workers and serves to promote democracy and human rights.

For market-building companies, globalization means growth. Such companies view contemporary China as presenting a historically unique growth opportunity. To companies as diverse as BASF, Boeing, Motorola, Coca-Cola, Sony, Unilever, and General Motors, the China market might represent only a small percentage of current revenues. However, because of the saturation and relatively slow growth of markets in the United States, Europe, and Japan, and because the Chinese economy has been growing at a 9 percent average for almost fifteen years, these companies are hoping that China will fuel their future growth. For example, Seattle-based Boeing is facing slow growth in its traditional American and European markets, as well as increasing competition from the European consortium Airbus. In China, however, Boeing is increasing sales dramatically in one of the fastest-growing air transportation markets in the world, with traffic growing by almost 20 percent per year during the 1990s. Boeing has produced 288 of the 400 airplanes that operate commercially in China, giving it a 72 percent market share. In the first two decades of the twenty-first century, Ron Woodward, president of Boeing's Commercial Airplane Group, projects a total market for approximately eighteen hundred commercial jets worth more than $125 billion.[17] Similar dizzying projections have already lured telecommunications firms and insurance companies, as well as detergent, soft drink, and cereal companies, to invest massive sums of capital in China. Even more multinational corporations are likely to enter the fray if China opens more of its market sectors as a result of WTO membership.

It is tempting to begin and end an analysis of the Chinese consumer market with the number 1.3 billion. Some naïve business executives who were early entrants into China had visions of the riches awaiting them "if only" they were able to capture the same percentage of China's customers as in their home markets. The fallacy behind this thinking is, of course, that China is a developing country. The vast majority of its citizens remain extremely poor, and most are unable to afford anything but the most basic consumer goods. This is changing, however, and thus a more accurate measure of China's attractiveness as a consumer market must take into account not only its large population, but also the personal wealth that has been generated by its extraordinary economic growth rate. Conghua Li of Deloitte & Touche Consulting Group has estimated that by the turn of the twenty-first century 450 million people in China will have annual household incomes in excess of US$3,000, and that 100 million will have annual household incomes exceeding $9,000.[18] Thus, although still poor by Western standards, China is beginning to develop a sizable middle class. For those companies willing to be patient and make substantial investments of capital, the Chinese consumer market does indeed offer tremendous opportunity. Success will not come easily, however, and it will not come overnight.

A few companies already have successfully exploited the consumer market opportunities in China. U.K.-based Unilever has formed a joint venture with a Shanghai company that sells more than 550 million tubes of toothpaste each year.[19] However, Unilever's success has been hard won. Even though Chinese consumer markets are growing, they are highly competitive. In virtually all of the major industries in which multinational corporations do business in China, strong competition is presented by other foreign companies, as well as by domestic firms. Unilever competes with Procter & Gamble and numerous well-established domestic brands. Coke battles Pepsi and the Chinese Jianlibao. Ford battles Volkswagen. Some markets for higher-priced consumer goods might even be characterized as *hypercompetitive* (i.e., technology and capital intensive, and with many entrants). For example, Motorola has invested billions of dollars to develop state-of-the-art factories to manufacture cellular telephones. Nonetheless, it has formidable European competitors in Ericsson and Nokia as well as the South Korean Samsung.

Why Global Companies Must Go Local

To be successful in China's competitive markets, a company must invest not only financial capital and technology, but also human capital. Firms relying too heavily on expatriate workers are at a twofold competitive disadvantage. First, expatriate workers are extremely expensive to pay and house in comparison to local workers. The average expatriate compensation package costs between US$250,000 and $300,000. Add to that housing costs of $100,000 a year and private school fees of $30,000 per child, and it becomes clear why Western companies are so anxious to replace expatriates with local managers, whose annual salaries usually average between $10,000 and $20,000.[20]

Even more important than the cost savings they generate is the understanding native workers posess about Chinese consumers and business markets. Companies that want to expand their market share in China must recruit, train, and retain local workers to assume technical, administrative, and managerial roles. Doug Thomson, Hewlett-Packard Asia Pacific's director of human resources, flatly states that "if you want to build a long-term sustainable business you can't build it on foreign nationals—you need local people in the top spots to be successful in the long run."[21] James Bruce, Unilever's chief strategist in the East Asia and Pacific region, explains that "a core strategy in the developing markets is to ensure the business is run as soon as possible under local management."[22] A Beijing-based U.S. diplomat reports that "every single company lists getting better qualified local managers as a top priority."[23]

Motorola presents a good example of how economic prosperity in China is inextricably linked to the development of human resources. The Chinese market accounts for approximately 11 percent of Motorola's worldwide sales, but the company is betting heavily on China as a source of future growth. Motorola has invested more than $1.5 billion in China, making it the country's largest American investor. However, Motorola is investing far more than financial capital. It understands that to compete successfully against Samsung, Ericsson, and Nokia, it must invest heavily in training. Each of Motorola's ten thousand employees receives an average of seventy hours of training a year. As of 1999, more than one-half of Motorola's middle managers were Chinese.[24] Motorola has opened a branch of Motorola University in China to train employees, customers, suppliers, distributors, joint venture partners, and government officials in managerial and technical subjects. The company spends $5 million a year on corporate education in China. Lois Webster, director of Motorola University in China, says that "the business environment is changing so fast. We believe we have to invest in our people so we can stay on top."[25]

The German-based chemical giant BASF has invested $1.5 billion in diverse enterprises and joint ventures in China. The company has complemented its financial investment with a significant investment in human resources. Dr. Jurgen Hambrecht, a member of BASF's board of directors, declared that training and developing local employees and cooperating with the Chinese scientific community was an "especially crucial measure" for the company. To fulfill this mandate, BASF built a Management Development Center at the prestigious Jiao Tong University in Shanghai, where the company has provided training for more than 650 local managers in the Asia-Pacific region.[26]

Companies such as Motorola and BASF are also contracting with independent consultants to conduct local training. Ira Cohen, the head of UI China Training Services, estimates that foreign firms are currently spending approximately $30 million on external consultants to train their Chinese workers. Cohen calls this a "drop in the bucket" and predicts that it will grow to a $300 million business in the first decade of the twenty-first century.[27]

Market Building as a Global Force Promoting Human Rights

Companies pursuing a market-building strategy have a very different impact on Chinese society than do companies that are in China to minimize costs. Whereas the pressures of globalization tempt cost-minimizing firms to abuse the human rights of workers, an entirely different set of forces emanating from the same global economy compels market-building companies to invest in training their workers to assume managerial roles. In other words, the forces of globalization compel multinational companies that want to capture market share in China to do good in order to do well.

Companies such as BASF and Motorola are putting down deep roots in Chinese society. Their fortunes are inextricably entwined with those of China, and vice versa. They are primarily concerned with attaining a significant and profitable market share five and ten years down the road, and they are not as preoccupied by this month's production costs as are cost-minimizing companies. These companies represent the other face of global capitalism in China, and it is a more attractive one than that presented by cost-minimizing companies. Market-building companies are not likely to be paying minimum wages in sweatshop factories. This would be inconsistent with their purpose in China. To pursue a market-building strategy in China, companies must make substantial investments of both financial and human capital. They must use a long-term time horizon to measure their success, because it takes many years to understand Chinese tastes, establish reliable sources of supply, obtain government approvals, and master all the many other factors that are critical to conducting effective operations. They must make a strong commitment to the Chinese market and to the Chinese people because their resolve is likely to be tested by unexpected setbacks. Most important, they must invest in training their workers.

The localization of management creates learning opportunities in two directions. Multinational firms learn about Chinese culture and society from their local managers. However, to be successful in a global company, local managers must also learn certain values and behaviors from their corporate employers. As later chapters show, the particular values and behaviors that local managers learn in training programs and on the job have a positive impact on human rights and the process of democratization in China.

Moral and Public Policy Issues Raised by Cost-Minimization and Market Building

The cost-minimization strategy raises a number of moral and policy questions. Without a doubt, a great temptation exists for a corporation trying to cut costs to engage subcontractors and suppliers and then to turn a blind eye to how those business partners run their factories. These kinds of practices are, in part, an attempt by firms to avoid moral responsibility for the human rights violations committed by business partners while still deriving economic benefit from the relationship. Companies that pursue a cost-minimization strategy in this way raise some sharp moral issues. Is a multinational corporation responsible for human rights violations committed by its business partners? What monitoring practices should multinational corporations follow to make sure that their subcontractors honor the human rights of their workers?

The cost-minimization strategy also raises a number of public policy questions. Most of these concern the best way of ensuring that subcontractors follow good labor practices. What minimum standards should manufacturers be expected to adhere to? Should self-monitoring and self-reporting by corporations of the activities of their subcontractors be relied on? Or are independent certifying agents needed to ensure compliance with human rights norms? Should worker rights and free trade be linked? Does the WTO have a role to play in protecting the human rights of workers?

Just as the cost-minimization strategy raises distinctive moral and public policy questions so too does the market-building strategy. In pursuing self-interest, do these companies contribute any benefit to Chinese society? In particular, do they help in any way to promote democracy and human rights? The answers to such moral questions have important public policy implications for foreign relations between the United States and China. If it is true that multinational corporations, by pursuing their own self-interest, can act as a catalyst for human rights, then this would serve as a powerful moral argument favoring China's entry into the WTO. In later chapters, all of these moral and public policy questions are addressed in the context of a broad "fair share" theory of moral responsibility for the protection of human rights.

CONCLUSION

At the dawn of the new millenium, many scholars, journalists, and other writers are grappling with the meaning of *globalization* and its human consequences. For some, such as John Gray, the very idea of a global capitalism is anathema for humanity.[28] For others, such as Tom Friedman, globalization means creating a global village in which culture, community, and tradition occupy space uneasily with capitalism, technology, and the free flow of information.[29] As this chapter illustrates, however, globalization unleashes economic forces that have both positive and negative consequences for humanity. Each of the two business strategies examined repre-

Table 2.1 Comparison of Cost-Minimization and Market-Building Strategies

	Cost-minimization strategy	Market-building strategy
Primary attraction to China	Bountiful supply of low-wage labor	An economy growing at 9% each year with consumers eager to buy new goods
Level of investment and operations in China	Little physical presence in China; act mostly through subcontractors	High capital and human investment; high investment in worker training
Wages and working conditions	Pay minimum wages; tempted to produce goods in factories with minimum levels of safety and very few amenities	Pay many times prevailing wages for the most talented and best educated workers; high-quality working environment
Commitment to China	Would leave quickly if better terms could be found elsewhere	Long-term commitment to the country and workforce
Time horizon	Month to month	Measured in years
Examples of companies following this strategy	Nike, Liz Claiborne	Motorola, General Motors, BASF
Most significant moral question	Are multinational corporations responsible for human rights violations committed by their subcontractors?	Does self-interested behavior really indirectly promote human rights?
Most significant public policy question	Should labor standards be enforced through the World Trade Organization?	Is engagement an effective way to make a positive impact on human rights?

sent rational, indeed necessary, responses by multinational corporations to the competitive dynamics resulting from the free flow of trade and capital across borders that characterizes globalization. Yet the two strategies have distinctive social impacts, as well as different investment objectives, different time frames for success, and different operational requirements. As a consequence, they raise very different moral and public policy questions. (These differences are summarized in Table 2.1.)

Obviously, the two strategies are what Max Weber would term *ideal types*. They are idealized, pure constructions, and they have been drawn up as "heuristic devices" to help us to classify and make some sense out of the many varieties of more complex strategies that multinational corporations actually pursue in China. As Weber wrote, "An ideal type is formed by the one-sided accentuation of one or more points of view and by the synthesis of a great many diffuse, discrete, more or less present and occasionally absent *concrete individual* phenomena, which are arranged according to those one-sidedly emphasized viewpoints into a unified *analytical* construct."[30] Very few absolutely pure types exist (even companies that are predominantly concerned with building market share must to a certain extent be concerned with cost minimization, and vice versa). Some companies defy easy classification and appear to be pursuing a hybrid of both strategies. Moreover, some companies that come to China primarily to take advantage of its cheap labor invest a lot of money in training and attempt to be good corporate citizens in China.

Despite these obvious caveats, these categories are useful in helping to sort out two very different sets of moral and public policy questions that arise from the activities of multinational corporations in China. These two sets of questions form the organizing principle for the remaining chapters of this book. The moral and public policy issues raised by market-building companies are discussed in Chapters 3, 4, and 5. Chapters 6 through 9 are primarily concerned with the practices of cost-minimizing firms. In Chapter 10, the moral and public policy questions common to companies pursuing either strategy are examined.

In Chapter 3, the causal connection between making money and promoting human rights is considered, and the positive "spin-off" effect on human rights of profit-making activities is described. Chapter 4 contains some real-life examples of how this spin-off phenomenon manifests itself—how, that is, doing well often necessitates doing good.

CHAPTER THREE

★

Doing Good While Doing Well:
A Theory of Human Rights Spin-Off

The claim is often made that multinational corporations promote human rights in developing countries. This claim is expressed in a number of ways, all of which imply a vague causal relationship between business activity and sociopolitical change. It is sometimes said, for example, that multinational firms are "exporting" human rights values to developing countries. The common idea behind all of these formulations seems to be that when multinational firms do business in developing nations, they somehow indirectly help to improve human rights conditions. There is what one might call a *human rights spin-off* from the normal, day-to-day operations of corporations.

The major problem with such claims is that they tend to be so vague that they cannot be tested against experience. That business activity has a beneficial effect on human rights conditions must be taken on faith, even though the precise nature of the effect remains mysterious and undefined. Because of such vagueness, many observers are understandably skeptical about the spin-off hypothesis. The idea of human rights spin-off also has an undeniably self-serving aspect. As a result, human rights advocates regard it as a thinly veiled pretext for multinational corporations to pursue profits without regard for the rights and welfare of the citizens of developing countries. The facile and often half-hearted manner in which the idea sometimes is invoked by business executives and politicians also serves to discredit it.

This is too bad, because there is actually much more to the idea of human rights spin-off than at first might meet the eye. In the case of China, considerable evidence, albeit anecdotal, supports the idea. However, before empirical support for the hypothesis can be mustered, a plausible explanation of how it might work must be developed. This chapter attempts to elucidate the theoretical connection between the activities of multinational firms and progress in democracy and human rights. It identifies a set of factors that are influenced by business, factors that, in turn, have a positive impact on human rights and sustainable democracy. The reader is forewarned that the bulk of this chapter is highly theoretical. In the next chapter, this theoretical framework is used to evaluate interview data supporting the spin-off hypothesis.

FOREIGN POLICY IMPLICATIONS OF THE SPIN-OFF HYPOTHESIS

There are a number of reasons why it is important to determine whether the human rights spin-off hypothesis is valid. Perhaps the most significant implications concern foreign policy toward China and other developing nations with poor human rights records. The rationale for the U.S. policy of "comprehensive engagement" with China rests partly on the existence of human rights spin-off. The Clinton administration has spoken of the need to form a broad "strategic partnership" with China because of the many economic, military, and geopolitical interests about which the two countries need to cooperate. However, public tolerance for the policy in the United States is predicated on the hope that economic engagement will also serve to improve human rights conditions. President Clinton no doubt had this in mind when he declared that "the more we bring China into the world, the more the world will bring freedom to China."[1] The human rights spin-off hypothesis is thus "wired in" to U.S. foreign policy. If the human rights spin-off hypothesis is not valid, considerable doubt would be cast on the policy of engagement. As a Beijing-based U.S. diplomat put it, "Our whole policy depends upon whether American companies are indeed transferring moral principles that will make a difference in terms of values related to human rights."[2]

If trading with China does not create any positive human rights effects, it would confirm the suspicion that foreign businesses are making a lot of money in China but not doing anything to improve human rights conditions there. It would mean that the United States has sacrificed its human rights ideals at the altar of economic expediency. If human rights spin-off is a ruse, then human rights advocates would have a legitimate argument that the United States should reconsider using the threat of trade sanctions to pressure China. The invalidity of the spin-off hypothesis would also be a powerful argument against further expanding trade relations with China through the WTO. Many would argue, again with some justification, that we should wait until China changes its human rights practices before engaging in normal trade relations. In short, a lot rides on whether the human rights spin-off hypothesis is true or false.

SOME QUALIFICATIONS AND LEGITIMATE REASONS FOR SKEPTICISM

The putative relationship between the normal profit-making activities of multinational corporations and human rights is a felicitous instance of "doing good by doing well." The social benefits supposedly generated by multinational firms do not result from a conscious effort by corporate executives to promote democracy and human rights. Nor do they depend on the adoption of an explicit human rights agenda. Rather, the benefits result collaterally from the pursuit of standard business objectives—that is, making profits. In other words, the pursuit of self-interest leads indirectly to a social good.

It should be said that not every foreign-owned enterprise doing business in China creates positive human rights spin-off. A company that sets up a sweatshop factory in China to produce a product cheaply will not have much of a positive indirect effect on human rights conditions. On the contrary, the economic interests of such cost-minimizing companies are in many respects antithetical to the human rights of workers. For such firms, a great economic incentive exists to, among other things, cut corners on safety and environmental protections and to pay low wages. Therefore, it is axiomatic that pure profit-maximizing behavior by cost-minimizing firms is not going to result in positive human rights spin-off. In the case of multinational corporations attempting to establish a long-term presence in the Chinese market, however, a much greater alignment of interests exists between profit-maximizing behavior and human rights. When we speak of a human rights spin-off, it is the latter, market-building firms that we generally (although not exclusively or universally) have in mind.

Claims that business generates social benefits by unabashedly pursuing selfish objectives are, of course, nothing new. Contemporary economists might term this phenomenon a *positive externality*, in which one person's self-interested behavior creates unintended benefits for others. The general idea dates back to Adam Smith's theory of the "invisible hand," which asserts that overall social welfare is enhanced by selfish behavior.[3] In the 1980s, the American financier (and later convicted felon) Ivan Boesky expressed this idea in its most perverse form when he declared famously to an audience of business students at Berkeley that "greed is all right, by the way. I want you to know that. I think greed is healthy. You can be greedy and feel good about yourself."[4]

There is a natural suspicion about such statements in their most extreme and categorical form. Experience tells us that self-serving behavior by corporate executives is very often socially harmful. Indeed, we have, among other forms of social regulation of business, antitrust, environmental, and occupational safety laws, precisely because the interests of corporations very often conflict with those of the public. In economic parlance, business behavior generates a great many "negative externalities" (i.e., self-interested behavior results in collateral negative consequences for society). Because such "negative externalities" result in "market failures," virtually all economists concede a valid regulatory role for government. When the benefits of regulation outweigh the costs, government controls business by preventing selfish behavior or by redirecting it through market incentives in ways that are welfare enhancing.

The claim that large, multinational corporations such as BASF, Hewlett-Packard, and Ford are the primary generators of human rights spin-off sends out additional cautionary alarms. Such arguments have been made before in the form of statements such as "what's good for General Motors is good for the country." We have learned through experience that the interests of "Big Business" do not always coincide with those of society. In the case of developing countries, there are special reasons to be skeptical about claims that multinational corporations do good by doing well. In developed countries, corporations operate within a highly regulated environment designed, however haphazardly and imperfectly, to minimize the social costs and enhance the social benefits of business activities. By contrast, in developing countries, where the regulatory environment is much looser, multinational corporations have much greater latitude to engage in self-interested activities that don't always benefit the citizens of their host countries.

Indeed, the loose regulatory environment is one of the things that attracts multinational corporations to developing countries in the first place. It is one factor that keeps labor and manufacturing costs low. What a pleasure it must seem at first to companies that are able to set up shop without having to worry about the U.S. Occupational Safety and Health Agency, the Environmental Protection Agency, or the Justice Department. Freed from the perceived regulatory excesses of their home country, multinational firms must surely be tempted to maximize their own profits at the expense of the citizens of their host country. Governmental corruption exacerbates this divergence between corporate interests and social interests. In China, for example, numerous laws and regulations exist to protect workers. Chinese labor activist Han Dongfang laments, however, that local officials often fail to enforce these rules because of graft or because they have a financial interest in the law-evading factories.[5]

To be fair, not all multinational corporations seek to take advantage of the loose regulatory structure by acting in accordance with the lowest legally required standard of social responsibility. Although the absence of clear standards is in some respects a boon to multinational corporations, it can also place enormous demands on the time and attention of conscientious corporate executives. Many firms in developing countries work hard to ensure that they meet health, safety, and environmental standards that are, if not at the level found in Western countries, at least above the legal minimums of the host countries. Corporate executives with a sense of social responsibility often agonize over where to draw the line between what is legally required in the West and what they can get away with in developing countries. One Shanghai-based general manager reported having to spend a number of days traveling to each of her subcontractors to decide, among other things, how many fire extinguishers were enough for each plant.[6]

For all of the foregoing reasons, the human rights spin-off hypothesis might engender reasonable skepticism. However, just as it is wrong to think that the interests of corporations always complement social welfare, it is also wrong to think that the two are in perpetual warfare. The most obvious, and perhaps most important, social contribution business makes by engaging in profit-maximizing behavior is to enable society to make the most efficient use of its scarce resources. Businesses that don't produce a product that consumers want in an efficient manner soon find themselves out of business.

In China, the link between profit maximization and social welfare extends beyond the satisfaction of consumer preferences. Companies that seek to sustain long-term gains in Chinese markets create positive social benefits for the Chinese economy and society. As Debra Spar has written, "simply by following their own self-interests, [multinational corporations] may influence the local environment in positive ways. They bring jobs, capital, technology, know-how, management techniques, labor relations, and administrative structures that are unlikely to depart too dramatically from U.S. standards."[7] Many of the influences that Spar cites have important positive effects on human rights and democratization. In fact, it is the best-run and most successful market-building companies that have the biggest positive impact. Before these effects can be observed in practice, however, we need to develop a better understanding of the theoretical connection between corporate profits and human rights.

FORMULATING A HUMAN RIGHTS SPIN-OFF HYPOTHESIS

Some Complicating Factors and Definitional Issues

To validate an empirical connection between the operations of multinational corporations and human rights, it is necessary to formulate an empirically testable hypothesis. One must identify a dependent variable (i.e., something that needs to be explained or predicted). One must also identify an explanatory variable (i.e., something that bears a relationship—causal, catalytic, or otherwise—to the dependent variable). One then can formulate a theory of the relationship between the explanatory and dependent variables that can be tested by evidence and thereby either validated or disproved.

Discerning an empirical connection between the operations of multinational business and human rights is especially difficult in a complex society such as China. As we try to understand the situation from the West, it is important to keep in mind that domestic political and social forces mostly will determine China's future. Nonetheless, although multinational corporations will have only a relatively modest impact on the course of human rights, they are by far the most important foreign influence within China. The purpose of developing a coherent human rights spin-off hypothesis is to help to confirm and explain this influence.

It is not only the unique complications presented by China that make the connection between multinational corporations and human rights an elusive one to pin down. Formulating a testable hypothesis is especially difficult in the case of a dependent variable as multifaceted and complex as human rights. Complications arise from the many kinds of human rights that are said to exist and the difficulty of measuring them. To begin with, the idea of human rights encompasses not only civil and political rights but economic rights as well. (Chapter 7 explores the distinctions among the various types of human rights more fully.) In the case of the spin-off effect, the influence of multinational corporations on civil and political rights is of most concern. However, even this delimitation leaves a very complex dependent variable.

The language of human rights overlaps imperfectly with the language of political theory. Some basic definitions and simplifying assumptions will allow us to move on a sounder footing between human rights theory and political theory and to describe more precisely the dependent variable we are trying to understand. A *liberal* political system is one in which "individual and group liberties are well protected and in which there exist autonomous spheres of civil society and private life, insulated from state control."[8] In other words, a liberal political system is one in which civil rights are protected. *Civil rights* include the right to free expression without interference from the state, the rights to organize and to demonstrate, and freedom of religion and travel. A *democracy* protects the political rights of all adults to vote and compete for public office at free and fair electoral competitions at regular intervals, and the right of elected representatives to have a decisive vote on public policies. We are trying to develop a spin-off hypothesis that allows us to determine whether the operations of multinational corporations are influencing China to move toward a *liberal democracy*— a mixed system of government in which democracy and civil liberties both flourish.

Theoretically, one can have political rights (democracy) without civil rights (liberalism) and vice versa. Fareed Zakaria writes about the existence of "illiberal democracies"—a prime example is Peru under President Alberto Fujimori—that violate the civil liberties of their own citizens, and goes so far as to suggest that for many transitional societies, autocratic governments that protect the civil rights of their citizens represent a better and more stable form of government than illiberal democracy.[9] However, except for a very few tiny island states, no liberal autocratic governments exist in the world. The evidence, on the contrary, is that political rights and civil rights go hand in hand. As Larry Diamond has observed, countries that hold free elections are overwhelmingly more likely to be liberal than those that do not, and "the more closely countries meet the standards of electoral democracy (free and fair, multiparty elections by secret and universal ballot), the higher their human rights rating." Of course, countries that meet the standards of electoral democracy would, by definition, have higher human rights ratings—at least in so far as political rights are concerned. Diamond makes clear, however, that the connection he is describing is between democracy and civil rights. He writes, "there is a powerful association between democracy and liberty."[10]

Measurement Issues

Because both the explanatory and dependent variables are so complex, measuring them can be highly problematic. Different proxies for measuring the activities of multinational firms and for measuring gains in human rights protection can yield radically different results. For example, one study purported to find a positive relationship between the activities of multinational corporations with civil and political rights. As a proxy for the activities of multinational corporations, this study used a measurement of direct foreign investment flowing from the United States, and as a measure of human rights conditions, it used the annual Freedom House survey of civil and political rights. The study found that levels of foreign direct investment correlated *positively* with both civil and political rights—that is, the more foreign direct investment, the better were human rights conditions.[11] When another group of researchers applied the same methodology on a different data set, however, they reached an opposite result. This second study used a different measurement for foreign direct investment that reflected non-U.S. as well as U.S. investment flows. It also used a different measurement for civil and political rights (one alleged to be less "politically biased" than the Freedom House survey used by the earlier study). The authors of this second study found that the activities of multinational firms correlated *negatively* with human rights—that is, the more foreign direct investment, the worse were human rights conditions.[12]

Whether either study could possibly control for the many other variables, in addition to foreign direct investment, that might affect human rights in any particular country is questionable (no attempt appears to have been made). However, the most significant problem with both of these studies is that they were conducted at such a high level of aggregation that neither study supports or refutes what might properly be considered an explanatory theory. Establishing whether foreign direct investment correlates positively with human rights is not the same as formulating and testing a theory of how the activities of multinational corporations may cause or otherwise affect improvement in human rights conditions. One positive step toward developing such an explanatory theory would be to make some distinctions about the kind of foreign direct investment under discussion, a distinction that has more salience than the source of such investment. As Chapter 2 discussed, foreign direct investment can be either of the market-building or the cost-minimizing type. Market-building investments have a positive effect on human rights. By contrast, cost-minimizing investments can have some very serious negative effects on human rights. A prediction of the impact of foreign direct investment on human rights should depend, in other words, on the type of investment under consideration.

The discrepancy in the two studies might also be attributable to the fact that foreign direct investment from the United States and Western Europe is more likely to be of the market-building sort than of the cost-minimizing sort. However, at least in the case of China, there is no reliable way to interpret existing data to test this hypothesis. Eventually, we come back to the same issue: we need a theory to explain what is happening. We need, in other words, to be able to explain why market-building firms and investments have a positive impact on human rights conditions and why, conversely, cost-minimizing firms and investments do not. The answer to this kind of question cannot be found in a study in which the explanatory variable is as vague as "foreign direct investment flows" and the dependent variable is as elusive to observe as the crude measures of human rights used in both surveys. To develop such an explanatory theory, we need to identify some intermediate dependent variables that have a relationship to the ultimate human rights variables. We also need to have some plausible explanation for, and way of observing, how multinational corporations affect these intermediate variables.

Intermediate Variables and Causality Issues

The human rights spin-off hypothesis proposed here identifies a number of intermediate variables affected by the activities of multinational corporations. The crux of the theory is that when these intermediate variables change, they indirectly help to bring about a change in the dependent variable of human rights. We are describing a two-step process, and the empirical connections in each of the two steps are different. The relationship between the operations of multinational corporations and the intermediate variables is causal—that is, the activities of multinational corporations directly effect a change in the intermediate variables. However, the relationship between the intermediate variables and human rights is not causal.

The relationship between intermediate variables and human rights that is suggested here is of the sort that Max Weber called "elective affinity." Weber wrote, "Historical causality determines the unique circumstances that have given rise to an event. Sociological causality assumes the establishment of a regular relationship between two phenomena, which need not take the form 'A makes B inevitable,' but may take the form 'A is more or less favorable to B.' "[13] In *The Protestant Ethic and the Spirit of Capitalism*, for example, Weber theorized that the religious tenets of Calvinism had an elective affinity with the mental outlook required to be a successful capitalist. He used this theory to explain why capitalism took root in Protestant areas of Europe but not in Roman Catholic ones.[14]

Weber was trying to explain the rise of capitalism. He did so by identifying the Protestant ethic as the explanatory variable that had an "elective affinity" with or was "more or less favorable to" the emergence of capitalism, the dependent variable. Our next step in formulating a testable theory is to identify a set of intermediate variables that have an "elective affinity" with or are "more or less favorable to" human rights. Once these intermediate variables are identified, we can then begin to think about what facts, behaviors, and changes we need to observe to confirm (or invalidate) a connection between the operations of multinational corporations and human rights.

One important intermediate variable linking multinational corporations and democracy is *economic prosperity*. Multinational firms contribute to the development of democratic rights in developing countries simply by increasing the material wealth of society. What does wealth have to do with democracy? Quite a lot, it turns out. Statistically, for reasons not completely understood by political scientists and economists, a certain level of per capita gross domestic product—the magic number appears to be $4,000 in U.S. purchasing power parity—is a reliable predictor of sustainable democracy (i.e., in countries in which a certain level of wealth has been achieved, democracy is more likely to survive).[15] Multinational corporations help to raise gross domestic product levels in the countries in which they operate. By investing in developing countries, multinational firms thus not only help to alleviate poverty, but also help to establish a fertile soil for democracy.

In addition to creating personal wealth for Chinese citizens, multinational corporations, through their formal worker-training programs and informal on-the-job learning opportunities, are changing the values and behaviors of their workers. These effects, in turn, are helping to change the social and political values of Chinese society in ways that have an "elective affinity" with liberal democracy. One social value with salience for human rights is the idea of *individual merit*. By paying workers higher wages than they would otherwise earn, and by paying such salaries on the basis of merit, multinational firms are promoting the radical—radical in China, at least—idea that individual merit matters. In the process, these firms are helping to create a middle class with power and interests independent of the state. What this means is that, for the first time in modern Chinese history, a young man or woman can achieve financial and career success without joining the Communist Party. This sense of the worth of the individual is a cornerstone of a culture that respects individual civil and political rights.

Multinational firms also are teaching their employees about the importance of *information sharing* and *teamwork*. Such ideas about the free flow of information are difficult to confine to the realm of business. The ideas workers learn in foreign companies are helping to change the way the information is viewed in Chinese society generally. By emphasizing the importance of sharing and disseminating information widely, multinational corporations are thus indirectly promoting the idea of openness and accountability in government, essential characteristics of a liberal democracy.

Finally, by empowering their employers to take *initiative* and assume *leadership* roles, and by emphasizing the need for continuous learning and *change*, multinational corporations are changing fundamental Chinese ideas about the relationship between the leader and the subordinate. By helping to shape the values of their employees about these issues, multinational corporations are contributing to the development of a social and political culture in which liberal democracy can thrive.

Conclusion

Despite the understandable skepticism about such claims, the normal profit-seeking activities of multinational corporations do have a positive human rights spin-off effect. This effect is inadvertent (it does not depend on the deliberate adoption of a human rights agenda), and it is indirect (multinational corporations do have an impact on a set of intermediate variables that, in turn, have an impact on human rights). In Chapter 4, human rights spin-off is examined in action, through a set of interviews with Chinese and Western managers who work for multinational corporations.

✷

CHAPTER FOUR

Human Rights Spin-Off in Action

"Foreign capital . . . will bring some decadent capitalist influences into China. We are aware of this possibility. It's nothing to be afraid of."

—Deng Xiaoping, August 1980

Multinational corporations with the long-term goal of penetrating the Chinese consumer and business markets are helping to improve human rights conditions. They are doing so inadvertently as they strive to maximize their profits. This contribution is an indirect "spin-off" of the human resource practices they must follow to be successful in China. This chapter demonstrates, through a series of interviews with Chinese and Western managers, how multinational corporations are having an effect on four sets of factors: economic prosperity, merit-based hiring practices, information-sharing and teamwork, and leadership style. The implications of these four factors for the future of human rights and democracy in China are also considered.

WEALTH AS AN INTERMEDIATE VARIABLE:
PROSPERITY AND DEMOCRATIC RIGHTS

Perhaps the most obvious contribution foreign companies make in developing countries is purely economic. There are, unfortunately, too many examples throughout the world and in China of companies that profit at the cost of exploiting their host countries, but this is far from universally the case. By investing capital and technology in developing countries, multinational corporations often enrich their host countries even as they enrich themselves. This has certainly been the case in China, where the government has worked assiduously to ensure that China reaps some of the economic rewards of foreign investment.

Since China began economic reforms in 1978, it has averaged more than 9 percent annual growth. Multinational firms have played a huge part in this wealth creation. Even companies that come to China to engage in low-cost production in most instances create job opportunities that improve the lot of their employees. However, the positive economic and noneconomic impacts of companies with a long-term commitment to the Chinese market are much more profound. These companies bring major technological advances to China, and in the process they create hundreds of thousands of high-paying managerial and technical jobs. They are helping to create a middle class that does not owe its prosperity and status to the state. The emergence of this middle class is essential to the future of democracy in China.

Almost all of the conversation in the West about working conditions in China has focused on sweatshop factories run by foreign joint ventures. Such abuses are indeed all too common, and they raise important moral, legal, and policy questions that later chapters examine. However, the focus on the dismal conditions in sweatshops should not obscure the fact that many, if not most, of the Western-based multinational companies operating in China pay wages that are significantly higher than prevailing local wages and very comfortably beyond what is necessary to survive. Unfortunately, reliable data concerning the number of jobs in foreign enterprises paying above the minimum wage are not available. Nor are data showing how wages for similar work differ among American, Japanese, European, and Asian firms. However, the few data that are available strongly support the view that many multinational firms in China, particularly those from the United States and Europe, pay far greater wages than those earned by the average Chinese worker.

According to official government statistics, the average monthly wage (not including housing or health benefits) in Shanghai is approximately 889 renminbi (RMB) (approximately US$110). In a survey conducted in 1997 by the Shanghai Manufacturers' Business Council, the average monthly wage for *unskilled* workers in American enterprises in Shanghai was approximately 2,400 RMB (approximately US$300) a month. For a foreman, the average monthly wage was more than 3,000 RMB. The income disparity is even greater among the white-collar employees in high demand among foreign enterprises. An entry-level marketing associate, for example, makes on average 4,000 RMB a month. A marketing manager makes approximately 10,000 RMB. A Chinese director of operations for an American company takes home on average 20,000 RMB (US$2,400) a month.[1]

Salaries for talented technical and managerial workers in the major metropolitan areas are likely to rise even higher in the near future. Although China has an abundance of cheap, unskilled labor, Daniel H. Rosen has observed that in major urban areas, "labor costs have skyrocketed (especially for skilled and semiskilled workers), the relative size of the talent pool has dwindled as demand has grown, and competition among [foreign-invested enterprises] for competent English-speaking accountants, finance directors, marketing managers, and the like is fierce." Rosen's research reveals that although wage increases have abated somewhat from their 1996 highs, increases for local managers in the major cities of Beijing, Shanghai, Guangzhou, and Tianjin continue to average between 16 percent and 12 percent per year.[2] In short, although the available data are incomplete and imperfect, there can be no doubt that foreign companies in China are helping to create a significant wealth effect among their workers—especially among those with technical, managerial, and language skills.

Statistics don't tell the full story of how multinational firms have materially enriched the lives of ordinary Chinese citizens. People who have visited China over a period of decades marvel at the positive changes economic development has brought to the lives of hundreds of millions of Chinese citizens. The opportunity to wear stylish clothes; to own a washing machine, refrigerator, and television set; or to go out to a good restaurant has dramatically changed the lives of ordinary people. Beyond any doubt, the economic activities of multinational firms have been an extremely important element of this transformation.

"Very nice," the human rights advocate might say of the new prosperity in China, "but what has all this to do with human rights and democracy?" Is prosperity being chosen over liberty? By choosing to engage China and contribute to its economic upswing, are we at the same time abandoning hopes of influencing China to become more democratic and to improve its human rights record? Worse yet—are we contributing to the economic power of a corrupt authoritarian regime? Such insinuations are based on the mistaken presumption that fueling China's prosperity has no positive political consequences. Contributing to the misunderstanding is the even more insidious notion that prosperity in China must come at the cost of political repression.[3] In fact, research shows that the relationship between prosperity and democracy is a positive one in that economic prosperity is a necessary precondition for stable democracy. Thus, by contributing to China's economic rise, multinational firms are not only materially enriching themselves and ordinary Chinese citizens, they are in the process laying the groundwork for democratic rights to prosper.

A certain level of national economic performance vastly increases the chances that democracy will flourish. The Yale political scientist Seymour Martin Lipset is credited with the modern articulation of this idea, which has been around in various forms since antiquity. As Lipset writes, "from Aristotle down to the present, men have argued that only in a wealthy society in which relatively few citizens lived in real poverty could a situation exist in which the mass of the population could intelligently participate in politics and could develop the self-restraint necessary to resist the appeals of irresponsible demagogues."[4]

Political scientists and economists have confirmed the "Lipset thesis" in various empirical studies. Political scientist Adam Przeworski reports that among the thirty-three democracies that have attained per capita income of US$4,000, in only two cases—Argentina and Uruguay—was the democratic regime subverted.[5] The economist Robert Barro also concludes that "increases in various measures of the standard of living tend to generate a gradual rise in democracy. In contrast, democracies that arise without prior economic development . . . tend not to last."[6] There are exceptions—most notably India—but economic prosperity generally is a precondition for a strong democracy.

Although serious and widespread poverty still exists in China, particularly in rural areas, average per capita annual income has reached $2,750 in terms of purchasing-power parity, making China "middle income," according to the World Bank,[7] and it is fast approaching levels that would sustain democracy. By lifting the wages of Chinese citizens, multinational firms thus help to build a strong foundation for democracy. Economic prosperity is good for its own sake, but it is also a key factor in sustaining democratic rights. As they contribute to China's prosperity, therefore, multinational firms are acting, however inadvertently, as agents of democratization.

THE NEW "MERITOCRACY CADRE"

Multinational corporations are not only creating individual prosperity in China. More important, they are doing so in the private sector according to private-sector rules. By hiring, firing, and promoting on the basis of merit, multinational corporations have two kinds of impacts on Chinese society. First, they are changing the mindset of their workers, who are learning that individual worth and talent matter. Second, this emphasis on individual worth is helping to create a well-heeled and highly-educated social class in China with power and interests separate and distinct from those of the state. Although at the moment it is a relatively small and fragmented group, this new meritocracy could someday pose a threat to the authoritarian rule of the Communist Party.

For decades, the traditional path to power and wealth in China has been to join the Communist Party, to work for an SOE, and to establish good relations with superiors. Being well-connected to the party and *literally* knowing and professing the "party line" on various issues has been the most important key to career success. Multinational firms are helping to break down this equation in dramatic ways. They are helping to create a whole new "meritocracy cadre" of Chinese citizens who are acquiring wealth, status, and power through individual merit and hard work rather than through connections to the state and the party.

The tremendous opportunities available in foreign joint ventures have caused a sea change in the ambitions and career paths of university graduates. In contemporary China, the M.B.A. has replaced party membership as the blue-chip credential of choice for upwardly mobile young men and women. Moreover, the emphasis that foreign companies place on technical qualifications and merit has brought a new dignity and sense of self-worth to many Chinese workers. As an American manufacturing executive puts it: "Working for a foreign company is a major change for the Chinese individual. You are respected as an individual and a human being."[8] The emphasis on merit has also freed Chinese workers from espousing political views to improve their job prospects. One Shanghai-based executive who has been doing business in China for more than a decade explains that "foreign companies put a premium on talent as opposed to what you think politically."[9]

Foreign companies make a positive contribution to human rights and democratization simply by hiring and promoting on the basis of merit. In China, the best jobs traditionally have gone to those with the best connections, or *guanxi*. "Lily," a Chinese woman working for an American investment bank in Shanghai, exemplifies the plight of young workers in this system. "When I graduated from university," Lily confides, "I would have liked to work for a Chinese commercial bank. The pay is good, and it is a very prestigious job. My parents, though, didn't have powerful connections."[10]

There is a sense of injustice as Lily reflects on less-talented schoolmates who landed plum jobs because of their parents' *guanxi*. However, the injustice is accompanied by an equally strong sense of relief. Lily says she feels fortunate that, unlike her parents, who work for an SOE, she will receive salary increases and promotions based on her abilities, rather than on how well she gets along with her boss. Lily recalls with sadness how as she was growing up her whole family's life was turned upside down when her parents were getting along especially badly with the head of their work unit. (Though she adds with puckish humor, "I understand that good relations with your boss can be a little important in America, too.")[11]

Workers inside SOEs confirm Lily's account of the arbitrary and political factors that go into promotions and raises. "Dong," a veteran of China's SOEs, attests to the traditionally politicized nature of promotion in most SOEs: "In the traditional Chinese SOE, you are always a small potato no matter what you do. If you work harder, do a good job or what not, there is no extra bonus, no wage increase, and no promotion."[12] Another veteran worker, "Chen," works in a state-owned insurance company and says the situation has worsened since the late 1980s, when the government began allowing SOEs to go bankrupt. He says that mass bankruptcies cut loose a large number of middle-aged Communist Party members who have flooded the management positions of existing Chinese enterprises and, by doing so, eliminated any hope of upward mobility for younger Chinese workers with no party affiliation. "A lot of the young guys like me did our work very well," Chen says, "but the bosses thought we were too young for promotions. And anyway, there were no spots up top. All the top-level positions had been taken by middle-aged managers who joined our company in the late 1980s when their own SOEs closed down. Many of them didn't have any ideas about insurance, but they were given management positions because of their age and because they were Communist Party members."[13]

Dong maintains that, even in contemporary China, it is still party membership that wins promotions in the Chinese SOE. He says that with party affiliation, "you can do poorly and not lose your job. You can even lose clients and work carelessly and you won't be punished or demoted." "Louisa," an extremely sharp young woman in Shanghai who graduated from one of China's most prestigious universities, adds that promotion on the basis of connections rather than merit starts early on: "I was a member of the college class that began in 1991. This was the first class after Tiananmen, and they took all incoming freshmen and sent us to a military school for brainwashing for a year before we started our formal undergraduate studies. When I was in military academy, you needed to have good relations with the officers. They didn't evaluate you based on performance; rather their evaluations were based on their subjective sense as to what kind of person you are. This meant that you needed to spend a lot of time endearing yourself to them. It wasn't good enough to do well; if you did well and didn't flatter them then you still didn't do well. For example, at the academy there was a college scholarship that was supposed to go to the best three students. It was supposed to be based on academic performance. I was the in the top three in my class but the people who got the scholarship were all party members and student leaders selected by the teaching staff. Their grades were poor to mediocre but they flattered the right people. . . . This is what happens in many Chinese companies."[14]

Louisa hastens to add: "I think it's very natural to do *some* politicking. Everyone wants compliments. I think it's normal to flatter people. For instance, my boss just got a promotion, and I sent him an e-mail congratulating him. I think I was sincere in doing this. But at the military academy there was a group of students who went to our superiors' homes to clean their windows. All the superstars at the academy did this regularly. So, yeah, at my company, we flatter our bosses as well, but it's less contrived. I would be ashamed to get a promotion because I washed the windows of my boss, and that's what happens at Chinese SOEs, not just the military academy."

For well-educated Chinese workers, the option of working for a multinational may even embolden them to pay less attention to political connections in their schooling than they otherwise might. Louisa describes how she came to be recruited on campus by an American consulting firm: "There are two sides of every university in China. There are the professors and academic staff and then there's the administrative staff. It is very important to get along with the administrative staff, because they determine what jobs you will get when you graduate. . . . That's especially true with placements for Chinese companies because all the Chinese companies simply ask for referrals each year from the administrative office. Now, I never made it a point to be the administrator's good girl, in fact I never got along with them so well, so I knew they would never appoint me to a good Chinese company. My only choice was a foreign one. . . . Simply knowing I would have that opportunity to find a job with a 'politically insensitive' multinational helped me to act more like an individual in college. Indeed, when the foreign companies came to recruit students on campus, I made sure to interview with them and ended up getting my present job."

A slightly different view is expressed by the SOE veteran Dong, a cigar-chomping man favoring suspenders and bright ties who is given to enthusiastic outbursts of nationalistic pride. He believes that the best opportunities for Chinese workers are in Chinese companies that have adopted some of the characteristics of western companies. Dong offers that "Chinese prefer to relate with Chinese rather than foreigners because foreigners are foreigners. If you are in a foreign company, the boss will never regard you as part of the company's society. Have you ever seen any Chinese in a really senior position in a foreign company? Of course not. All of my experience tells me that foreign people don't really believe in domestic Chinese. Most of my friends who work for foreign companies believe this way. They believe if you are really going to work hard, it's best to work in a Chinese company, not a foreign company. In a foreign company you will always be a foreigner. Of course, many Chinese want to work in foreign companies because they can learn Western management and technical skills. They do this until they have learned these skills, and then they try finding a position in a Chinese company as their final destination. In my current SOE, the managers are very progressive-thinking, in part because they all spent many years working for American companies."

Notwithstanding Dong's optimistic view of his own firm, personnel decisions in SOEs continue to be dominated by Communist Party members who are as interested in political correctness as in skill and talent. The human resources departments of SOEs are one of the means by which the Communist Party exercises control over the lives of Chinese citizens. Political dissidents are often punished for their views by being fired from their jobs. Others whose political views are suspect don't receive promotions they might otherwise deserve. SOEs maintain a *dang an* for each employee. The *dang an* is a dossier file that contains both work-related and personal information. Daniel H. Rosen writes that the *dang an* is "established as early as primary school and maintained by employers thereafter. It tracks an individual's political and professional record, from academic grades to performance reports, from problems with authorities to marriage and child bearing. This dossier is an essential record needed before an employer can hire or provide pension or insurance benefits for the individual."[15]

Western human resources professionals who have worked on personnel issues in joint ventures with SOEs report that their Chinese counterparts have very little professional training.[16] Since the onset of economic reform, many Chinese SOEs have begun to attempt to incorporate Western management techniques. Some Chinese universities are moving to fill the need for professional human resources managers. Ira Cohen of UI China Training Services reported in 1999 that "there are now less than half a dozen reputable universities—including Beijing University ('Beida'), Nankai University-Tianjin, and the University of International Business and Economics—offering a variety of courses on Western HR [human resources] practices. Motorola has sponsored an HR-focused M.B.A. with Nankai and Beida. The entire HR function has been under review in the SOEs for the past few years. The focus was on retraining of the workforce and instituting promotions based on professional criteria versus the traditional relationship concepts. Since the restructuring of government entities and SOEs, the closure of failing enterprises, and the drastic reduction in ministry personnel, the HR functions are making some movement toward more professional practices. They still, however, have a long way to go."[17]

For the SOE that is looking to meet foreign competition by beefing up its training in Western management practices, communist propaganda and capitalist ideology can find themselves at cross-purposes. This became comically poignant to an American professor teaching an M.B.A. business course to mid-level executives in an SOE. She was startled one day to hear loud chanting and applause from a classroom next door. When she inquired about the source of the noise, a student told the business school professor that it was a Communist Party training program for the company's human resources professionals. Later, one student expressed a sense of superiority and distaste for the comparatively brief and highly political training being conducted for the human resources managers. The same teacher reported being mystified one day when many of the students in her class were handed a piece of paper that they all carefully put away. When she inquired, she was told that they were certificates of good standing with the Communist Party and that about 80 percent of the students in her class were members. It seemed, she thought, that her M.B.A. students were hedging their bets on the best way to advance within the company![18]

Beyond the humor of these stories is a more fundamental issue involving the incompatibility of professional ideas about merit-based hiring and promotion with Communist Party control techniques that use job actions as a means of social control. If, to become more competitive with foreign-owned enterprises, the SOEs adopt more professional human resources practices that are focused more on merit than on political correctness, it would represent a significant loss of control for the Communist Party and another step in the direction of democratic reform. There is, in fact, evidence that SOEs are changing many of their business practices in response to Western competition.[19] In his research on SOEs in the Shanghai area, for example, Doug Guthrie found that with respect to commercial relations between companies, "the growing importance of price, quality, and service is rendering *guanxi* unimportant."[20] It is hard to imagine, however, that SOEs will stop altogether the use of political correctness as a significant criteria for hiring and promotion. Personnel practices are simply too important as instruments of social control. The conundrum facing the Communist Party is that if SOEs don't change their personnel practices, then company performance is bound to suffer and talented employees are bound to become disgruntled, particularly when they see their friends and counterparts in foreign-owned companies achieving success on the basis of their talents. Internal power struggles between traditional Communist Party managers and Western-trained managers seeking to professionalize SOEs are also likely. In either case, the idea and practice of merit-based hiring by foreign-owned companies in China represents a radical challenge to the power of the Communist Party, a challenge for which there are no simple answers. Merit-based hiring and firing are not ideas that can be easily assimilated into Communist Party thinking. The standard personnel practices of Western companies are fundamentally antithetical to Communist Party ideology and practices. Therefore, such practices will always remain a radical threat to the Party's control, either from outside or within the SOE structure.

For SOEs, hiring on the basis of merit presents a difficult choice between economic and political viability. Foreign firms, however, which must answer to the bottom line, simply cannot afford the politically based, personal, and sometimes abusive management style that prevails in SOEs. To be sure, even in the West, being connected and well-born gives you a substantial leg up. But Western firms must answer to the discipline of the market—if they don't hire, pay, and promote for performance, and if they don't manage employees in a professional and respectful manner, they will lose their most talented employees and eventually go out of business. Enlightened firms looking for long-term success in China must play by the same rules. The result is a positive spin-off effect for human rights. By following professional, up-to-date personnel practices in China, multinational firms foster the radical notion that individual merit matters and should be rewarded. This sense of the worth of the individual and the accompanying idea of procedural fairness are essential characteristics of a culture that respects human

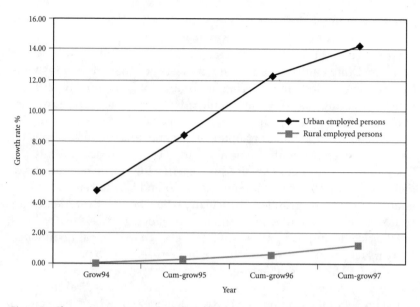

Figure 4.1 Change in percentage of urban/rural employment in China, 1994–97. Growth rate percentage is the value of cumulative percentage starting from 1994. (Data from *China Statistical Yearbook*, China Statistical Bureau, 1998.)

rights. Thus, by managing the personnel policies of their organizations effectively and efficiently, multinational corporations help to promote values that underpin human rights.

Through their meritocratic hiring and promotion practices, multinational corporations in China also are helping to create a middle class with power and interests independent of the state. As foreign companies rapidly move to localize their workforce and put Chinese managers in charge of their operations, they are contributing to the creation of a social class of white-collar and technical workers who have achieved their position through hard work and talent. This class also includes China's new entrepreneurs—men and women who have tossed aside the bland security of working for state-owned enterprises in favor of striking out on their own. Although the number of Chinese citizens who are working in foreign owned enterprises and as entrepreneurs is still relatively small, these are by far the fastest-growing sectors of the Chinese economy.

This "meritocracy cadre" is rapidly becoming a force to be reckoned with. In fact, if the demographic trends of the 1990s continue for the next two decades (admittedly a heroic assumption, but worth pondering

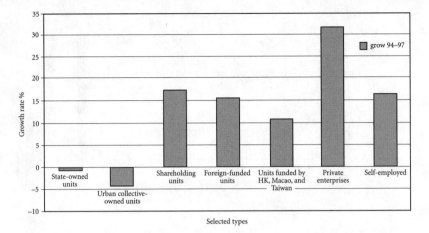

Figure 4.2 Rates of change in various types of urban employment in China between 1994 and 1997. Growth rate percentage for each type of urban employment is the average of three years' growth: 1994–95, 1995–96, and 1996–97. HK, Hong Kong. (Data from *China Statistical Yearbook*, China Statistical Bureau, 1998.)

nonetheless), most of the urban workers in China will be either self-employed or working for locally owned and operated private enterprises.[21] (A related overall trend is the rate of urbanization of Chinese workers [Figure 4.1].) By contrast, employment in SOEs and collective-owned enterprises will decline. China's economy and society are, in other words, changing dramatically. Although foreign-owned enterprises make up only a small statistical element of this change, they are an important source of ideas for the new social classes likely to emerge from this period of rapid change (Figures 4.2 and 4.3). Even if, for a variety of possible reasons, the rate of change in urban employment patterns is not as rapid as projected in Figure 4.3, a sizable class of urban private-sector workers will emerge in China. No one can predict the precise effects of such a large and well-heeled social class on the dynamics of Chinese society and politics, but it is very likely to be destabilizing.

Although traditional communist ideology regards capitalists as "despicable" creatures, a 1999 amendment to the Chinese Constitution concedes that private business is "an important component of the socialist market economy." As one successful Chinese entrepreneur observes, however, "There's a tension here between ideology and reality in our changing society."[22] A time will come in China when the self-made men and women who have risen as entrepreneurs and employees in foreign-based corpo-

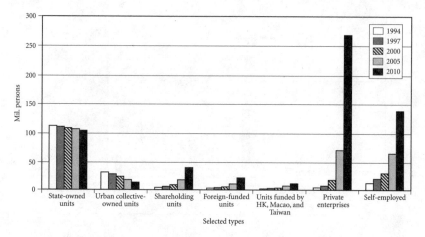

Figure 4.3 Projected changes in various types of urban employment in China, 1994–2010. The values for year 2000, 2005, and 2010 are author's projections, based on the assumption that the growth rate of the previous three years (1994 through 1997) continues. HK, Hong Kong. (Data from *China Statistical Yearbook*, China Statistical Bureau, 1998.)

rations will occupy social and political space uneasily with the managers of SOEs who have acquired their positions through the old *guanxi* system. These self-made men and women are likely to have little patience for the shortcomings of those who have achieved material well-being and power by demonstrating loyalty to the Communist Party line rather than by dint of their talent. By providing an alternative avenue for social and economic mobility, multinational corporations in China are helping to create a middle class with interests and ideas that are quite distinct from those of the Chinese state. Ironically, the Communist Party accentuates this sharp divide in circumstances and attitudes by prohibiting private businesspeople from even applying for membership in the Party.[23]

It is not, however, only the idea of merit that is being instilled into workers at foreign companies. The management toolkit of the modern multinational firm is loaded with other radical—radical for China, that is—values and perspectives that are bound to spill over into the society at large.

CHANGING STYLES OF LEADERSHIP AND OPENNESS TO CHANGE

Multinational corporations are helping to redefine power relationships within China. Many aspects of their management styles are inherently radical influences in the context of traditional Chinese culture. The pioneering Dutch scholar Geert Hofstede has observed that the power relationships that characterize any culture tend to be congruent—that is, the same pattern is found between parent and child, teacher and student, boss and subordinate, and political leader and citizen.[24] In the traditional Chinese Confucian pattern, the good subordinate obeys and respects the boss. The boss gives orders and makes decisions. The good boss, in turn, looks after the subordinate. In contrast, more conversation, conflict, and shared decision making exists between boss and subordinate in the Western style of management. Thus, when multinational corporations inculcate Western ideas about power relationships in their workers, they are doing more than accomplishing business objectives. They are, in the process, injecting radical new ideas about power relationships into Chinese society that can help to foster a political culture in which democracy can thrive.

Chinese workers in foreign companies learn that a subordinate may exercise initiative and take responsibility. As one human resources director said, "foreign companies are teaching that work is the mutual responsibility of every person. Don't say 'it's not my job.' "[25] A young woman working for a European company in Shanghai observed that "We learn . . . to speak out and say what we think."[26]

Multinational corporations don't view the need to increase initiative among their workers as a cultural or political matter. They see it as a matter of economic survival. Foreign companies teach that it is everyone's responsibility to do something about a problem, or at least to bring a problem to the attention of a manager. Western corporations well understand that unless their workers learn to take individual responsibility, their businesses will not be successful. An American manufacturing executive observes that "a person working in an SOE doesn't care if something goes wrong. He will walk past smoke in a plant."[27]

German-based chemical giant BASF, which employs more than two thousand people in China, has set up a Management Development Center at Shanghai's elite Jiao Tong University. Seeking, among other things, to teach "leadership and communication," the BASF program calls for its local executives to "share their thoughts, insights, and experiences in a distinctly proactive way."[28] This emphasis on leadership and proactive communication is in marked contrast to the management style prevailing in SOEs, where, as the old Chinese proverb goes, "the nail that sticks up will be hammered down." To be sure, companies such as BASF are out to develop business, not political, leadership, but it would not be too surprising to discover that one day a successful private businessperson—perhaps one with extensive exposure to Western management practices—will emerge in China with quite radical ideas about how to exercise political power.

Working in foreign companies, Chinese workers are learning a style of management that is very different from that in SOEs. A human resources administrator for a U.S. company says that they are learning "how to supervise and still respect the dignity and esteem of subordinates."[29] One Chinese manager said that a big part of making the transition from an SOE to an American company was the "need to think more about how to get the most out of the people who work for you."[30]

As the Tiananmen Square events of 1989 dramatically demonstrated, Chinese citizens, particularly young students, have from time to time challenged authority. Still, the dominant pattern of power relationships in China has been one with great distance between leader and subordinate. To introduce a competing cultural pattern in their operations, foreign companies thus have had to undertake a deliberate cultural reeducation of their workers. Given this need to change leadership values, it is no surprise that foreign companies have a strong preference for younger workers in China. To be sure, younger workers—those in their twenties and thirties—possess educational backgrounds and foreign language skills (particularly English) superior to those of their older, "lost generation" counterparts in their forties and fifties, who are suffering the consequences of the dismantling of the higher education system during the Cultural Revolution. But there is a much more important consideration behind the preference for younger workers—their willingness and ability to change how they think, something that is hard for older workers to learn. For foreign managers, change, responsiveness to the market, and continual innovation have become a way of life in competitive markets. The need to change quickly to survive is as real in China as it is in the United States or Europe. One French manager of a multinational public relations firm observes, "Shanghai changes every day. There is more and more competition. The challenges change every day."[31]

To succeed in a foreign company, Chinese workers have to learn how to change. Time after time, when young people are asked about the key to succeeding in a foreign company, they reply "attitude"—the willingness to learn how to do things differently. One young woman said that foreign companies require you to "take full responsibility" and "think differently." Ultimately, the most radical notion foreign corporations introduce in China may be the importance of change itself.

If Chinese bosses, according to Confucian ideals, are supposed to follow the model of a good father or philosopher king, this is hardly the role that is emphasized in the everyday affairs of SOEs. Rather, the overriding characteristic of employee-employer relations in Chinese enterprises is mute obedience on the part of the employee. Dong reports that, in his first SOE, young employees never ventured to share opinions or speak freely with their superiors. "In my old SOE, the boss was the boss. You don't correct him. Even if he does something that is really wrong, you can't say it . . . because if you do, your boss will find ways to punish you, like demotions or public humiliation."

Chen offers a similar description: "In my first job with an SOE you couldn't criticize bosses at all. Once, when my colleague offended someone in power, the boss called a public meeting to criticize him in front of one hundred people. He was punished in front of over one hundred of his colleagues. . . . At the end, each of us was supposed to comment on the meeting and I said that I didn't think it was appropriate to criticize my colleague. At the time, the boss just smiled and said thank you for your comment. But everyone was afraid for me, and sure enough I was demoted soon afterwards. I had been working in marketing and was demoted to room checking brigade. My job was to go from one house to another and make sure everything was in order before tenants moved in."

Louisa also notes that female workers are expected to maintain their mute obedience even when confronted with unwelcome sexual advances. In the week she was interviewed, Louisa reported that two of her female friends needed to deal gingerly with their bosses' sexual advances for fear of losing jobs. Another woman, "Milly," attests to the prevalence of sexual harassment in SOEs. In fact, she says that such situations are so common that they have served as a special motivator for many of her female friends to seek jobs with American companies. She says, "In Chinese . . . firms, the boss can do and say what he likes. He doesn't care if his advances are unwanted because he's the boss. In an American firm, I feel well protected from that. I know my rights."[32]

Foreign companies, particularly American companies, are helping to break down the distance between boss and subordinate in everyday settings. "You cannot help but have an impact on the people that you are working with," explained an American diplomat in Beijing. "It happens every day. Chinese workers learn in a team meeting that someone younger can tell their boss they are wrong. Every time we have a staff meeting, the point is made. We don't have to make the point. The point is made in action."[33] Chinese employees for foreign companies enthusiastically attest to this. As Louisa notes: "Relationships between colleagues and bosses are much better in American companies. Here, I can really open up and act on my opinions. The open environment allows me to be creative and work according to my instincts."

Louisa says that, unlike in a Chinese SOE, she feels perfectly comfortable disagreeing with her American boss. "Right now, my boss is driving me crazy these days, but I can tell her she's driving me crazy. I can also tell her she doesn't make any sense when she's wrong about things. This is because the environment in American companies is more open. You make friends with your bosses; you don't simply fear them. Everyone is equal."

Ironically, Louisa believes that in some ways the open environments created in Western companies don't equip their Chinese employees to deal with the hard realities of the world outside their office door. As Louisa puts it, "if anything, there is too little politics in this firm. In the senior management of my state-owned clients, there is a lot of heavy-handed politics, and I feel in a certain way I really need to be exposed to this if I am going to do well in the outside world or in a Chinese company. In some sense, my friends who work in Chinese companies think I am naïve. They say I feel like good work will be rewarded and that my job hasn't prepared me for the soft side of human relations—manipulation or even motivational skills. What they mean is that I won't know how to motivate people when they are not willing to do the work. In a Western firm, we don't have this problem—everyone is hard working."

One U.S.-based company with more than two thousand workers in Asia puts each employee through a training program coordinated from Hong Kong but conducted by local trainers in the local language. Because it is in the manufacturing sector, the company places primary emphasis on technical skills and safety, but the training also teaches the importance of innovation and change. These are not values likely to be learned in the typical SOE. Listening to the company's regional director of training and education explain the training program, one can grasp right away how the training can have a political dimension: "We change a lot and we change very quickly. We don't do things the same every time. We improve. We bring people in and out on assignments. We're not focused on the past. We value open and direct communication."[34] This company is, of course, interested in profits, not politics, but receptivity to change is an idea that can't be confined to the workplace. As workers in foreign companies assimilate such values, they are bound to spill over into the broader society.

Multinational firms also promote human rights and democratization by stressing the importance of information sharing and teamwork. Corporations encourage such behaviors because they are essential to optimal decision making and operational effectiveness, but teamwork and information sharing are hard to confine to the workplace. By teaching the importance of these ideas in a corporate context, foreign corporations in China are helping to put in place values and practices that in the long run can help to promote human rights and sustain democracy.

The modern corporation thrives on the free flow of information up, down, and across organizational structures. In addition to sharing information freely, workers in the modern corporation must work cooperatively to solve complex problems in teams drawn from diverse parts of organizations. Companies that hope to maximize their profits must design their organizations and train their workers to share information and work together in teams. One of the prime reasons for the resurgence of American business in the 1990s was the massive investment that companies made in information technology, including telecommunications equipment and computer hardware and software. Among other things, this investment in technology has made possible the sharing of information among workers within an organization and with other organizations. The emergence of the Internet and of various business models of "e-commerce" have accelerated this trend. As a result of this technological quantum leap, the ante has risen sharply for companies that want to compete in the global economy. Sharing information throughout an entire network of organizations has become an indispensable key to survival. This is as true in Shanghai and Chengdu as it is in New York and Peoria. In China, however, the notion of speedy and open access to information is a radical concept that poses a threat to the power of the Communist Party, which throughout the history of modern China has maintained social control by controlling information.

Ironically, when it comes to learning about cooperation and teamwork, a kind of Asian boomerang effect is at work. The emphasis on teamwork in Western firms is a relatively recent development in management theory. After the ascendancy of Japanese companies in the 1970s, Western companies reinvented themselves to meet the competition. One thing that Western companies learned from Japanese firms was the importance of teamwork. American firms, in particular, have worked quite deliberately to break down bureaucratic, hierarchical management structures and replace them with fluid, horizontal team structures. For individualistic Americans, this new style of working together did not come as naturally as it did for Japanese workers, who are part of a more collectivist, cooperative culture.

Now it is Western companies that are attempting to teach their Asian workers in China about teamwork and cooperation. At first blush, this might seem like a preposterous notion. But it is a very real phenomenon. Western companies are spending tens of millions of dollars on training programs for Chinese workers, and one of the biggest items on the training agenda is teamwork. It would hardly seem possible that Chinese workers are not team-oriented in a work context. Chinese culture, after all, is highly collectivist. However, this collectivism does not automatically translate into cooperation, especially interdepartmental cooperation in the workplace. The management scholar Chao Chen attributes this paradox to factors such as *guanxi*, particularism, factionalism, and familism. Chen believes that Chinese people can be highly loyal and cooperative, but only with people with whom they have a relationship and whom they trust, the so-called "in-group members."[35]

One Western manager believes that there are other deep-rooted impediments to getting her staff to work as a team. "We have a phenomenon developing in China called the 'only child phenomenon.' It's going to have an incredible effect on the Chinese social structure. On the surface, these only children are smart and outgoing. If they are shy by nature, an only child is going to be more outgoing than a third or fourth child, who is shy but is protected by older brothers and sisters. However they want to be independent. And it is difficult to teach them that you can't be independent in a company—you are part of a team."[36]

For Western companies, it is critical that Chinese workers learn to practice teamwork and share information on the job. Wall's, the ice cream subsidiary of U.K.-based Unilever, offers a good example of how teamwork affects the bottom line. Wall's general manager for China, Duncan Garood, is a businessman concerned about market share and profits, not politics. Shortly after taking over his assignment, Garood dispatched a cross-functional team to cut the costs of a particular product whose costs, he thought, were getting out of line. He was rewarded with a 10 percent cost reduction without loss of quality.[37]

To accomplish Garood's assignment, Wall's workers had to work together, share information, and think creatively about re-engineering a product. These are the trendiest ideas in modern management science.

Any firm not practicing them is unlikely to be competitive for very long. Information sharing and teamwork are also, however, the hallmarks of a healthy democracy. In his study of Italian regional government, the political scientist Robert Putnam found that trust, cooperation, and civic and community associations all contribute to effective and sustainable democratic institutions.[38] Only after opinions and facts have been aired and considered can a democratic people effectively deliberate about public issues. The right to free speech and the right of the press to publish freely are essential enablers of public deliberation. Without these rights, the information flow in a society is stunted and democracy cannot work. In the same way that information sharing is essential to good decision making and operational effectiveness in a corporation, free speech is essential to good decision making in a democracy. It is hard to imagine that ideas about the importance of information flow can be confined to corporate life. Inevitably, those who work in foreign corporations will wonder why their government restricts the flow of information.

Teamwork and information sharing are common areas of emphasis for foreign companies operating in China. When an expensive piece of machinery was delivered to Motorola's cellular telephone manufacturing facility in Tianjin, it immediately began malfunctioning. No one could understand why. A cross-functional team was formed from the manufacturing and engineering departments. Some members of the team were sent to Austin, Texas, to confer with Motorola personnel there. The group achieved an outstanding result that led to the adoption of modifications on the machine throughout Motorola's worldwide manufacturing facilities. One Chinese worker summed up what he learned from the experience: "One person cannot solve all the problems."[39]

Enlightened companies such as Edelman are helping to create a new class of communications professionals in China. In 1990, Edelman general manager Jean-Michel Dumont, a Frenchman who speaks English as effortlessly as he does Mandarin, managed the first communications joint venture to open in Shanghai. "The media did not even know what a press kit was. We had to devise new ways of communicating in a new environment." Edelman's office is organized around four groups, but Dumont insists that the teams cooperate with each other. In addition to learning to work in different styles, the cross-functionality encourages them to share information about media suppliers and contacts. Dumont says, "In the communication field, you need to work as a team and share information."[40]

The efforts of multinational corporations to increase the flow of information in their corporate offices complement other trends that lead to greater flow of information. Although official news outlets are still tightly controlled, the proliferation of private publications, the fax machine, the Internet, and foreign travel have all made it more and more difficult to control the flow of information within China. It is estimated that more than 3 million people in China have access to the Internet. Not only is it getting harder to control the free flow of information in China, it is getting harder to suppress the idea that the free flow of information is good for society. Already, for example, Internet chat rooms have become hotbeds of political debate. One Western diplomat observed that "the outspokenness of the people posting these messages is startling. No topic seems to be taboo."[41]

The impact of foreign companies on information flow within Chinese society is not limited to office policies and practices. Foreign companies need to operate in a legally transparent environment. To operate effectively, they must understand and have confidence in the fair enforcement of rules about property rights and other regulatory concerns. In many developing countries such as China, however, such rules are often unpublished and arbitrarily administered. In China, the foreign business community has been successful in persuading the government to agree to publish laws and administrative regulations that pertain to business activity.

Multinational corporations in China are promoting the rule of law in other ways. Chinese businesspeople are learning that to do business with Westerners, they must operate within the confines of law. As one U.S. businessman stated, "Chinese businesspeople are learning how to sell to people who will insist on doing business in a certain way, for example, letters of credit. Commerce has a common language. It was new to the Chinese, but they are educating themselves quickly."[42] Some of the most tragic events in Chinese history have been fueled by the tight strictures on the flow of reliable information. In the late 1950s, during the Great Leap Forward, for example, gross overestimates of agricultural production were not corrected for three years, during which time between 20 and 30 million people died. In contemporary China, however, the flow of information is much freer, thanks in part to the influence of foreign corporations. If China is to progress as a nation and avoid such catastrophes in the future, the current trend of easing information flow must continue. Through their training programs and office practices, multinational corporations are contributing to this trend in a small but important way.

The forces being unleashed by foreign businesses in China complement other trends in contemporary China. In addition to those whose prospects have risen while working for foreign companies, other groups that have emerged from China's economic reforms include rich peasants, entrepreneurs, and professionals. These developments are positive steps toward democratization and progress in human rights. But where, exactly, are these steps heading? Are they leading to the emergence of the kind of pluralism and civil society that led to the downfall of communism in Eastern Europe? This is hard to predict.

Pluralism and civil society are characterized by a multiplicity of overlapping, competing intermediary organizations representing the interests of their social constituencies and acting autonomously of each other and the state.[43] In the former Soviet bloc, the emergence of a civil society and organizations such as trade unions proved to be the bulwark of change and, ultimately, revolution. The Chinese leadership is well aware of this phenomenon. Former premier Li Peng is said to have commented at the height of the Tiananmen Square uprising in 1989 that "if we recognize the College Students Autonomous Federation just because the students insist on it, then we will be most likely to recognize a solidarity trade union if the workers insist on their demands, won't we?"[44]

As Li Peng's sarcastic comment reveals, the leaders of the Communist Party in China understand the threat posed to them by an emerging civil society with interests and bases of power distinct from those of the state. For some of the hard-line elements within the Party, this threat is perceived to be great enough to call into question the whole process of reform in China.

The Chinese leadership is determined not to make the same mistakes as its now-defunct Eastern European counterparts. They want economic reform, but they don't want to lose power. The traditional means that the Communist Party has used to control the population are losing force. As many have observed, Chinese citizens have more personal freedom than ever before. Many workers in SOEs are quitting their jobs—including the subsidized housing, medical care, schooling, and social security benefits that go along with those jobs—to become entrepreneurs or to work for foreign companies. Peasants are leaving the countryside to find better-paying jobs in cities. The Communist Party has not, however, permitted this new occupational and geographical mobility to be accompanied by the emergence of independent representative organizations.

On the contrary, the government continues to restrict and keep close tabs on autonomous organizations. Gordon White reports that by late 1993, although there were more than 1,460 national social organizations, 19,600 at the provincial level, and more than 160,000 at the county level, the independence of these organizations was undercut by "not only the need for each social organization to obtain formal approval by registering with the appropriate Department of Civil Affairs, but also the requirement to 'link up' . . . with a specific government agency which acted as its 'superior department' or official sponsor." White also reports that more than thirteen hundred such organizations have been banned in China.[45] His assessment of the ultimate impact of China's policy of incorporating and repressing independent social organizations is a bleak one: "As pressures from below have mounted yet not found adequate channels for expression, and the tension between state and society has increased in consequence, the force of incipient civil society has increasingly taken on the form of spontaneous and sporadic bursts of activity—demonstrations, riots, protests, sit-ins, beatings, and fights—in both urban and rural areas. This can itself be seen as an index of the lack of a fully institutionalized civil society in which organizations have the ability not merely to form and operate autonomously within an orderly regulatory framework, but also have the legally guaranteed right to represent the interests and concerns of their constituencies to the authorities. The image of a boiler building up a dangerous level of steam pressure is an apt one."[46]

The volatile forces White describes can most readily be found in the increasing numbers of unemployed workers in China. The Chinese Academy of Sciences estimates that urban unemployment in China has reached more than 16 million. The numbers are swelling as millions more are laid off from SOEs restructuring to become more efficient and meet foreign competition. Added into this mix are tens of millions—the "floating population"—of displaced farmers who have migrated to the cities in search of jobs. These desperate workers can be seen huddled hundreds deep with their belongings around the train stations of China's major cities. So far, there have been only scattered reports of violence among these workers. The Chinese government has tried to quell discontent by dispensing emergency aid and arresting the most vocal labor leaders, but the potential for violent upheaval is real. Apo Leung, director of Hong Kong's Asia Monitor Centre, which studies labor issues, reports that "we're sitting on a volcano." Orville Schell has commented that "you get the feeling of some very flammable liquid just being dripped all around the place waiting for someone to light the match."[47]

At this stage in the country's history, it is unclear whether China will develop the kinds of pluralistic institutions that characterize civil society. What is clear, however, is that multinational corporations are making an important contribution toward that goal. The values and behaviors that workers are learning in foreign companies are helping to form the bedrock on which the institutions of civil society can be constructed. It is important to bear in mind, however, that foreigners will have a relatively minor role to play in the drama that is to come. Only the future will tell whether political developments within China will embrace or seek to reverse the radical ideas being let loose in multinational corporations.

FIVE CAVEATS

The case for the positive human rights role of foreign companies in China should not be overstated. At least five caveats should be kept in mind. First, as noted earlier, not every foreign company in China or elsewhere is a positive force for democracy and human rights. The Western and Chinese managers quoted in this chapter work for world-class companies that are market leaders in their respective fields. These companies are sending their best managers to China and using the most advanced management techniques. The positive spin-off effects of business activity on political and social change in China flow primarily from these kinds of companies that invest in their workers, pay them well, and treat them decently. In other words, although human rights spin-off is a byproduct of profit-seeking activities, it is by no means an inevitable byproduct of any and all profit-seeking activity. Companies that go to China only to find a cheap source of labor and achieve this goal by exploiting and mistreating their workers do not create human rights spin-off. They remain part of the human rights problem in China.

A second important caveat is that the phenomenon we have been discussing affects only a tiny fraction of Chinese citizens. Even after twenty years of economic reform and foreign investment, less than 1 percent of the Chinese labor force is employed in foreign-invested enterprises. It is important to emphasize, however, that foreign-invested enterprises, along with private companies, are the fastest-growing segments of Chinese society. In time, therefore, the impact of human rights spin-off will grow in importance. Moreover, although at the moment the number of workers exposed to these radical ideas constitutes only a tiny fraction of

Chinese society, the contributions of market leaders can have a significant ripple effect. As Ken Grant of Hong Kong–based Market Access noted, "Who's to say what the impact will be when a couple of guys are talking over beer after work and comparing their experiences of working in a state-owned company with those in a foreign company?"[48]

A third caveat is that, despite the substantial overlap and relationship between business and politics, they are still in many respects distinct spheres. As "Sophie", a highly sophisticated, European-educated native Chinese manager in Shanghai, sarcastically responded when asked whether she thought business was contributing to the democratization of China: "Does this mean that we will get to elect our general manager?"[49] The answer, of course, is no, but at least she will be able to leave her job if she is unhappy—something not possible before foreign companies arrived in China. As a Western human resources manager said, "Skills give you personal freedom. You can't choose who your boss is at work, but you can choose to leave."[50]

Sophie's point, although on the surface merely amusing, addresses a more serious concern about the human rights spin-off hypothesis. The common thread that holds politics and business together is culture. One way of thinking about the spin-off hypothesis is that business has an effect on certain cultural patterns—ideas about individualism and collectivism, styles of leadership—and this cultural change in turn has an effect on politics. But some might question whether cultural patterns that run so deep in a society and are learned at such a young age can be much undone by influences that come later in life in a localized context. Geert Hofstede, for example, has argued that "values are acquired in one's early youth, mainly in the family and the neighborhood, and later at school. By the time a child is ten years old, most of its basic values have been programmed in its mind. Organizational practices, on the other hand, are learned through socialization at the workplace, which most people enter as adults, that is, with the bulk of their values firmly in place."[51]

Societies, however, change. Political and cultural change tends to accompany economic change. Taiwan, a country that shares cultural traditions with China, offers an apt example of how even cultural patterns with long histories can change significantly over a relatively short period. Larry Diamond writes that "what is most striking about Taiwan is the generally steady increase since democratization began in the mid-1980s, in the proportions of the public expressing pro-democratic sentiment and rejecting the paternalistic, collectivist, illiberal norms associated with the 'Asian values' perspective. Between 1985 and 1991, support for authoritarian political norms declined, and on some measures the change was huge. . . . [H]istory and early socialization constitute a powerful determinant of culture. But they are not destiny."[52]

A fourth caveat is that one must be careful not to overstate the potential impact of foreigners on Chinese culture. As the example of Taiwan demonstrates, Chinese culture is capable of rapid change, but foreign business will be only a small part of this change, the bulk of which must come from elements within Chinese society. The siren call to change China is nothing new. The historian Jonathan Spence has sagely warned of the folly of Westerners who adopt a superior attitude toward China. Since the sixteenth century, Western advisors have traveled to China as advisors about a panoply of subjects. These advisors have typically betrayed a fatal Western bias about China. As Spence colorfully recounts, under the guise of advising about subjects such as astronomy, engineering, and military tactics—one might now add capitalism to that list—Western advisors came to regard their mission as being that of "civilizing" China.[53] In this respect, Westerners have been and will continue to be sorely disappointed.

Chinese culture has endured nearly a thousand years of Western influences and remained remarkably intact. One should, therefore, take a very sober view of the potential transformative power of capitalism in China. China is very likely to adapt what it finds useful from the Western management toolkit and dismiss the rest. One ethnically Chinese American businessman expressed this idea in the following way: "China will not achieve economic success along the lines that we dictate."[54] Moreover, if China does change and adopt greater democracy and respect for human rights, it will mostly be as the result of China's internal sociopolitical dynamics. The influence of foreigners on this transformation will be marginal. Foreigners must therefore learn to temper the zeal to transform China with the flexibility to understand and deal with the multifaceted, nuanced China that is likely to emerge as a world power in the twenty-first century.

A fifth and final important caveat concerns the ability to generalize from a single case, particularly from the case of China. As has been noted, the economic situation in China is unique among developing countries. Because of China's population size and economic growth rate, multinational firms are extremely eager to establish a foothold there. The firms that come to China perceive high, long-term stakes. Therefore, they enter the China market with their best technology and their top managers and use up-to-date management practices. As we have seen, the exigencies of the free market drive the kind of corporate practices that have beneficial effects on human rights and democracy. However, competitive circumstances won't necessarily be the same in other developing countries. One must, therefore, wonder whether less competitive market pressures in other countries would lead to the adoption of different kinds of management practices. It could be argued that the incentives for investing and training workers in the ways described earlier would apply to multinational firms regardless of the particular competitive situation. However, that companies operating in less competitive environments will perceive less of a need to localize the training of their workers is also plausible. Therefore, a special positive human rights role could exist for multinational firms in China that might not transfer to other developing nations.

China also may be distinctive because it is precisely the cultural factors described in this chapter that are holding back the country's progress on human rights and democracy. Accordingly, the fact that multinational firms have a cultural impact on China enables them to make an impact on the human rights situation and democratization. In other countries, the sources of human rights problems may not be a function of cultural norms. In such cases, multinational firms are less likely to have a significant human rights spin-off effect.

Conclusion

Notwithstanding these caveats, this chapter has presented some evidence, albeit anecdotal, that multinational corporations are making a significant contribution to the process of democratization and human rights in China. Ultimately, whether or not cultural learning within a business organization can have a significant effect on cultural patterns in the larger society is an empirical question that must be tested by far more extensive and systematically collected data than have been assembled in this chapter. Nevertheless, this chapter has attempted to make the case that Chinese citizens are learning many ideas in Western companies that are quite radical in the context of Chinese society.

The contribution that multinational corporations are making to human rights and democracy is not a result of any conscious intention to make a political impact in China. It is an inadvertent human rights spin-off resulting from the self-interested pursuit of profits. Multinational corporations are influencing four sets of factors—economic prosperity, merit-based hiring practices, information-sharing and teamwork, and leadership values—that have an "elective affinity" with human rights and democracy. These values are being transmitted to mostly young Chinese workers through both formal and informal learning channels. The ultimate outcome of these influences on the future course of democracy and human rights is unclear because so much depends on the far greater domestic forces driving social and political change in China. What is clear, however, is that because of human rights spin-off, multinational corporations are playing an important human rights role. In the next chapter, the implications of this human rights spin-off for American foreign policy are examined.

CHAPTER FIVE

☆

Comprehensive Engagement Plus: Human Rights and Foreign Policy

In the previous chapter we observed that multinational corporations unintentionally foster human rights and democracy in China simply by acting in their own self-interest. This chapter considers the implications of this human rights "spin-off" for U.S. foreign policy. One subtle but important consequence of human rights spin-off is that it exposes the need to develop appropriate criteria for measuring the success or failure of the U.S. policy of comprehensive engagement with China. Many observers point to the continued arrests of political dissidents in China as evidence that economic engagement with China is a mistake—at least as it concerns human rights. Such sentiments have even led some human rights activists to oppose China's entry into the WTO. Tallying the number of released dissidents is not, however, an appropriate criterion to judge the merits of economic engagement as a human rights policy. This chapter suggests a better way to do so.

A formidable obstacle to forging and sustaining an effective human rights policy toward China is the absence of an appropriate lens for understanding and measuring how various policy options work. As a result, American politicians do a very bad job of choosing appropriate intermediate objectives and an even worse job of judging whether those objectives are being achieved. A tendency to overlook the obvious and immediate was manifest in President Clinton's overly ambitious attempt in 1993 and 1994 to pressure China into making dramatic societal changes by threatening to revoke Most Favored Nation (MFN) trading status, a policy that was much better suited to attaining discreet, short-term objectives, such as the release of political dissidents. By contrast, too much focus has been placed on the immediate, near-term effects of "comprehensive engagement," a policy that produces subtle and little-understood effects that will require years of patience to run their course. Each of these policies is capable of achieving particular kinds of intermediate objectives, but each also is wholly unsuited for the achievement of other sorts of intermediate objectives. We will much improve our judgments about these policies if we think through what we need to observe to accurately assess the respective capabilities and shortcomings of economic pressure and economic engagement.

There are five questions that need to be answered in order to evaluate and compare various human rights policies:

1. What factors within China is the policy trying to change? The release of dissidents? Social and political values and attitudes? Institutional transformation?
2. How does the policy hope to accomplish this change? Through pressure? Influence? Cooperation?
3. How long will it take for the policy to have an effect?
4. How do we know in the short run if the policy is working? What are the things we can observe and measure to determine whether the policy is having its intended effect?
5. If the policy is successful in changing these factors, how will human rights conditions in China change? What are the long-run implications of a change in these factors on Chinese society in general and on human rights in particular?

Within this framework, it is apparent that the MFN sanctions policy and comprehensive engagement are two very different foreign policy tools. Although each may share, in a very general sense, the ultimate goal of improving human rights conditions in China, each has its own distinct intermediate objectives and each uses its own distinct means to attain those objectives. Because the two policies have different intermediate objectives and means of accomplishing them, we need to focus on different factors and evaluate them over different time frames to determine whether either policy is successful. These differences, which are discussed later in this chapter, are summarized in Table 5.1.

The debate is not, however, simply a matter of perception and evaluation. The ultimate goals of American foreign policy toward China are also very much at issue. The question of how best to address human rights is embedded in a larger debate about the best way to manage overall relations with China. This interplay between human rights and other national interests has been a recurring issue in U.S.-Sino relations since the Tiananmen Square massacre in 1989. The debate over China's

Table 5.1 Comparison of the Policies of Economic Sanctions and Comprehensive Engagement

	Economic sanctions	Comprehensive engagement
What factors within China is the policy trying to change?	Release of dissidents	Social and political values and behavior
How does the policy hope to effect this change?	Economic pressure	Formal and informal learning by young workers in American companies
How long will it take for the policy to have an effect?	Short-term, months	Long-term, years
How do we know in the short run whether the policy is working?	Dissidents are released and allowed to speak and organize.	Values and behaviors of young workers change.
If the policy is successful in changing these factors, how will human rights conditions in China change in the long run?	Dissidents are able to build support for their political positions, putting pressure on government to change or leading to a change in government.	As social values change, political values also change. Ultimately, the political structure must change to incorporate these new values.

accession to the WTO has raised this issue anew. Many Sinologists and foreign-policy experts have developed the consensus view that other national interests are too important to burden with concerns about human rights.[1] This point of view stems from a deeply rooted presumption—a geopolitical relic of the Cold War, really—that human rights must inevitably conflict with other national interests. I will argue that this dichotomy is not valid, at least in the case of U.S.-Sino relations. On the contrary, because the phenomenon of human rights spin-off described in the previous chapter is real and discernible, the expansion of economic interactions with China through its entry into the WTO will serve to improve human rights conditions.

The United States has followed a policy of engagement with China roughly since 1994. That year, President Clinton, in one of the stunning reversals that marked his early presidency, reneged on a campaign pledge to stop "coddling" China's leaders and declared his intention to form a "strategic partnership" by seeking out areas of cooperation. In one form or another, engagement also has become the official policy of the European Union, Japan, Australia, Canada, Sweden, Brazil, Norway, and other nations.[2] Engagement has replaced multilateral censure and bilateral economic pressure as the preferred foreign policy for addressing China's human rights violations. This chapter offers support for this policy. However, it also argues that the United States and other Western nations should pursue a "comprehensive engagement plus" strategy— that is, increasing friendly cooperation with China but, at the same time, being willing (when circumstances warrant) to criticize China on human rights and other matters.

It was after the events in Tiananmen Square that the world first became preoccupied with human rights conditions in China. After the Tiananmen massacre, the rest of the world was left with a difficult dilemma. How should it deal with a rising economic and political power that commits serious and pervasive human rights abuses against its own citizens? As the twenty-first century begins, the United States and other nations are still struggling to fashion the best answer to this question.

THE TIANANMEN MASSACRE: CHINA SHOCKS THE WORLD

In the spring of 1989, what began as a student protest in Beijing galvanized diverse social groups throughout China.[3] Spurred by the death of the popular prodemocracy Politburo member Hu Yaobang, university students began a series of protests in Beijing's Tiananmen Square, the civic and cultural heart of China. The students camped out in Tiananmen Square, listening to speeches, chanting slogans, and singing songs of freedom and protest. Print and broadcast media covered the lofty pronouncements of the charismatic student leaders. After some weeks, the students held the entire nation of China in thrall, threatening the ideological hold of Deng and the other octogenarian Communist Party leaders.

Traditionally, the people of China have viewed student protests respectfully. The students, in fact, consciously sought to associate themselves with the May 4th Movement, a popular and patriotic pre-republic protest against foreign domination. At the core of the students' concerns was a hope for greater democracy. Indeed, one of the most enduring symbols of the Tiananmen Square protests was the erection of a large-scale statue— the "Goddess of Democracy." In 1989, the economic reform initiated by Deng was a decade old, and many within China—even at the highest levels of government—believed that it was time for political reform as well.[4]

By May, the protests had expanded to nearly forty cities throughout China. The students drew support from many elements of Chinese society—from journalists, intellectuals frustrated by the Communist Party's tight control over free expression in the press and academic institutions, urban workers concerned about growing inflation (nearly 27 percent in the first four months of 1989), and even bureaucrats upset about government corruption. The participation of workers in the protests was especially galling and worrisome to Communist Party officials. The party was, after all, supposed to be the vanguard of the workers. Moreover, as events in Tiananmen Square were unfolding, party leaders were aware that Lech Walesa had recently led the independent trade union Solidarity in a call for political reform and free elections in Poland.

By chance, in mid-May the state visit of former Soviet leader Mikhail Gorbachev to Beijing brought hundreds of foreign journalists to Beijing. As a result of the press entourage accompanying Gorbachev, images and accounts of the student demonstrations in Tiananmen Square were transmitted throughout the world. The young, photogenic student leaders, such as Chai Ling, were joined in a hunger strike by pop singer Hou Dejian. Publicly embarrassed and frustrated, Chinese leaders were divided over how to deal with the protesters. Deng and Prime Minister Li Peng advocated taking a hard line with the students. They were mindful not only of China's historical susceptibility to chaos, but also of the rapidly unfolding upheavals of communist governments in Eastern Europe. At one point Deng was reported to have flown to Wuhan to set up a military command post in Central China, just in case Beijing was lost.

Deng called the student protest an "organized conspiracy to create chaos."[5] The *People's Daily*, the official Communist Party newspaper, published an editorial accusing the students of plotting to overthrow the government. The editorial shocked and angered the students, who viewed their actions as patriotic. Ambitious moderates such as Politburo member Zhao Ziyang, however, advocated an open dialogue with the students, declaring that "political reform and economic reform should basically synchronize; it won't do to lag behind in political reform."[5]

By the end of May, the hard-liners led by Li Peng won out and the decision was made to remove the students remaining in Tiananmen Square. On May 20 martial law was declared in Beijing. One hundred and fifty thousand People's Liberation Army (PLA) troops were mobilized. But when they tried to enter Beijing, citizens heroically stopped them and pleaded with them to turn back. A PLA officer told citizens as his troops departed, "We are soldiers of the people and will never suppress the people."[6]

Communist leaders were humiliated by the people's defiance of the PLA. Deng reportedly commanded his generals to "recover the square at any cost." Just before midnight on June 3, spearheaded by the 27th Army, the PLA smashed through civilian barricades, fired into the crowds, and made their way to Tiananmen Square. Shortly before dawn, tanks and troops stormed into the square. According to some accounts, the tanks mowed down students, along with civilians trying to remove casualties. The official Chinese government account of the massacre claimed that no blood was shed in Tiananmen Square itself and that only a small group of civilians was killed when they attempted to recapture the square.[7] Independent estimates of total deaths ranged from 700 to 2,600. However, contrary to many published reports by Western journalists who did not witness events firsthand, most of the carnage occurred as the troops made their way to the square. An estimated 2 million ordinary Chinese citizens took to the streets attempting to ward off the PLA. When the troops actually arrived in the square, reports and images of the carnage in and around Tiananmen Square were transmitted throughout the world. Perhaps the most poignant and enduring moment came shortly after the massacre. A solitary man stood face to face with a tank, defiantly attempting to prevent it from moving. (In a bold effort at "spin control," the Chinese authorities later cited this incident as an example of the restraint of the PLA!)

Almost universally, other nations swiftly and unambiguously condemned China. Some multilateral institutions such as the United Nations Human Rights Commission and the International Labor Organization also voiced criticism, as did nongovernmental organizations such as Amnesty International and Human Rights Watch. A month after the Tiananmen massacre, each of the Group of Seven nations—the United States, Canada, Great Britain, France, Germany, Italy, and Japan—suspended ministerial contacts and arms trade with China, requested the postponement of new loans by the World Bank, and extended the visas of Chinese students.[8]

In January 1990, China, stung by international criticism and seeking to reverse economic sanctions, lifted martial law in Beijing and released nearly nine hundred of the estimated thousands of prisoners taken during and after the Tiananmen massacre.[9] Over the next year, international economic sanctions were lifted and China again became eligible for World Bank loans. Although eschewing further political reforms, China resumed its program of economic reform and privatization.

In years past, the death of three thousand Chinese citizens and a few months of political turmoil in Beijing would have attracted little world attention. Indeed, it could be argued with some justification that political repression in contemporary China is mild in comparison to what it was, and that Tiananmen Square was only one of several horrifying modern Chinese political catastrophes. During the Great Leap Forward in the late 1950s, tens of millions of people died of famine when politically correct forecasts of crop yields turned out to be grossly overstated. In the

1960s, during the Cultural Revolution, millions of Chinese were humiliated and tortured in a mass movement of ideological purity engineered by Mao and the notorious "Gang of Four."

Although historically such catastrophic events have gone little noticed in other parts of the world, Tiananmen Square ignited a maelstrom of international scrutiny and criticism that continues in the present time. Some Chinese citizens believe that Western criticism of its human rights record is part of an effort to contain China and prevent it from assuming its rightful place as a world power. However, a more benign explanation is that China has only recently reached out to the world in the form of trade and foreign investment. Traditionally, the "Middle Kingdom" remained aloof from international affairs.[10] The Opium War and the neocolonial experiences of the nineteenth century were shocking and brutal intrusions into an ancient, inward-looking, and self-sufficient civilization. Even after Mao assumed power, China remained closed to the rest of the world (with the exception of Soviet influence in the 1950s and early 1960s). This inward-looking attitude began to change with the dramatic visit of U.S. President Richard M. Nixon to China in 1971. It was only after Mao's death and Deng's subsequent ascension to power, however, that China began in earnest to seek significant economic and political world power.

As a result of increased economic interaction with the world, China has attracted attention to human rights practices that went unnoticed even as late as the 1970s. In addition, as was dramatically illustrated during the Tiananmen massacre, modern telecommunications technology has vastly increased the flow of information coming out of China, thereby further increasing worldwide scrutiny of Chinese political repression. Also contributing to the international attention have been tens of thousands of Chinese expatriates, including many veterans of the Tiananmen protests, who have been granted political asylum in the West. Although fragmented both geographically and ideologically, these overseas Chinese have helped to keep the world focused on human rights developments in China. Finally, the heightened scrutiny is also due to the increasing visibility and effectiveness of nongovernmental organizations, such as Human Rights Watch and Amnesty International, that have worked to document and publicize human rights violations in China and elsewhere.

THE MOST FAVORED NATION DEBATE: A WASHINGTON RITE OF SPRING

In the immediate aftermath of the Tiananmen massacre, the United States attempted to use economic sanctions to pressure China into improving its human rights conditions. Since 1990, it has become an annual rite of spring for Congress and the President to debate whether to grant MFN treatment to China. In the spring of 2000, the annual debate over China's trading privileges will take on added significance as Congress debates whether to grant China permanent MFN status in connection with its entry into the WTO. MFN status, now referred to as *Normal Trade Relations*, is a centuries-old concept originating in international commercial agreements in which signatories extended to each other's trade no less favorable import duty treatment than that given to a nation which was the "most favored."[11] Under the General Agreement on Trade and Tariffs (GATT) treaty, the United States was contractually obliged to extend MFN treatment to other GATT signatories. However, because China was not a signatory to the GATT (or to the successor treaty that created the WTO), the United States is not required to grant MFN treatment to China. Moreover, the 1974 Jackson-Vanik amendment stipulates that nonmarket economies such as China are ineligible for MFN trading status with the United States unless the President determines—and certifies annually— that such countries allow their citizens the right of free emigration.

In the early 1990s, President George Bush vetoed a number of legislative attempts by the Democrat-controlled Congress to condition MFN renewal on China's progress in human rights. In the 1992 presidential campaign, candidate Bill Clinton made an issue of these vetoes, accusing President Bush of "coddling the dictators in Beijing." On May 28, 1993, President Clinton, using the Jackson-Vanik amendment in a creative fashion, issued an executive order renewing China's MFN status for another year, but conditioning renewal in the following year on the achievement of a broad laundry list of improvements in human rights. Sending a confusing and ambitious threat, the executive order also required Chinese officials to "pursue resolutely all legislative and executive actions to ensure that China abides by its commitments to follow fair, nondiscriminatory trade practices against U.S. businesses, and adheres to nonproliferation principles." In a speech announcing the executive order, Clinton was clear about the connection between trade issues and MFN. "[W]e have concerns," he stated, "about our terms of trade with China. China runs an $18 billion trade surplus with the United States—second only to Japan. In the face of this deficit, China continues practices that block American goods."[12]

Even the purely human rights aspects of the executive order were wildly ambitious, overly broad, and impossible to achieve in the allotted one-year time frame. The order included an "absolute condition" that China guarantee the right to emigrate, patterned on the original intent of the Jackson-Vanik amendment. However, there was no suggestion that the United States was prepared to take in the tens of millions of émigrés adherence to such a policy would likely generate. A second "absolute condition" was compliance with a 1992 bilateral agreement on prison labor. But China's offer to open five prisons to inspection was dismissed by human rights groups as a "token gesture" because it did not allow unannounced inspections.

The executive order also called for "overall, significant progress" in five other areas. The first—"taking steps to begin adhering to" the Universal Declaration of Human Rights—was either so vague as to be meaningless or so specific as to be truly monumental. In either case, compliance with such a sweeping demand was elusive to measure. Other areas in which the executive order called for "overall, significant progress" were the release of dissidents, humane treatment of prisoners, protection of the religious and cultural heritage of Tibet, and allowing international radio and television broadcasts into China. Although these are laudable human rights goals, they constitute a motley blend of demands on which to condition MFN renewal.

The multiple concerns and broad sweep of the executive order reflected the fact that, in addition to being a focal point for human rights, MFN had become a lightning rod for debate on the full panoply of issues in U.S.-Sino relations. This lack of focus was in no small measure responsible for the demise of the policy. It turned compliance with the executive order into a cat-and-mouse game. China, not knowing what was required, did as little as it guessed would satisfy the United States. The United States, in turn, not really sure what it wanted from China, greeted each new concession with disappointment. Both sides ended up frustrated with their efforts.[13]

Although caught flat-footed by the original executive order, the U.S. business community, under great pressure from China, lobbied heavily to de-link MFN and human rights. While Secretary of State Warren Christopher and Assistant Secretary for Human Rights John Shattuck continued to press China for progress on human rights, other members of the Clinton cabinet began to signal their opposition to the MFN policy at the end of 1993. Treasury Secretary Lloyd Bentsen, Commerce Secretary Ron Brown, and Agriculture Secretary Mike Espy, as well as U.S. Trade Representative Charlene Barshevsky all publicly stressed the importance of trade with China. Ultimately, President Clinton, fearing the threat of Chinese retaliation, was unwilling to place American economic interests at risk to pursue human rights objectives. Further forcing President Clinton's hand was the fact that the European nations, which stood to gain lucrative contracts from China's retaliation against American companies, refused to join the United States in pressuring China.[14] On May 4, 1994, less than a year after issuing the executive order, President Clinton renewed China's MFN status unconditionally, citing the fact that $8 billion of exports to China in 1993 supported more than 150,000 American jobs.

Clinton made the decision to de-link MFN renewal from human rights despite the fact that by his own admission "the Chinese did not achieve overall significant progress in all the areas outlined in the executive order." Clinton noted some modest success, including the establishment of a memorandum of understanding about prison labor and the release of some prominent dissidents. "Nevertheless," President Clinton conceded, "serious human rights abuses continue in China, including the arrest and detention of those who peacefully voice their opinions, and the repression of Tibet's religious and cultural traditions." Citing the desire to avoid "isolating" China, President Clinton announced what he called "a broader strategy of engagement with China."[15]

For all of the policy's flaws, the decision to de-link human rights and MFN had little to do with the failure of the policy vis-à-vis human rights. A more decisive factor was that the Clinton administration—with some prodding from the business community and foreign policy elites—concluded that human rights should not be allowed to dominate the relationship between the United States and China. The China experts in the academic-policy community were also united in support of the de-linking. David Shambaugh's view was typical. He wrote:

> Comprehensive engagement with China evolved out of the need to repair the deteriorated relations that had existed since 1989, and to provide an overarching framework to guide America's ties with China. Since the Beijing massacre of that year, America's China policy had been captured by a host of special interest groups, with the result that the Clinton administration found itself pursuing a fragmented policy that was largely reactive to independent domestic interests. Competitive and contentious elements came to dominate the relationship, restricting cooperation in important areas where national interests converged. The new policy was thus driven by the need to stabilize the deteriorating relationship and to work together where possible.[16]

Let us, for the moment, remain agnostic about whether, as Shambaugh suggests, a China policy with a strong human rights focus unwisely jeopardizes other important interests. It is worth revisiting whether threatening to revoke MFN was a failure *as a human rights policy*. One view is that the threat was a failure because all it actually accomplished was to secure the release of prominent dissidents, whereas it had ambitions of causing quick and fundamental change in a broad array of matters—some related to human rights, some not. This, however, is less a critique of the use of sanctions per se than of the unrealistic notion that they could work in the simultaneously expedient and grandiose manner imagined by the Clinton administration.

All that the MFN policy could reasonably be expected to accomplish was what it did accomplish, namely the release of some prominent dissidents. Expecting more was unreasonable. However, considering this an unimportant accomplishment also was wrong. The Chinese government puts dissidents in jail because it doesn't like what they have to say and because it perceives them as a threat to its rule. If, as a result of external pressure, the government releases dissidents, it should not be dismissed as a meaningless gesture. The ability of a dissident to get back out into society and express his or her views is a key human right. By being able to speak out publicly, dissidents can help to bring about changes that might secure other rights. (In the late 1990s, the Chinese discovered that it was wiser to release dissidents such as Wei Jingsheng and Wang Dan only if they agreed to leave the country.) The collapse of communism in the former Soviet Union and in Eastern Europe was in part made possible by the fact that the West pressured those countries to release dissidents. Much of that pressure came in the form of economic sanctions.[17] The fact that threats to its MFN trading status pressured China into releasing dissidents was a significant accomplishment. Thus, although abandoning the policy arguably may have enabled the United States to achieve other objectives, as a human rights policy MFN was in fact modestly successful, and its success was about all that reasonably could have been expected. The disparagement of the policy as a human rights policy was mostly a function of the Clinton administration's unrealistic expectation that Chinese society would change virtually overnight as a result of American economic pressure.

COMPREHENSIVE ENGAGEMENT: THE ACCIDENTAL HUMAN RIGHTS POLICY

In the fall of 1994, U.S.-Sino relations reached an all-time low when U.S. and Chinese naval forces came dangerously close to military engagement in the Yellow Sea. In China, the reaction to deteriorating relations was a virulent government-engineered strain of anti-American xenophobia. Chinese officials complained that the United States was trying to "contain" China and prevent it from reaching its rightful role as a world power. When Beijing lost its bid to host the Olympics in the year 2000 because of its human rights record, the resentment of foreigners, particularly of Americans, intensified.

In much the same way that some American politicians use anti-communist rhetoric, Chinese leaders have from time to time skillfully stoked anti-American sentiment to shore up hard-line domestic constituencies. In late 1994, this scripted xenophobic outrage paid a handsome bonus when many China-watchers in the United States began to warn of the dangers of trying to "contain" and "isolate" China. The political scientist Lucien Pye has observed that the highly calculated and characteristically Chinese style of bold, fearless confrontation and finger-pointing finds a perfect foil in the American guilt culture. As Pye writes, "Whenever the Chinese declare that the 'relationship is in trouble' they can always count on some American voices being raised in self-criticism—indeed providing more sophisticated rationalizations for the behavior of the Chinese than they themselves could produce."[18]

In the mid-1990s, the Clinton administration slowly came to the conclusion—reinforced by a second perilous naval stand-off in the Taiwan Straits in 1996—that U.S. interests required more cordial relations with China. The solution was very simple and politically expedient: stop making such a big issue over human rights and start emphasizing those areas in which America could expand cooperation with China. From this realization came the current policy of comprehensive engagement with China.

Beginning in 1997, Clinton officials began to give public speeches enunciating the new China policy. As significant as anything else was the fact that everyone seemed to be reading from the same script. Previously, there were deep and open disagreements among cabinet officials. Former Secretary of State Warren Christopher was a strong advocate for pressuring China on human rights. Simultaneously, the late Commerce Secretary Ron Brown was an advocate of expanding business contacts and playing down human rights. In 1997, by contrast, the administration presented a consistent message. Ambassador to China James Sasser, Assistant Secretary of State for East Asian and Pacific Affairs Stanley Roth, Under Secretary of State for Economic and Business Affairs Stuart Eizenstat, and finally President Clinton himself all gave major policy speeches that could have been written by the same speechwriter.[19]

Notably, Secretary of State Madeline Albright did not give a major policy address in support of the policy of comprehensive engagement. It is unclear whether, in light of her oft-stated commitment to human rights, she had misgivings about the policy or whether she was simply preoccupied at the time with events in the Middle East and the Balkans.

The term "comprehensive engagement" was used deliberately by Administration officials in lieu of "constructive engagement," the phrase used to describe the Reagan administration policy toward South Africa. Comprehensive engagement is meant to be a broader policy, involving more areas of interaction than merely trade and investment. The fundamental premise of the policy is the idea that cooperation is preferable to confrontation. The sensible and pragmatic notion is that engaging and expanding areas of cooperation with China constitute the best way to advance American interests. A second element of the policy is the clear articulation of U.S. interests. China's cooperation is essential to world and Asian peace and stability, nuclear and chemical weapon nonproliferation, control of drug trafficking, global trade and investment, and preservation of the environment. Added up, this is an impressive list of what's at stake in the U.S.-Sino relationship. A third critical aspect of comprehensive engagement is that no one area of disagreement, in particular human rights, should be allowed to dominate and sour the relationship between China and the United States. The principle would appear to be a simple instrumental calculation of "foreign policy utility"—that is, maximizing aggregate gains and minimizing losses across all of the many areas in U.S.-Sino relations. In practice, the underlying agenda was to jettison human rights as an important consideration in formulating U.S. foreign policy.

The clearest indication of how comprehensive engagement downgrades human rights can be seen in the terminology applied to it by administration officials. It is a subtle but telling fact that, in all public speeches, administration officials never refer to human rights as an "interest." Instead, human rights are consigned to the putatively lower status of "values"—important in some vague idealistic sense, but not worth making a fuss over like "interests" such as trade and military considerations. In the most important speech about China of his administration, President Clinton made this point quite clear. He referred to various "profound interests" of the United States at stake in relations with China. One "profound interest" was world peace. Another "profound interest" was Asian peace. In all, Clinton used the phrase "profound interest" seven times to refer to some aspect of U.S.-Sino relations. Human rights was not one of these "profound interests." Later in his speech, Clinton declared in rhetorical doublespeak—apparently lost on his audience, who gave him a rousing ovation—that the "United States must and will continue to stand up for human rights . . . To do otherwise would run counter to everything we stand for as Americans."[15] The message Clinton was delivering was clear. Human rights would be relegated to a secondary status in foreign policy toward China and would no longer be allowed to stand in the way of America's "profound interests."

Because of the obvious downgrading of human rights that comprehensive engagement implies, to refer to it as a human rights policy is a misnomer. Nonetheless, as we saw in the previous chapter, comprehensive engagement does result in a significant human rights spin-off because of the influence of foreign business. One might appropriately call comprehensive engagement an "accidental human rights policy" because, at least from the public record, it would seem that the Clinton administration really had very little idea about how and why comprehensive engagement would lead to progress in human rights. It seems fair to say that human rights progress in China is the unintentional byproduct of the Clinton administration's pursuit of other "profound interests" in the same way that human rights spin-off is an unintentional byproduct of the pursuit of self-interest by businesspeople. As it turns out, this accidental policy is a pretty good human rights policy, although many regard it as a failure either because they don't understand it or they undervalue what it is accomplishing.

Evaluating Comprehensive Engagement

Although comprehensive engagement is responsible for some positive human rights developments, the policy also has resulted in some backtracking. By 1998 and 1999, when the policy of comprehensive engagement was in full flower, the arrests of dissidents in China were increasing. In July 1999, the government arrested more than five thousand adherents to the Falun Gong religious sect.[20] The U.S. State Department report on human rights practices in China for 1998 offers the following bleak summary:

> The Government's human rights record deteriorated sharply beginning in the final months of the year with a crackdown against organized political dissent. The loosening of restrictions on political debate and activism by authorities for much of 1997 and 1998, including toward public calls for

political reform and expressions of opposition to government policies, abruptly ended in the fall. The Government continued to commit widespread and well-documented human rights abuses, in violation of internationally accepted norms. . . . Abuses included instances of judicial killings, torture and mistreatment of prisoners, forced confessions, arbitrary arrest and detention, lengthy incommunicado detention, and denial of due process. . . . In many cases, particularly sensitive political cases, the judicial system denies criminal defendants basic legal safeguards and due process. . . . The Government continued restrictions on freedom of speech and of the press, and tightened these toward the end of the year. The Government severely restricted freedom of assembly, and continued to restrict freedom of association, religion, and movement. . . . [A]n unknown number of persons, estimated at several thousand, are detained in violation of international human rights instruments for peacefully expressing their political religious or social views.[21]

As a result of the stepped up oppression of political dissidents, many members of the U.S. Congress and the public have called for a re-evaluation of U.S. policy toward China. As it did during the MFN debates, once again the public discussion of human rights became mixed up with other concerns. During the summer of 1999, dissatisfaction with comprehensive engagement was fueled by revelations that Chinese spies had been stealing nuclear secrets for more than a decade, continuing reports of possible Chinese attempts to influence the 1996 Presidential election through illegal contributions, and the siege of the U.S. embassy in Beijing after the accidental bombing of the Chinese embassy in Belgrade. Later that same summer, U.S.-Sino relations were dealt a further blow when outgoing Taiwanese President Lee Teng-hui proposed that the Republic of China might seek independent nation status, thereby creating military tensions with the mainland and putting the United States in the awkward position of having to reaffirm its delicately balanced "one China" policy. As a result of the deterioration of relations on so many fronts, some China skeptics in the United States were beginning to question the whole idea of a "strategic partnership" with China.[22]

The most significant potential casualty of this skepticism might well become the agreement reached late in 1999 between the United States and China regarding the terms of China's entry into the WTO. As Congress began to consider the agreement early in 2000, China skeptics were joined in opposition by a number of organized labor and industry groups that are likely to lose jobs and market share as a result of increased competition from Chinese imports.

The problem with dismissing comprehensive engagement as a human rights policy and holding up China's entry into the WTO because of the increased arrests of dissidents is that it misses the contribution of trade and investment to human rights and democratization. The short-term emphasis on political dissidents may have been an appropriate way to measure the success of the MFN policy; that policy was capable of having, and did have, an immediate, demonstrable impact on the release of political dissidents. The right way to judge the MFN policy, therefore, was by the number and prominence of dissidents released from prison. However, comprehensive engagement has vastly different aims, uses different means, and should be evaluated according to different criteria and over a different time span. Comprehensive engagement should be measured by the degree to which multinational corporations, simply by following their own self-interest, have an indirect human rights spin-off effect on human rights and democracy in China. This will take time and subtle observation, two commodities not always abundant in American political discourse.

The stepped-up jailing of dissidents should not be viewed so much as a failure of the policy of comprehensive engagement as the inevitable fallout of the abandonment of the MFN policy. This characterization is not intended as a clever play on words but rather to suggest a subtle but important distinction. Without any credible threat of economic sanctions, China's leaders have felt emboldened to step up political repression of dissidents and religious figures as it suits them. At the same time, China's exposure to foreign ideas is helping to inspire many Chinese citizens to speak out and exercise their civil liberties. Thus, the short-term result of the replacement of the economic sanctions policy with comprehensive engagement is that the number of dissidents is increasing and that the current government has more latitude to repress them. So, as strange as the notion might seem to some, the increased political repression in China, rather than being an indication that comprehensive engagement is not working, is actually an indication that the policy is working by emboldening more citizens to speak out. As time goes on, the winds of change brought on by China's entry into the WTO will encourage even more voices of freedom. Eventually, something has to give in this increasing tension between social change and government repression.

It would be nice to have the best of both worlds—the human rights spin-off effect of comprehensive engagement and the leverage to release dissidents that comes with the MFN policy. Unfortunately, the two policies are mutually exclusive. One policy has hostile overtones and works quite bluntly, the other works subtly through a friendly embrace. One cannot credibly assume both postures simultaneously; the United States and other nations must choose one policy or the other. At this point in time, the wisest decision for the United States is to stay the course of comprehensive engagement, to strike a deal on WTO, and to find other ways—other than the threat of economic sanctions—to put pressure on the government to release prisoners of political and religious conscience.

COMPREHENSIVE ENGAGEMENT PLUS:
WHY AND HOW TO RAISE THE PROFILE OF HUMAN RIGHTS

Although the policy of comprehensive engagement "accidentally" fosters human rights, U.S. foreign policy can and should do more to influence human rights policies in China. The United States should have a strong human rights policy not only because as a nation it has a moral obligation to do so. (The moral claims of human rights on nation-states and other actors are discussed in Chapter 8.) It is also in the long-term national interest to promote human rights in China. Put simply, the United States has a very "profound interest" in the geopolitical emergence of a China that are democratic and respects the human rights of its citizens. If, by contrast, China develops as an illiberal, undemocratic power, it would present an inherently destabilizing and dangerous situation for the whole world.

There is a deep-rooted and long-standing belief among many foreign policymakers that it is inappropriate and perhaps even dangerous for nations to pursue moral objectives such as human rights because such pursuits expose altruistic nations to the power of states acting purely in their own self-interest. According to this view, "states cannot afford to be moral."[23] Arguably, in the dangerous and uncertain nuclear age that overlapped with the Cold War, this dichotomy between the national interest and human rights might have made some sense. But the dichotomy has considerably less salience at the beginning of the third millennium. The one big lesson that humanity should have learned in the last half century of the second millennium is that liberal democracies do not go to war with one another. If there is to be hope of peace in the twenty-first century, the democratization of China needs to be a high priority for any foreign policy. Thus, human rights, rather than weighing down the national interest, is at the very core of our concerns—even our security concerns.

China's willingness to abide by international human rights norms is also a telltale sign of its willingness to abide by other international norms. Conscious of its status as a rising world power, China is integrating itself slowly but steadily into global economic and political institutions. This integration, however, although a positive development, does not necessarily signal an era of harmony and cooperation. China is as likely to change those institutions as it is to be changed by them. Very real conflicts on a broad array of issues are sure to persist well into the twenty-first century as China's vision of the world comes into conflict with that of the United States. A crucial issue the United States must address is where and how to draw the line on the changes that will inevitably occur in the principles and dynamics of the world international order. In this context, that the policy of comprehensive engagement downgrades the importance of human rights is alarming. It is not only a bad sign for human rights; it is also a bad sign of what is to come in other areas of "profound interest."

In addition to needlessly, indeed foolishly, de-emphasizing human rights, another fundamental flaw of comprehensive engagement is that it is based on a false dichotomy about the future of China. In all of the major speeches delivered by President Clinton and other administration officials, the economic, military, and geopolitical rise of China in the twenty-first century is viewed as having only two potential outcomes—each the polar opposite of the other. In the positive scenario, China emerges as a stable, open, nonaggressive "strategic partner" that embraces free markets, political pluralism, and the rule of law and that cooperates with the United States to build a secure international order. The alternative is that China "turns inward" and confrontational and becomes a dangerous, possibly even military, adversary of the United States.

One of the ironies of comprehensive engagement is that, try as we might to avoid the Manichean mental constructs of the Cold War, we are doomed apparently to repeat them. The impulse to see the world in terms of darkness and light is seemingly ineluctable. In the Cold War, the darkness was the evil empire of the Soviet Union and the light the torch of democracy held aloft by the United States. In the case of China, the hostile, alien, inward-looking China is one side of the coin. The friendly, pluralistic China learning the virtuous habits of capitalism and democracy from the United States is the other side.

Although each extreme is certainly a possible eventuality, the most likely scenario is much more complex and nuanced. The economic and political transformation of China is likely to take decades, and the system liable to emerge will not necessarily be perfectly congruent with American values. The most probable scenario, in other words, is that China and the United States will be allies in certain respects and rivals in other respects. A sensible China policy must therefore be capable of successfully managing both cooperation and conflict.

Comprehensive engagement accentuates the cooperative elements of the relationship, but it overstates the breadth and depth of the "strategic partnership" that is possible between the two global rivals. As a result, when the inevitable serious conflicts emerge, as they did in the spring of 1999, the feel-good mood is quickly replaced by profound hostility. This pattern is reminiscent of how the short-lived interval of détente was succeeded by a grave chill in U.S.-Soviet relations after the Soviets, not surprisingly in retrospect, invaded Afghanistan. The issue of human rights belongs at the forefront of U.S.-Sino relations precisely because it is one that divides the two nations most deeply. Ignoring that conflict is dangerously wishful thinking. Learning how to deal with the conflict is essential to a healthy and sustainable relationship.

Although it is a mistake to overemphasize the possibility of a "strategic partnership" with China, it also would be a mistake to overemphasize confrontation. Thus, in considering the options available to raise the profile of human rights, we should endeavor to do so within the framework of a relationship that enhances mutual understanding, trust, and cooperation. We should concede at the outset that returning to the use of sanctions is not a viable option. Contrary to what some may believe, the United States does have the economic power to make sanctions hurt China significantly. If the United States revoked MFN status, China would retaliate, and many American jobs would be lost. Nevertheless, the U.S. economy would survive. China, however, would suffer greatly. It could even result in an economic and social catastrophe. Perhaps five or ten years ago, revoking MFN was a viable policy option, but today it is unthinkable. Having encouraged China to open its markets, it would be inhumane to reverse course now and leave China to suffer the dire economic consequences. Moreover, engagement and economic sanctions are mutually exclusive policies. The United States cannot encourage China to open up to the world and at the same time constantly threaten to turn its back on China. Having begun the process of engagement, there is now no retreating. It would also be a mistake to backpedal on China's entry into the WTO. Drawing China into the world trading system and increasing economic interactions will serve as powerful forces of liberalization and democratization. The United States should welcome China's entry into the WTO enthusiastically and choose its battles with China more wisely.

Foreign nations can strengthen the human rights emphasis of their foreign policies within the general policy paradigm of comprehensive engagement. What is needed is a policy of "comprehensive engagement plus." One factor that can be combined with comprehensive engagement is the force of rhetoric by political leaders who are not afraid to speak up about human rights. In his 1998 trip to China, President Clinton did just this. Unfortunately, the impact of his words was undermined somewhat when Clinton acceded to China's demand that he drop three Voice of America reporters from his press entourage. Nevertheless, his frank comments about human rights were accorded unusual attention in the Chinese press. Ideas do matter, and the publication of Clinton's comments mattered in China. Even a year later, during a trip to China, I encountered a number of Chinese citizens who wanted to discuss the points raised by Clinton. U.S.-Sino relations survived his televised dialogue with Chinese President Jiang Zemin. In fact, one could say the relationship was strengthened by the frank and honest talk. Other public officials traveling to China should follow the President's lead and find opportunities to express concern about human rights conditions in China. The more voices of international leaders that join in the chorus of criticism of China's human rights record, and the more often these voices are heard, the greater the effect of the criticism will be. Brewer Stone, an American businessman with longstanding ties and experience in China and a Ph.D. in government from Harvard, put it this way: "Constant and repeated criticism by foreign leaders will have an effect. It can simply drive home the point that China is not living up to its own stated ideals, and in the end most people find themselves uncomfortable with hypocrisy."[24]

A second way in which the United States can emphasize human rights in its foreign policy within the paradigm of comprehensive engagement is to press the case against China more forcefully in nontrade multilateral institutions such as the United Nations Commission on Human Rights. In a thoughtful testimony before Congress, Michael Posner, the executive director of the Lawyers Committee on Human Rights, explained the rationale for a multilateral approach:

Having adopted seven of the major international human rights treaties and announced its intention to accede to the International Covenant on Economic, Social, and Cultural Rights and the International Covenant on Civil and Political Rights, China is increasingly entwined in the international human rights system. By encouraging the international human rights bodies to exercise their power to examine China's human rights performance, the United States can help produce critiques that due to their multilateral character command greater respect in China and at the same time strengthen the long-term capacity of these institutions to monitor China's human rights performance.[25]

Unfortunately, the multilateral approach suggested by Posner presents some challenges. As is discussed in greater detail in Chapter 7, deep-rooted and systemic problems exist at the Human Rights Commission that hamper its capacity to monitor or enforce human rights. The most formidable obstacle to the Commission's effectiveness is the excessive politicization of its deliberations, which was unmistakably evident in its 1996 vote refusing to debate human rights violations in China. In April 1996, the Human Rights Commission narrowly passed a "no action motion" pre-empting the Commission from even debating a resolution introduced by the European Union and the United States to engage an independent committee of experts to prepare a survey of human rights practices in China. A year earlier, a similar resolution had been debated and narrowly defeated. China was, however, embarrassed by the debate surrounding the resolution. Its victory on the "no action motion" prevented any such debate from taking place the following year. Geraldine A. Ferraro, leader of the U.S. delegation to the Human Rights Council, called the Chinese maneuver "an act of censorship."[26]

China's successful opposition was made possible by the support of other developing nations, including Pakistan, India, and all but one of the African representatives on the fifty-three-member Commission. In a fiery speech referring to the United States as "the superpower" and the "imperial" power, Chinese delegate Wu Jianmin warned that "what is happening to China today will happen to any other developing country tomorrow." China did not limit its campaign to anti-imperialist rhetoric. Using heavy-handed "commercial diplomacy," China offered foreign aid packages—including, reportedly, sports stadiums and highways—to small African nations in return for favorable votes. Ms. Ferraro found such tactics particularly ironic in light of China's long-fought battle with the United States to de-link trade from human rights: "We don't impose trade and aid into the Commission. China does. China says, 'Don't take human rights and impose them on trade.' But they turn around and impose trade on human rights." Joanna Weschler, the U.N. representative of Human Rights Watch, offered an even more somber assessment: "It's really appalling that this Commission was not given a chance to vote on the merits of the resolution, that one exception was made on behalf of a very powerful country. It really puts into question the future of the Commission if it is not able to take on extremely serious issues."[27] Amnesty International issued a report declaring that "human rights lost out to political horse-trading . . . as governments backed off from tackling violations committed by their trading partners."

Another formidable obstacle to a multilateral approach is the weak resolve of European nations. Already reluctant to confront China directly about human rights for fear of losing out on commercial contracts,[28] nations such as Germany and France have become afraid to press such concerns even in international forums. As Amnesty International observed, "trade contracts worth millions of U.S. dollars are determining the European Union's policy on human rights in China. The European Union lacked a commitment to condemn China's human rights record."[29]

To avoid a similar debacle in the future, one option is for the United States to take off the gloves and fight harder to win the vote at the United Nations. If political maneuvering is the order of the day, then the United States should try to use tougher, or at least more clever, tactics. A better course is to pursue a long-term strategy of encouraging institutional reform of the Human Rights Commission to make it into a less political and more professional and technical body. This strategy has the added virtue of strengthening the long-term prospects of human rights not only in China, but also in the rest of the world. Such significant institutional reform is, of course, easier said than done. However, unless this goal is achieved, the Commission will never have the requisite neutrality and independence to become an authoritative voice for human rights.

CONCLUSION

A "comprehensive engagement plus" policy is admittedly difficult to implement. It requires some finesse to have open trade and investment with China and simultaneously find credible and effective ways to exert pressure on it to release dissidents. The former *New York Times* Beijing correspondent Patrick Tyler refers to this task as the "unfinished work" in American foreign policy toward China.[30] In an editorial, the *Wall Street Journal* observed that "from the standpoint of Washington, the task is to balance yin and yang without going to either extreme."[31]

The task of balancing the yin and the yang is not made easier simply by taking a multilateral approach. Even if criticism is undertaken through international institutions, China will resent American human rights initiatives, and this creates the possibility of conflict and hostility. Despite the difficulties involved, however, finding ways of combining pressure with economic engagement is essential. The most important reason for doing so is to support the cause of reformers within China. As the Sinologist Andrew Nathan has written, "confluence with domestic currents makes it even more probable that future foreign pressures will exert continued or enhanced influence on the evolution of China's domestic human rights regime. Conversely, relaxation of Western pressures would weaken the ability of liberal domestic forces to influence developments."[32] In this very practical sense, multilateral external pressure complements what is happening within China as a result of the human rights spin-off effect. The changes in values and perspectives that foreign companies are bringing to China will not by themselves carry China to democracy. The Chinese people must do that themselves. The most America can do, and what it must do, is to lend its full support to the efforts of internal reformers. Any foreign policy that fails to do so because of other supposedly "profound interests" is self-defeating and unworthy of support from the American public.

The "plus" aspects of "comprehensive engagement plus" would require the United States to take a principled stand in favor of human rights. The proposed "plus" initiatives—speaking out in public forums and in international institutions and pressing for the release of jailed dissidents—are not as hostile and confrontational as threatening economic sanctions. Nonetheless, they require a willingness to put human rights on a par with other national interests. In the long run, as noted earlier, human rights and national interests are complementary, but in the short run taking a principled stand on human rights might threaten other national interests. For example, the possibility always exists that China will be so upset at American criticism of its human rights record that it will try to retaliate against American economic interests. Such a possibility, real as it is, should not intimidate the United States from taking a principled stand on human rights.

☆

Human Rights on the Factory Floor: When Principles Collide with Profits

Thus far, we have observed how, propelled by some of the positive forces unleashed by global capitalism, multinational corporations inadvertently promote democracy and human rights simply by following enlightened self-interest. The management practices of successful market-building firms impart radical—at least in the Chinese context—values to their white-collar and technical employees. These values, in turn, help in various ways to foster sustainable democracy and human rights. This human rights spin-off is an instance of "doing good while doing well"—it is an unintended byproduct of the self-interested pursuit of profits.

Profits and human rights are not, however, always in harmony. They come into conflict in at least two ways. First, companies seeking to maximize profits by tapping into China's reservoir of cheap labor are propelled by a different set of global economic forces that put the human rights of workers at risk. Second, any company doing business in China inevitably faces difficult moral issues as a result of operating in a country in which there are serious and pervasive abuses of civil and political rights. For example, even companies that studiously avoid the issue of human rights may have it thrust on them if the government attempts to sanction one of their employees for exercising his or her civil or political rights.

These kinds of situations can create career- and life-defining moments and decisions for multinational executives. They are defining moments because the decisions managers make reveal their personal character and brand the public image of their firm. These decisions pit human rights principles against profits in ways that challenge a manager's moral fiber and business acumen simultaneously. In such situations, a manager who tries to do the right thing may wind up threatening the company's commercial prospects. Conversely, a manager who ignores the moral considerations in such situations risks not only offending his or her own conscience, but also exposing the company to public outrage. There is no comfort zone. Making good decisions in morally challenging situations can become as crucial to a company's survival as making good marketing and finance decisions.

Whether or not they are inclined to think about moral responsibility, managers in multinational corporations must develop skills in moral reasoning that will help them make these tough decisions. Managers must learn to answer difficult moral questions about corporate responsibility for human rights. What, in particular situations, should a company do to act in a morally responsible way? Can a company fulfill its moral duties while minimizing the possibility of economic loss? What significance should the potential of economic loss have in assessing moral responsibility for human rights? These are among the questions addressed later using the fair share theory of corporate responsibility for human rights developed in Chapter 8. This chapter sets forth in greater detail the two kinds of situations in which human rights and profits most often collide in the Chinese political and economic environment, and it gives critical consideration to three alternative frameworks that have been suggested as potential guides to resolving the moral and operational issues created by the clash of profits and human rights.

GLOBAL ECONOMIC INCENTIVES TO ABUSE THE HUMAN RIGHTS OF WORKERS

Dear Comrade Editor:
We are staff and workers of Guangdong's Zhaojie Company. The company docks our pay, deducts and keeps our deposits, beats, abuses and humiliates us at will.

Zhaojie Company is a joint venture. It sends people to Sichuan, Henan and Hunan to recruit workers. Even children under 16 are their targets.

We people from out of province only knew we had been cheated after getting here. The reality is completely different from what we were told by the recruiter. Now even though we want to leave, we cannot because they would not give us back our deposits and our temporary residence permits, and have not been paying out our wages. This footwear company has hired over 100 live-in security guards, and has even set up teams to patrol the plant. The staff and workers could not escape even if they had wings. The only way to get out of the factory grounds is to persuade the officer in charge of issuing leave permits to let you go. A Henan worker wanted to resign but was not allowed to by the office. So he climbed over the wall to escape, but was crushed to death by a passing train. Although it means forfeiting the deposits and wages and losing their temporary residence permits, each year about 1,000 workers somehow leave this place. Being beaten and abused are everyday occurrences, and other punishments include being made to stand on a stool for everyone to see, to stand facing the wall to reflect on your mistakes, or being made to squat in a bent-knee position.

The staff and workers often have to work from 7:00 A.M. to midnight. Many have fallen sick. . . . It is not easy even to get permission for a drink of water during working hours.

Signed: Guangdong Zhaoxing City Zhaojie Co.,

Yang Shuangqi, Li Shaohua, and 20 others

—Letter to the Editor of the *Workers' Daily* (1995)[1]

In addition to unleashing positive forces leading to positive human rights spin-off, global capitalism also unleashes negative forces that create powerful economic incentives for corporations to abuse the human rights of their workers. The free movement of capital and goods across borders fuels what some have called a "race to the bottom" in labor abuses. As this phrase implies, global economic forces can place various private and governmental actors in a position in which survival must be secured at the cost of human rights. Retailers and manufacturers locked in price competition must perpetually seek out the lowest-cost suppliers. Suppliers compete for contracts. Developing countries compete to attract foreign capital. Even within developing countries, regions, towns, and villages compete with one another to capture the jobs and tax revenues that accompany foreign investment. All of these competitive forces, taken together, create a powerful, synergistic set of perverse incentives to violate the basic rights of workers. When factory owners and operators respond to these forces with unfettered greed and moral depravity, when government officials turn a blind eye to violations of law, and when workers are not allowed to organize and bargain collectively to protect themselves from abuse and exploitation, the results can be horrific, as epitomized by the Zhaojie shoe factory in the southern Chinese province of Guangdong.

Because of its large supply of inexpensive labor, China possesses a "comparative advantage" in labor-intensive manufacturing. In the 1990s, China—particularly the southern and coastal provinces of Guangdong, Zhejiang, Fujian, and Jiangsu—has attracted billions of dollars in foreign direct investment geared toward labor-intensive manufacturing. Hard as it may be for some in the West to understand and accept, for millions of impoverished and poorly educated rural Chinese people this influx of foreign capital and the openness of foreign markets to Chinese-manufactured goods have been a major blessing. This promise of a better life is why tens of millions of former farm workers from interior rural provinces have migrated to the coastal provinces in search of a factory job. By Western standards, the pay these migrant workers receive in foreign-run factories seems shockingly low—$35 to $45 a month. Nevertheless, when compared to the life of rural poverty they left behind, the factory jobs represent a real improvement for many of these workers. For millions of others, however, the promise of a better life in a foreign-run factory is a cruel hoax.

In flagrant violation of the most basic international norms and Chinese labor laws, untold numbers of foreign-funded factories in China violate the most basic human rights of their employees. Among the most serious human rights abuses one can readily find are the following:

- Forced, bonded, and prison labor
- Physical mistreatment and control of bodily functions
- Violations of local minimum wage and overtime laws
- Unconscionable health and safety risks

Although the full extent of these abuses is unknown, enough examples have been documented to conclude that the problem is serious and pervasive. Given the sensitivity of the subject matter, it should come as no surprise that no academic research systematically assessing human rights violations in the labor-intensive, foreign-owned manufacturing facilities in China exists. Because we have no way of knowing for sure, the best we can do is speculate about whether foreign-owned factories in China meet applicable local and international standards, even if they do not adhere to the more stringent labor standards prevailing in developed countries.

The number of stories circulating about factories that fail to meet even local standards is disquieting, to say the least. Han Dongfang, a prominent Chinese labor activist, reports that in the South China region around Shenzhen, the first and still the largest special economic zone for foreign investment, "I don't think anyone will find *any* factory where workers work less than 10 hours a day, even though according to Chinese law they should only be working 8 hours a day."[2] Dorothy J. Solinger, a Sinologist who has researched migrant labor in China, offers the following assessment:

> The foreign firms . . . have often invested at the behest of local governments anxious for the extra taxes they will yield, and their state regulations are frequently ignored altogether. There have been numerous reports both in the Chinese and the foreign presses of the litany of abuses suffered by migrants in these overseas-financed enterprises. These range from sixteen-hour days to an absence of toilet breaks, kicking, beatings, lock-ins, and even being penned up in a dog cage and being made to stand in the rain as penalties![3]

Of course, not all low-wage, labor-intensive manufacturing operations in China are as horrible as those that are described here. In many cases, Chinese factories are run in a safe, clean, and humane manner. Certainly, many business executives take very seriously their responsibility to run factories with the welfare of their workers in mind. Factories that are run professionally and humanely create important work opportunities for Chinese migrant workers, and as such, they make a significant contribution to the welfare of Chinese society. Nevertheless, the press and human rights nongovernmental organizations (NGOs) have uncovered enough examples of egregious abuse to suggest that toys, apparel, shoes, and other labor-intensive goods are often manufactured in China with reckless disregard of the most basic international norms and local laws. Although the full extent of the abuses that do take place will never be known, it is clear that very strong economic incentives entice manufacturers to abuse the human rights of workers and that equally strong economic incentives encourage governmental authorities to be lax in enforcing existing legal protections. The economic incentives to exploit and mistreat unskilled workers in China, when combined with the desperation and vulnerability of these workers, creates a fertile ground for abuse.

Factory owners possess tremendous leverage over the vulnerable workers they lure from the countryside. These migrant workers often are not able to leave a job without forfeiting a month's pay "deposit" and losing their work and temporary residence permits. As the Zhaojie shoe factory illustrates, however, the line between forced labor and prison labor can often become blurred. In addition to being virtually imprisoned, many Chinese factory workers are physically mistreated and subjected to humiliating control over their bodily functions. Anita Chan, who has done extensive fieldwork at factories in southern China, reports that in one Shenzhen factory, a worker who goes to the toilet more than twice a day is fined 60 yuan—about $7.50, or one-sixth of their monthly income. "In some factories," Chan observes, "they are not allowed to talk during work hours, or even while eating; employees have to walk following a particular route in the factory compound; and they are not allowed to get married, to 'talk love,' that is to have a steady serious relationship with someone of the opposite sex or, of course, to be pregnant."[4] Mary Gallagher, a political science doctoral student at Princeton, describes another outrageous example at a factory in Hubei Province:

> A compound surrounded by four-meter-high walls, with two guards and two dogs watching over the iron entry gates. Inside, security guards have hand guns, rifles, and machine guns as well as shock batons. This is not a prison but a factory. . . . The workshops all have overseers because the workers "tricked" into working there, both male and female, are not allowed to go out nor to write letters to their families. They work over 12 hours a day, in which time they are allowed to go to the toilet twice (three minutes for urination, seven minutes for defecation). The toilet is 100 meters from the workshop, so they have to run. After hours their dormitories are locked from the outside. Their diet is rice gruel and pickles. When two Sichuan workers were caught stealing rice from the kitchen, they were beaten by the factory head.[5]

Wages paid to Chinese factory workers are often below legal levels. A survey conducted by the Guangdong Provincial Labor Union found that 35 percent of the workers interviewed were not paid for overtime and 32 percent were paid below the minimum wage of approximately $40 a month. Moreover, the desperation of workers in China leads them to work under unconscionably unsafe conditions. In the Xiamen Jiamei Cutlery Company, for example, one-fourth of the four hundred workers have been maimed or injured. Eighty-seven workers died in a Shenzhen toy factory fire in which all the doors were locked and the windows barred.[6] The full extent of the health and safety problems in China is hard to gauge, but the Hong Kong–based Committee for Asian Women offered this dramatic conclusion in a research report about migrant women workers: "For most of [the women] life is nothing but a nightmare. Just what does it mean working in shoe, toy, and electronics factories where glues and solvents are commonly used? A gas chamber."[7]

Another point about these abuses that warrants emphasis is that these are not issues in which cultural factors might arguably play a factor in our moral judgments. There is no controversy about the fact that these are serious legal and moral transgressions under any moral standard. They violate China's 1994 Labor Law, as well as provincial wage and overtime regulations. They violate pertinent International Labor Organization conventions to which China has acceded. Finally, they violate provisions in the International Covenant on Economic, Social, and Cultural Rights. The plight of these workers is not simply a Western preoccupation. Even Chinese observers report and bemoan the terrible conditions in foreign-owned factories.[8]

The web of moral responsibility for conditions in Chinese factories ranges far and wide. At the epicenter, it needs to be said (at the risk of offending some) that labor leaders and researchers consistently report that the most egregious human rights violations occur in factories managed by Asian investors from Taiwan, Hong Kong, and South Korea. Despite this fact, however, the moral problem is not an exclusively Asian one. Goods manufactured in these factories find their way into stores in the United States and Europe, and eventually into the hands of Western consumers. Asian investors act as the middlemen for Western companies that subcontract out manufacturing work and then market the final products in the West. As a result of this free movement of goods and capital, Western consumers have come to expect inexpensive clothes, shoes, toys, and household products. These consumer expectations feed back into the global economic system and thereby contribute to the enormous financial pressures on Western companies to turn a blind eye to labor standards in the factories of their subcontractors.

Increasingly, Western consumers, the press, and human rights NGOs are shining a spotlight on factory conditions in China and other parts of the developing world. The glare of this publicity is falling primarily on the multinational corporation. From this heightened scrutiny of labor abuses have emerged a number of moral and public policy questions with global implications. These questions are addressed in Chapter 9, but a few are worth noting briefly here. The most basic questions concern whether and how multinational corporations are morally responsible for human rights violations committed by their subcontractors. If uncertainty exists about the seriousness and pervasiveness of human rights violations, then a related moral question is whether this uncertainty is acceptable or whether multinational corporations have a duty to make certain that goods supplied by their business partners are manufactured without violating human rights. Another related question concerns how the responsibility for factory conditions is most effectively discharged. Some have suggested that independent monitors and unannounced spot checks are necessary, whereas other argue that companies are fully capable of monitoring factory conditions themselves.

Apart from the moral issues, a great deal of controversy exists over the best public policy to deal generally with the sweatshop issue. Some companies have drawn up their own codes of conduct for relations with business partners. Others have proposed industry-wide initiatives. In the United States, for example, the apparel industry has joined with the government and NGOs to establish a voluntary code of conduct for their subcontractors. Oxfam has proposed a similar code for large U.K. clothing retailers. Others believe, however, that voluntary codes are not sufficient to stamp out labor abuses and that a set of global labor standards must be implemented through a "social clause" in the World Trade Organization that can be monitored and, if necessary, enforced through trade sanctions. In Chapter 9, all of these moral and public policy questions and issues are considered within the framework of the fair share theory developed in Chapter 8.

CORPORATE RESPONSIBILITY FOR ABUSES OF CIVIL AND POLITICAL RIGHTS

A second inexorable conflict between human rights principles and corporate profits in China arises because of the government's frequent arrest or arbitrary detention of religious and political dissidents. When one of those dissidents happens to be employed by a multinational corporation, the issue of human rights insinuates itself onto the corporate factory floor and into office suite. The linchpin connecting the persecution of political dissidents to the corporate suite is the personnel office. It is common practice for the Chinese government to punish dissidents by firing them from their state-sector jobs. For example, Seth Faison of the *New York Times* reported that when the government clamped down on a popular religious movement in the summer of 1999, within a few short weeks "thousands of . . . work places around the country . . . carried out a purge of Falun Gong members."[9]

The ease with which the government was able to punish Falun Gong members by firing them was made possible by the highly politicized nature of human resource practices in Chinese companies. Communist Party representatives are involved in nearly every aspect of hiring, firing, and promotion, and political correctness is an explicit criteria used in these decisions. To have a worker fired or kept from employment because of his or her political or religious views is not difficult. A worker fired for such reasons has no legal rights or recourse under Chinese law.[10]

Given the prevalence of religious and political dissidents in China, it can safely be predicted that at least some foreign employers and joint venture partners will come under pressure from the government to take job actions against religious and political dissidents who are their employees.[11] When employees attract the attention of the Chinese government because of political or religious activities, multinational corporations find themselves in the middle of a thorny situation requiring them to make difficult moral decisions with potentially devastating economic consequences.

The Gao Feng case exemplifies the challenging issues and decisions that confront the multinational executives when the Communist Party wants to punish one of a corporation's employees for expressing his or her beliefs. In May 1994, Gao Feng, a devout Christian, was arrested in Beijing for planning a private worship service and candlelight vigil to commemorate the fifth anniversary of the Tiananmen Square massacre. Gao was a twenty-six-year employee of Beijing Jeep, Chrysler's joint venture with the Chinese government. He was accused of violating Chinese laws against the practice of religion outside of a state-authorized venue.[12]

Technically, Gao appears to have violated Chinese law. Article 36 of the Chinese Constitution nominally provides for freedom of religious belief. However, the government restricts religious practice to government-sanctioned organizations to control the growth and scope of activity of religious groups. State Council Regulation 145, signed into law by then Premier Li Peng in January 1994, requires all places of worship to register with government religious affairs bureaus and come under the supervision of official "patriotic" religious organizations. Nearly 85,000 approved venues for religious activities exist in China. Many religious groups, however, have been reluctant to comply with the regulation either out of principled opposition to state control of religion or because of fear of adverse consequences if they reveal, as the regulations require, the names and addresses of church leaders.[13]

According to press reports, Gao remained under administrative detention for five weeks. He was never formally charged. In early July, Gao returned to work at Beijing Jeep and told his supervisor that the Chinese Public Safety Bureau had imprisoned him for a month. Chrysler told Gao that it would fire him unless he produced proof of his detention. The Chinese police gave Gao a note that said he had been detained for three days and then released without trial. Chrysler, presumably reasoning that Gao had no documented reason for failing to report to work for the bulk of the time he was missing, thereupon fired Gao for poor attendance. Gao's case became widely publicized when the advocacy group Human Rights Watch (HRW) took up his cause.[14] Because of the personal intervention of Chrysler's chairman, Robert J. Eaton, Gao was eventually reinstated,[15] but his case dramatically illustrates the moral and financial pitfalls of operating in a country with the serious and pervasive human rights abuses found in China.

In contrast to the win-win aspects of human rights spin-off described in the previous chapter, the multinational corporation facing this type of situation is in a no-win situation. If it fails to yield to the pressure from the foreign power, it could jeopardize millions of dollars of invested capital. If the corporation cooperates with the government against the dissident, it compromises its own moral integrity and invites severe public condemnation.

Multinational corporations understandably are reluctant to speak openly about instances in which they have been asked to fire or take another kind of job action against a political or religious dissident. Therefore, it is difficult to estimate how often such situations arise and how executives have responded to such requests. However, off-the-record conversations with American business executives in China suggest that these kinds of situations arise frequently enough that it behooves managers to think in advance about how they should react.

Even when the employees of a multinational corporation are not involved in dissident activities, human rights issues can still occupy the agendas of multinational executives. Because human rights violations in China are serious and pervasive, some argue that multinational corporations should not be doing business there at all. Participation in the Chinese economy is seen as helping to keep a repressive government in power. Very few companies have reached this conclusion. One notable exception is the San Francisco–based jeans company Levi Strauss & Co. In a much-publicized move, Levi Strauss decided to sever most of its business ties in China to remain faithful to its "Guidelines for Country

Selection." That policy was drawn up out of concern that operating in certain countries would tarnish Levi Strauss's valuable brand name and be inconsistent with the company's long-standing values. The "Guidelines for Country Selection" stipulated that Levi Strauss would not initiate or renew contractual relations in countries in which human rights abuses were "pervasive." Reasoning that the company would have no power to affect the general human rights situation in China by doing business there, Levi Strauss executives believed they had no choice but to stop doing business in China.[16]

Although one should not criticize Levi Strauss for its decision (indeed, some might feel praise is appropriate), it is not one that other companies should feel obliged to emulate. Despite the undeniably repressive nature of the government, it is still possible for foreign companies—particularly those whose executives have thought through their human rights responsibilities and how they will discharge those responsibilities—to operate in China without becoming complicit in abuses by the government. Moreover, as has been shown, many companies doing business in China create positive human rights spin-off in the values they impart to their employees. In recognition of these factors, Levi Strauss decided in 1998 to allow its Asia Pacific Division to seek supply contracts in China (for products exported to the region but *not* back to the United States or Europe), provided that they could do so in accordance with the company's global sourcing guidelines.[17]

THREE VIEWS OF CORPORATE RESPONSIBILITY FOR HUMAN RIGHTS

There is no shortage of opinions, informed and otherwise, about what responsibilities corporations have for human rights conditions in China. Three of the most highly publicized of these views—those of the American Chamber of Commerce in Hong Kong (AmCham), HRW, and the Clinton Administration's "Model Business Principles"—are examined and compared in this section (Table 6.1).

The American Chamber of Commerce in Hong Kong

For most business executives, the very idea that their company should draw up and enforce vigorous human rights policies is threatening and confusing. The suggestion that companies should adopt a human rights code of conduct in China tends to elicit a strong negative response. As

Table 6.1 Selected Comparison of American Chamber of Commerce in Hong Kong
(AmCham), Human Rights Watch (HRW), and Clinton Codes

	AmCham	HRW	Clinton
Refuse to do business with business partners with unsafe and inhumane working conditions?	Yes	Yes, plus— includes unannounced check-ups	No—only "encourages" them not to follow such practices
Refuse to fire employees because of their political views?	Not addressed	Yes	Not addressed
Proactively raise human rights issues with Chinese government?	Not addressed	Yes	Not addressed

one business representative put it, "the impetus of laying on the American business community a corporate code of conduct simply gives credence to the idea that business is morally responsible for the human rights situation in China. We don't accept that."[18] Others believe that corporations should be expected to promote human rights only if they can do so by pursuing self-interest. This attitude seems to underlie the comments of a representative of the Chamber of Commerce when he said that, when it comes to human rights in China, "U.S. companies are part of the solution, not the problem."[19]

The most threatening aspect of dealing with human rights issues is the fear, unfortunately quite rational, that corporations stand to lose a lot of money by confronting the Chinese government. As we have seen, competition in China is fierce, as European, Japanese, and American companies vie with each other for a foothold in the world's fastest-growing and most populous economy. Moreover, one of the keys to success in the Chinese market is good relations with the Communist Party, which keeps rigid control over the economy. Multinational corporations spend years cultivating good *guanxi*, or connections, in China. They are thus extremely vulnerable to retaliation. Even powerful corporations such as Motorola, Hewlett-Packard, and General Motors are cognizant that they could jeopardize billions of dollars of investments if they take a position on human rights that angers the Chinese government. At the time of the Gao Feng incident, for example, Chrysler was well aware that failure to accede to the government's request could result in losing a valuable minivan contract to its German competitor Daimler Benz (the two companies have since merged). As a consequence, the basic survival instinct of most foreign businesspeople in China is to stay as far away from the subject of human rights as possible.

Business executives also tend to view human rights matters as political issues that are outside of their area of expertise and legitimate concern. The view of an executive at an American aircraft manufacturer is typical: "If we start getting involved in their internal affairs, then we've stepped over the line. As long as it's good for us and the airplane, that's fine."[20] When DuPont Chairman Edgar S. Woolard met with Chinese President Jiang Zemin in the summer of 1994, he did not broach the subject of human rights, observing that it "is inappropriate for businesspeople to be involved when governments are involved on this issue."[21]

The various negative and fearful attitudes of the business community concerning human rights coalesced in the model "Business Principles" issued in 1994 by AmCham (Appendix A). The most striking thing about the AmCham principles is that they do not dare mention the words "China" or "human rights." The omission is particularly glaring because the principles were drawn up specifically in response to President Clinton's pledge to propose model business principles regarding human rights in China. The stated reason for not formulating specific principles for China was an avowed desire for consistency. AmCham argued that any principles addressing human rights problems in China should be applied with equal force to other nations. Otherwise, such principles would unfairly single out China. Behind this ostensibly even-handed sentiment, however, it is obvious that an important factor in declining to issue principles specifically directed toward China was fear of reprisal from the Chinese government. For example, around the time that the AmCham principles were promulgated, an AT&T executive expressed the fear that "a code of conduct would be viewed by the Chinese government as another attempt to influence Chinese domestic politics and would be detrimental to U.S. business."[22]

The sad truth is, of course, that such fear is well founded. As the saying goes, just because you are paranoid doesn't mean that they are not out to get you. China has not been hesitant to flex its newly formed economic muscle to blunt criticism of its human rights record. For example, on the last day of his visit to the United States in November 1997, Chinese President Jiang Zemin announced that three Hollywood studios would be prohibited from distributing films in China because they produced films critical of its human rights practices. Moreover, despite the fact that China desperately needs foreign capital to continue its economic expansion, it has proven quite adept at pitting American, European, and Japanese suitors against one another. This further increases the pressure on multinational corporations to avoid human rights confrontations with the Chinese government.

To be fair, the AmCham principles have much in them to admire. They were clearly written by a group of companies that accepted responsibility for matters they felt they could control. The principles include an unqualified and direct pledge to "refuse to do business with firms which employ forced labor, or treat their workers in inhumane or unsafe ways." Also of note is the emphasis the principles place on training: "We shall endeavor to promote the highest possible standards of training and education for our employees. Training objectives derive from raising issues such as promoting self-confidence, independent and innovative thinking, self-improvement, and problem solving through teamwork." It is precisely these kinds of training programs that lead to the human rights spin-off effects discussed in Chapter 4.

In other respects, however, the AmCham principles must be counted a less than courageous effort. Most significant, they fail to address the role of multinational corporations in protecting the political rights and civil liberties of their employees. One might well imagine that the appetite for taking on such a controversial subject must have been very slight indeed. Nonetheless, AmCham missed an important opportunity. The failure to provide guidance on this critical issue stems in part from the hope that if the issue is not addressed, it will not come up. As a result of this head-in-the-sand approach, American corporations operating in China were deprived of guidance on the most difficult human rights issue they are likely to face in China from a knowledgeable group that was well suited to offer practical advice on the subject.

The Human Rights Watch Principles

In May 1994, the NGO HRW issued a "Working Paper" urging firms in China to take a "proactive approach" toward human rights.[23] The HRW proposal contained, as did the AmCham principles, a strongly worded provision concerning prison labor. HRW went a step further, however, and urged firms to make unannounced factory site visits to ensure that suppliers were not employing prison or forced labor. HRW also admonished firms to refuse to discriminate against workers for their political beliefs and to refuse to terminate workers who have been imprisoned for their political beliefs.

The most far-reaching and dubious HRW proposal urged firms to seek audiences with Chinese officials to raise concerns about human rights violations that are unrelated to business operations:

[S]enior management should raise concerns about respect for human rights with appropriate Chinese officials including the detention, arrest or conviction of people whose only "offense" is the nonviolent expression of their political views. . . . Often U.S. companies are well-placed to use their influence in the course of their dealings with central, provincial, and local authorities. Concern can be expressed discreetly and in a non-provocative manner, *and can be framed not as a criticism but as a problem threatening the expansion of a mutually beneficial business relationship* [emphasis added].

HRW publicized its proposal for "proactive" policies as an exercise in "enlightened corporate self-interest," noting that "none of these steps involves a violation of Chinese law, and the good faith standard ensures that there is considerable leeway to avoid taking action that could unnecessarily imperil business relationships." Nonetheless, the reaction of the U.S. business community to the HRW proposal was swift and predictably unenthusiastic. A representative of the U.S.-China Business Council remarked: "This may appear to be a harmless form of political expediency, but in fact such a code would cripple the prospects of many American companies in the Chinese market and undermine progress in human rights. . . . China will respond by severely restricting their activities or throwing them out altogether."[24]

The Clinton Administration's "Model Business Principles"

In April 1995, the Clinton administration released a set of voluntary "Model Business Principles," approximately one year later than they were promised (Appendix B). The Clinton principles were not, as originally promised, addressed specifically to China. Nor did they address in any meaningful way the civil and political rights issues in China that necessitated the promulgation of the principles in the first place.

The Clinton principles exhort firms to avoid child and forced labor as well as discrimination on the basis of race, gender, national origin, or religious belief. However, with regard to the employment practices of business partners, the Clinton principles are looser and vaguer than either the AmCham or HRW principles. Whereas the AmCham principles state unequivocally that firms should "refuse" to do business with partners that follow inhumane business practices, the Clinton principles say only that firms should be *"encouraging* [emphasis added] similar behavior by their partners, suppliers and subcontractors."

Although the Clinton principles urge "respect for the right of association and the right to organize and bargain collectively," they fail to mention discrimination in hiring and firing practices based on political belief. This failure is especially notable because by the time the principles had been announced, Chrysler's firing of Gao Feng for his religious views had already received significant publicity. The Clinton principles instead make a vague call for "maintenance, through leadership at all levels, of a corporate culture that respects free expression consistent with legitimate business concerns, and does not condone political coercion in the workplace."

The Clinton principles were intended to serve as a model that firms would voluntarily emulate. A year after their release, however, Mike Jendrzejczyk of HRW reported that he was unaware of any firm that had been influenced by the Clinton principles to adopt a code of conduct.[25] The failure to inspire U.S. firms to adopt ethical principles for operating in China can in part be explained by the lack of leadership provided by the Clinton administration. It is, after all, somewhat audacious to ask U.S. firms to take a strong stand on human rights when only a year earlier the government itself had backed down from its promise to condition MFN renewal on human rights progress. Thus, the fact that firms operating in China declined President Clinton's invitation to put themselves on the human rights hot seat is hardly surprising. U.S. firms also feared that any "voluntary" principles would, as did the Sullivan Principles for South Africa, travel a slippery slope to legal mandate. (In 1986, Congress passed the Comprehensive Anti-Apartheid Act, requiring U.S. firms doing business in South Africa to adopt the Sullivan principles.)[26]

CONCLUSION

Multinational executives face significant human rights challenges in China requiring them to make difficult decisions about their moral responsibilities. These decisions have potentially devastating economic consequences. It is, therefore, imperative that multinational executives develop the capacity to make morally sound decisions and implement those decisions in a way that minimizes the negative financial consequences. The three proposals examined here all attempt to provide a framework to resolve these moral and practical dilemmas. However, they all suffer from a common set of shortcomings and, as a consequence, they are ultimately not very helpful to corporate executives who want to cope successfully with the human rights issues they face in China.

First, all three proposals are virtually devoid of any sense of philosophical inquiry and moral reflection, both of which are indispensable in addressing issues of corporate responsibility for human rights. Even the HRW proposal, although perhaps "moralistic" in intent, sets forth no criteria for judging the moral obligations of corporations. It simply regards the corporation as a tool for advancing a human rights agenda without reflecting on what one can reasonably and justly require it to do. Predictably, the Clinton principles, which were spawned by an interagency effort headed by the National Economic Council, offer the worst example of this lack of moral analysis. It is self-evident from the result that the authors of the Clinton principles were not up to the task of making tough choices based on principle. Consequently, they failed to generate respect among either human rights advocates or the business community. A Chamber of Commerce representative called them "ambiguous and open to interpretation." An HRW official called the principles "far too vague and broadly worded to have any impact." John Kamm, a businessman long active in human rights, called them "a bowl of warm mush."[27]

A satisfactory and useful account of corporate responsibility must be grounded in a moral framework that distinguishes when duty requires corporations to act and when it does not. Such a moral framework must derive from deep reflection on the nature of human rights and the nature of the moral duties they imply. Where the line is drawn between what corporations are and are not morally required to do has very serious consequences. It is not sufficient to simply pull "a code of conduct" or "human rights principles" out of thin air. Most important, for a code or set of principles to have moral authority, it must be based on underlying moral values and reasoning that are clear and compelling. These values, and the reasoning process that accompanies the incorporation of the values into codes and principles, must be convincing to both corporate executives and human rights advocates, as well as to ordinary concerned people. This kind of "disinterestedness"—that is, this sense that the principles being advocated are right regardless of one's material interest, is perhaps the most important distinguishing characteristic of morality. As political ethicists Amy Gutman and Dennis Thompson write:

What distinguishes ethical principles from purely prudential principles common in politics is their disinterested perspective. Prudence asks whether an action or policy serves the interests of some particular individual group or nation. Ethics asks whether an action or policy could be accepted by anyone without regard to his or her particular circumstances such as social class, race, or nationality.[28]

None of these three proposals evinces that kind of disinterestedness. They are each products of particular points of view, sharing only minimal give and take with other points of view. Hence, it should come as no surprise that none of them carries any particular moral weight. In Chapter 9, we will consider a number of more recent efforts to draw up human rights codes of behavior. Because these efforts were joint industry-NGO efforts, they come much closer to achieving the disinterested moral perspective that is required if a code or set of principles is to have moral authority.

A second failing of these proposals is that they evince little understanding of the extent of the power possessed by multinational corporations to affect human rights conditions in China. In the case of the AmCham principles, corporate power to affect human rights outcomes is understated. In the case of the HRW proposal, the sense of what corporations can achieve is overblown. Only by considering how multinational corporations actually function in the Chinese setting can one appreciate the extent and limits of what they can and cannot do to positively affect human rights. This kind of analysis is an indispensable precondition for judging what corporations have a moral duty to do. It is often said in moral theory that "ought implies can." None of these proposals has an accurate sense of "can." Thus, the "ought" each of them proposes is off the mark.

A final problem with the three proposals is that they attempt to establish corporate responsibility in a vacuum. Corporations are not the only actors who can do something constructive about human rights in China. Many other actors in the international community, in addition to corporations, have human rights duties—for example, nation-states, intergovernmental organizations, NGOs, and individual consumers. Understanding who these other actors are and what human rights duties *they* owe are essential steps in coming to understand the human rights responsibilities of multinational corporations. We simply cannot expect that multinational corporations will do alone what all of the morally responsible actors must do together.

Chapter 8 proposes an alternative fair share approach to determining corporate responsibility for human rights in China. It endeavors to avoid some of the conceptual shortcomings that plague the three proposals considered in this chapter. From this general theory, principles about corporate responsibility for human rights are derived. In subsequent chapters, these principles are applied to answer the practical moral issues outlined in this chapter. Before turning to the task of constructing the fair share theory, however, Chapter 7 attempts to put the issue of human rights and all of the controversies that it engenders into some historical perspective. This historical perspective is essential to understanding why multinational corporations are coming under pressure to assume increasing duties in protecting human rights. Understanding the broad and long-standing historical controversies generated by the idea of human rights also will assist in the formulation of a realistic vision of the potential reach of corporate human rights responsibility.

☆

Human Rights in the Latter Half of the Twentieth Century: Ideological and Institutional Fragmentation

"What are human rights? They are the rights of how many people, of a majority, of a minority, or of all the people? What the West calls human rights and what we call human rights are two different things, with different standpoints."

—Deng Xiaoping

This book has already touched briefly at various points on some of the controversies engendered by the idea of human rights. This chapter explores the nature and historical genesis of these controversies in greater detail. The point of this historical account is to try to put the human rights responsibilities of multinational corporations into context. The political complexity and interculturally controversial nature of human rights are important factors that must be taken into account when we reason about the human rights duties of multinational corporations. In general, the more politically complex and culturally controversial an issue is, the less suited corporate executives are to taking an active advocacy role in resolving the issue. The subject of human rights is one of the most complex and controversial issues the world faces today. Powerful nations and world leaders have been perplexed by it for years and are often reluctant to take strong stands on human rights for fear of giving offense, losing commercial contacts, or creating international tension. These factors suggest some constraints that should be taken into account when discussing what multinational corporations can and ought to do about human rights.

To summarize, the complexities and controversies concerning human rights include the following:

- The idea of human rights is at odds with the notion of state sovereignty and the corresponding principle of noninterference by states in the affairs of other sovereign states.
- No real consensus exists about which rights qualify as human rights.
- Some regard an emphasis on civil and political rights as a Western bias and argue that these rights must be interpreted and enforced in the light of the unique cultural and economic circumstances of each particular nation.
- No consensus exists about the appropriate international institutional framework for enforcing human rights.

All of these controversies have deep historical roots dating back to the very beginnings of the human rights movement. As the third millenium begins, developing nations use the principle of state sovereignty as a shield to deflect human rights criticism that they regard as meddling in their internal affairs. It is sobering to bear in mind, however, that the developed nations also have exhibited fear of the consequences of internationalism and the loss of state sovereignty. Motivated by this fear, the members of the United Nations forged weak international human rights institutions with little power to monitor, punish, and prevent human rights abuses. This initial ambivalence about human rights was further fueled by two other historical factors: the Cold War and the rise of the Third World.

THE UNIVERSAL DECLARATION: A FRAGILE IDEOLOGICAL CONSENSUS

The concept of human rights has antecedents in liberal democratic theory arising in Western societies in the seventeenth century—most notably, John Locke's idea of natural rights and limited government.[1] However, it is more appropriate to think of human rights as a twentieth-century concept with specific historical roots. What makes human rights truly distinctive are their internationalist claims—that is, the notion that governments and other actors throughout the world might bear some responsibility for securing human rights. (This aspect of human rights is taken up in greater detail in Chapter 8.) Accordingly, it is not overstating the point to say that *human rights*, as we understand the term today, had their genesis on December 10, 1948. On that date, the General Assembly of the newly constituted United Nations passed a resolution endorsing the broad utopian ideals of the Universal Declaration of Human Rights.

In 1948, the appalling consequences of the world's failure to acknowledge and prevent the moral horrors of the Holocaust were still a fresh memory. Buoyed in large part by the desire to avert future tragedies, the Universal Declaration of Human Rights emerged in the fledgling United Nations as a noble moral vision of humanity. The Declaration is the most comprehensive catalog and unequivocal endorsement of human rights. This unprecedented document proclaimed itself to be "a common standard of achievement for all people and all nations." As the twenty-first century begins, however, the hope generated by the Universal Declaration has not led to substantial international consensus about either the meaning of human rights or an appropriate institutional framework for enforcing them. The consensus that flowered briefly in 1948 has given way to bitter division over the scope, meaning, and universality of human rights, as well as the institutional mechanisms for enforcing them.

The consensus embodied in the Universal Declaration was a fragile one brokered by a small group of elite diplomats, mostly from or educated in the West, who did not even have the full support of their respective nations. This fragility was evident as early as during the drafting of the U.N. Charter in 1945. Some nations, including Canada, Australia, and Mexico, called for the inclusion of a bill of human rights in the U.N. Charter itself. In the initial consultations among the "big four" nations—the United States, United Kingdom, Nationalist China, and the Union of Soviet Socialist Republics—Nationalist China argued for including nondiscrimination and equal rights provisions in the charter. The United States, however, resisted such efforts, primarily to avoid scrutiny of racial segregation practices in southern states. The United Kingdom similarly wished to avoid international criticism of its exclusionary immigration policies. The Soviet Union also vigorously opposed any attempts to create a human rights basis for intrusion on state sovereignty. Compromise language in Article 55 of the charter provided that the United Nations would "promote . . . universal respect for, and observance of human rights and fundamental freedoms for all without distinction as to race, language, religion, or sex." In Article 56, the members of the United Nations pledge to take "joint and separate action" to achieve these purposes.

Despite these pronouncements, however, Article 2(7) expressly placed human rights outside the military intervention powers of the United Nations. (Article 39 in chapter VII does provide, however, a justification for military force in the case of a "threat to the peace, breach of the peace, or act of aggression.") Except in the case of a gross human rights violation posing a threat of war, therefore, the charter left the realization of human rights ideals to a haphazard institutional framework that, even after nearly half a century, has yet to achieve coherence and effectiveness. Article 13 empowers the general assembly to initiate studies and make recommendations for "promoting and . . . assisting in the realization of human rights." Article 62 authorizes the Economic and Social Council to make recommendations promoting "respect for, and observance of human rights." Article 68 created the Human Rights Commission, although it failed to specify its power and authority.

The principle that individuals should be held accountable for violations of international law, even when acting in an official capacity, has been debated since the Nuremberg prosecution of Nazi war criminals. However, there has not been sufficient consensus within the United Nations to codify the Nuremberg principles. After the publicity given to atrocities in Somalia, Bosnia, Rwanda, Haiti, Kosovo, and elsewhere, support has been developing for the creation of an International Criminal Court with jurisdiction to try and punish individuals committing serious human rights abuses. (What qualifies as "serious" enough to trigger the jurisdiction of such a court is still a matter of some debate.) Special tribunals have been set up, for example, to prosecute war crimes in the former Yugoslavia and Rwanda. At the moment, however, no permanent international mechanism exists by which individuals can be held accountable for even gross violations of human rights.[2]

In sum, the U.N. Charter created little hope of establishing an institutional framework that would be capable of taking effective action against nations that violate the human rights of their citizens. The United Nations gave birth to human rights ideals without putting in place institutions to enforce those ideals. Without a strong and effective international human rights institution, the task of enforcement would be left to the uncoordinated and ill-defined efforts of individual states and nonstate actors. Eventually, the United Nations would give the Human Rights Commission monitoring powers but, as the case of the 1996 vote on China (described in Chapter 5) illustrated, the Commission's effectiveness has been limited by both institutional constraints and excessive politicization.

Between the founding of the United Nations in 1945 and the first meeting of the Human Rights Commission in 1947, a debate emerged about the powers and goals of the commission. At one extreme, some urged the commission to propose a binding bill of rights and the assumption of powers of inquiry to enforce such provisions. At the other extreme, some criticized the proposed Universal Declaration as a "cruelly deceptive" gesture that would raise false hopes for unachievable ideals. As Yale law professor Edwin Borchard wrote presciently at the time: "[T]he times seem hardly propitious for the much greater advance involved in affording the individual protection for the enforcement or international guaranty of his rights against his own state. . . . [T]he chances that the United Nations will implement their promises and hopes by provisions of positive law, and especially that they will enforce these provisions effectively, are rather less than rosy."[3]

Eventually, the United Nations directed the commission to draw up an international bill of rights and to make recommendations regarding other matters concerning human rights. The commission, responding to pressure from both Western nations and the Soviet bloc, declined to advocate the creation of institutions empowered to enforce human rights. It did, however, set about the task of formulating human rights standards. Within two years, the eighteen-member commission completed the drafting of the Universal Declaration of Human Rights. It was drafted by an eight-member committee that included Eleanor Roosevelt of the United States as chair, Harvard-educated Charles Malik of Lebanon, and Columbia postgraduate P. C. Chang of Nationalist China, as well as representatives from the Soviet Union, United Kingdom, France, Australia, and Chile.

The drafting of the Universal Declaration exhibited many of the controversies that exist today. As there had been in the drafting of the United Nations Charter, considerable disagreement arose over whether the commission should attempt to produce a hortatory declaration or a binding treaty with enforcement provisions. The Indian and Australian delegations, among others, favored the latter. But the Soviet Union and the United States favored the adoption merely of a nonbinding declaration. Indeed, after W. E. B. DuBois, writing on behalf of the National Association for the Advancement of Colored People, submitted a lengthy petition seeking U.N. redress for U.S. violations of the human rights of blacks, southern segregationist Senators opposed the adoption of any human rights document. Eleanor Roosevelt, in fact, was able to successfully campaign on behalf of the Universal Declaration only by assuring opponents that it would not create legal obligations for the United States.

Even as a strictly hortatory document, the Universal Declaration generated considerable controversy. Western nations sought to place the emphasis on political and civil liberties—due process and freedom of religion, expression, and association—whereas the Soviet bloc nations gave priority to economic and social rights—jobs, education, and social security. The Universal Declaration itself represented a compromise. The first twelve of its twenty-five articles concern civil and political rights. Five articles concern rights for criminal defendants, two affirm political rights, and six proclaim economic, social, and cultural rights.

Although traditional Western political and civil rights norms were those most forcefully and fully expressed in the Universal Declaration, these norms were subjected to minor but telling modification by distinctively non-Western ideas. The right to freedom of opinion and expression in Article 19, for example, arguably is subject to the limitation in Article 7's protection "against any discrimination in violation of this Declaration and against any incitement to such discrimination." Article 29 proclaims that "everyone has duties to the community in which alone the free and full development of his personality is possible." Concerned that the economic, social, and cultural provisions would lead to excessive state socialism, the American and Canadian bar associations declared the proposed Declaration "not in content or draftsmanship suitable for approval or adoption."[4]

On December 10, 1948, forty members of the United Nations General Assembly adopted the Universal Declaration of Human Rights without dissent, but eight nations, including the Soviet Union and South Africa, abstained because they were concerned that voting for the declaration would impose new legal obligations on them. It thus emerged as a "common standard of achievement," but it created no legally binding obligations for U.N. members. The task of drafting a legally binding treaty was put off for another day, reflecting a lingering ambivalence about internationalism in general and human rights in particular.

The Human Rights Covenants: Reluctant Formal Agreement

By 1954, the Human Rights Commission finally produced a follow-up treaty to the Universal Declaration, but by this time it had become necessary to propose not one but two treaties or "covenants"—one for political and civil rights and the other for economic, social, and cultural rights. A U.N. General Assembly resolution in 1950 declared that the commission should draft a single covenant reflecting both economic and political rights. At the insistence of the United States and Western European nations, however, the human rights treaty was split into two: the International Covenant on Economic, Social, and Cultural Rights and the International Covenant on Civil and Political Rights. Nevertheless, a close reading of the two documents reveals that they contain many overlapping provisions reflecting the persistent hope of the U.N. General Assembly (embodied in a 1952 resolution) that the two treaties possess unity of purpose. In any event, nations were slow to sign and ratify either of the covenants. As a result, the covenants were not opened for signature until 1966.[5]

In the United States, opposition to the human rights covenants was formidable. In the early 1950s, states-rights forces from the South feared that ratification of international human rights treaties would lead to the end of racial segregation. One of the perverse ironies of the championing of human rights by the United States is the country's own spotty record in ratifying human rights agreements. It was not until 1992 that the United States finally ratified the International Covenant on Civil and Political Rights, and it has never seriously considered ratifying the International Covenant on Economic, Social, and Cultural Rights. Adding insult to injury, when the United States finally did ratify the Covenant on Civil and Political Rights, it reserved the right not to undertake any treaty obligations inconsistent with the United States Constitution or that would cause or require a change in existing U.S. law or practice.

The legal scholar Louis Henkin has pointed out that "the United States apparently seeks to assure that its adherence to a convention will not change, or require change, in U.S. laws, policies, or practices, even where they fall below international standards."[6] At least ten nations and the Human Rights Committee have objected to the United States's ratification of human rights treaties with reservations. (The Human Rights Committee—not to be confused with the Human Rights Commission—consists of eighteen expert members who administer the International Covenant on Civil and Political Rights.) Professor Henkin writes that "the United States seeks to sit in judgment on others but will not submit its human rights behavior to international judgment. To many, the attitude reflected in such reservations is offensive: the conventions are only for other states, not for the United States."[7]

THE COLD WAR AND HUMAN RIGHTS

Simultaneously with the drafting and adoption of the Universal Declaration, the United States and the Soviet Union fell into the Cold War, a prolonged period of intense geopolitical hostility. In 1948, Soviet troops marched into Hungary. Within two years, the Soviet Union completed its military domination of Eastern Europe. In 1949, the Communist Party assumed complete control of mainland China. Mao Zedong's PLA marched into Beijing and founded the People's Republic of China. The U.S.-backed Kuomintang forces of Chiang Kai-Shek were forced to flee across the Taiwan Strait to the island of Formosa. Soviet domination of Eastern Europe and its sponsoring of Communist Party activities in Greece, France, and Italy eventually spurred the United States to pursue a foreign policy that was to be dominated, until the dramatic disintegration of the Soviet bloc, by an overriding concern with the military and political containment of communism.

Although the origins of the Cold War are complex, its intellectual birth can be located in a remarkable series of writings by George Kennan. In his "long telegram," composed in 1946 while he was still an obscure diplomat in Moscow, and in an article the following year in *Foreign Affairs* anonymously published under the name "X," Kennan offered a bleak vision of the Soviet Union. According to Kennan, the very nature of the communist philosophy and the Soviet system made tension with the outside world inevitable.

Kennan's view of the Soviet Union was modified by the Truman administration to convince the traditionally isolationist Republican Party to support military and economic aid policies such as the Marshall Plan for Europe. In announcing in 1947 what would come to be known as the Truman Doctrine, President Truman proclaimed a struggle between two fundamentally different ways of life: "One way of life is based upon the will of the majority, and is distinguished by free institutions, representative government, free elections, guarantees of individual liberty, freedom of speech and religion and freedom from political oppression. The second way of life is based upon the will of a minority forcibly imposed upon the majority. It relies upon terror and oppression, a controlled press and radio, fixed elections and the suppression of personal freedoms." Central to Truman's "evil empire" vision was the idea (articulated by Cold Warriors who reinterpreted Kennan) that Soviet communism was inherently expansionist and that U.S. foreign policy should contain this threat wherever and whenever it occurred. President Truman proclaimed that it was the "policy of the United States to support free peoples who are resisting attempted subjugation by armed minorities or by outside pressures."

Henry Kissinger has observed that criticism of America's containment policy "appeared at both ends of the intellectual spectrum: some protested that America was defending countries that, however important, were morally unworthy; others objected that America was committing itself to the defense of societies that, whether free or not, were not vital to American security. . . . American foreign policy has been obliged to navigate between those who assail it for being amoral and those who criticize it for going beyond the national interest through crusading moralism."[8] As Kissinger personally experienced, navigating between these two critical hazards is very difficult indeed. In its worst moments, such as the Vietnam War, in which tens of thousands of American lives were lost, the containment policy failed on both grounds as it sought to promote regimes of questionable strategic significance, led by morally dubious governments, located in distant lands.

As were most other foreign policy considerations, U.S. human rights policy during the Cold War was subordinated to and made a handmaiden of containment. Under the aegis of containment, the United States has at various times supported repressive military and civilian regimes in Bolivia, Chile, the Dominican Republic, Guatemala, Haiti, Iran, Liberia, Pakistan, Paraguay, Somalia, South Africa, Sudan, South Vietnam, South Korea, and Zaire. Jack Donnelly has observed that "the United States regularly equated anti-communism with pursuit of human rights. . . . The logic typically has run something as follows: Communism is (inherently) opposed to human rights. The United States is (almost by definition) in favor of human rights. Therefore, U.S. action against international communism is equivalent to action on behalf of human rights."[9]

MANIPULATION OF TRADE POLICY AND MILITARY AID

During the Carter and Reagan administrations, the United States attempted to use military aid and trade policy as weapons to promote human rights. In both administrations, however, the Cold War agenda continued in many cases to override human rights concerns. As a result, U.S. human rights policy has been inconsistent, selectively applied, and often hypocritical, further eroding the legitimacy of human rights ideals in the eyes of other nations.

The political scientist Lisa Martin has observed that the impetus to link aid and trade policies with human rights was initiated in the 1970s by a Democrat-controlled Congress that sought to influence the human rights policy of Republican presidents. These efforts grew increasingly bolder throughout the 1970s.[10] In 1973, Congress amended section 32 of the Foreign Assistance Act of 1961 (P.L. 93-189), providing that it was "the sense of the Congress" that the President should withhold military aid from countries that held political prisoners. A year later, after a number of high-profile hearings criticizing Republican human rights policies, Congress passed section 502B of the Foreign Assistance Act of 1974. Section 502B, as amended in 1976 and 1978, provided that, "except in extraordinary circumstances, the President shall substantially reduce or terminate security assistance to any government which engages in a consistent pattern of gross violations of internationally recognized human rights." Gross violations were defined as "torture or cruel, inhuman or degrading treatment or punishment; prolonged detention without charges; or other flagrant denials of the right to life, liberty, and the security of the person." In 1977, Congress created the position of Assistant Secretary of State for Human Rights and required the Export Import Bank to consult with the assistant secretary before facilitating loans in nations in which human rights were being abused.

On the basis of 502B, the Carter administration denied or cut military aid to countries such as Chile, Uruguay, Brazil, El Salvador, Guatemala, Nicaragua, Paraguay, Ethiopia, Argentina, and Bolivia. In a number of cases, however, Cold War geopolitical calculations continued to trump human rights in foreign aid decisions. Thus, in this same period, the "extraordinary circumstances" exemption was invoked to keep military aid flowing to repressive regimes in the Philippines, South Korea, Iran, Zaire, and Indonesia.[11]

The inconsistency of U.S. human rights policy was in part due to partisan changes in the control of the presidency. The Reagan administration reversed Carter's policy of opposing multilateral aid on human rights grounds to Chile, Argentina, Paraguay, and Uruguay. In the 1980s, Reagan routinely certified that El Salvador was making progress in human rights even as there were regular and reliable news reports of the activities of death squads in that country. President Ferdinand Marcos of the Philippines and President Chun Do Hwan of South Korea were praised by Reagan officials for their commitment to democracy and freedom.[12]

Reagan's U.N. ambassador, Jeane Kirkpatrick, in an influential series of articles, distinguished "authoritarian" right-wing governments amenable to democratic liberalization from "totalitarian" communist governments that were not. The "Kirkpatrick Doctrine" explicitly sanctioned the domination of U.S. human rights policy by the overriding concern with the military containment of communism.[13] As was often the case during the Cold War, the Reagan administration made strange bedfellows in the name of human rights. Reagan's economic sanctions policy reflected a Cold War agenda. The Soviet Union and other "totalitarian" states, such as Poland, became the targets of economic sanctions. "Authoritarian" regimes, which coincidentally were amenable to the U.S. geopolitical agenda, were embraced regardless of well-documented human rights violations.

The weapon of choice in attacking human rights abuses in the former Soviet bloc countries was the Jackson-Vanik amendment to the Trade Act of 1974. The Jackson-Vanik amendment took its name from its sponsors in the Senate, Henry M. Jackson (D-WA), and the House, Charles Vanik (D-OH). Jackson-Vanik prohibits extension of MFN status to nations with centrally planned economies that restrict emigration. Some have tried to use the Jackson-Vanik process to pressure China into adopting human rights reforms. In the 1980s, the Reagan administration used Jackson-Vanik to deny MFN treatment to Bulgaria, Czechoslovakia, East Germany, Hungary, and Romania.[14] As it has been so often, avowed U.S. concern for human rights was mixed with other political objectives. In a 1983 speech in which he attempted to describe the criteria for invoking the Jackson-Vanik procedure, then Vice President George Bush candidly acknowledged this overlap:

> We look to what degree countries pursue autonomous foreign policies, independent of Moscow's direction, and to what degree they foster domestic liberalization—politically, economically, and in their respect for human rights. The United States will engage in closer political, economic, and cultural relations with those countries, such as Hungary and Romania, which assert greater openness or independence.[15]

Whatever might have been the positive effects of containment on American security interests and the eventual demise of the Soviet empire, its consequences for human rights were unequivocally negative. Much of the contemporary cynicism of developing countries toward U.S. pronouncements about human rights can be traced to a history of using human rights as a pretext for geopolitical influence. In the wake of the Cold War, these misgivings continue, except that now U.S. human rights policy is often viewed in developing countries not only as a geopolitical tool, but also as a form of cultural imperialism and disguised economic protectionism.

In the 1990s, the attention of U.S. human rights policy shifted to Asia, and concerns included labor rights in addition to civil and political rights. But again accusations were made of a hidden agenda. Many developing nations have characterized the U.S. concern for labor rights as a thinly veiled form of economic protectionism. In September 1993, for example, a team of U.S. officials visited Indonesia to investigate working conditions, labor regulations, and wage levels. At stake was Indonesia's continued access to the United States Generalized System of Preferences, which allowed selected goods to be exported to the United States duty-free. (The U.S. Generalized System of Preferences, the Caribbean Basin Initiative, and the Andean Initiative give preferential duty treatment for selected products from eligible developing countries.) Indonesian officials viewed the U.S. delegation skeptically. Said one: "A poor and over-populated developing country cannot apply the same standards as a more prosperous nation."[16] Another official suggested that, with unemployment and competition from Asian imports becoming political issues in the United States, U.S. concerns about human rights were simply disguised protectionism. Seventeen other countries, including Malaysia and Thailand, also were being investigated.[16]

THE EMERGENCE OF THE THIRD WORLD: NEW VOICES AND CONCERNS

With the emergence of the Third World, new voices began to express reservations about the notion that human rights had one universal meaning. When the Universal Declaration of Human Rights was adopted in 1948, the United Nations consisted of forty-eight countries. By 2000, there were roughly three times as many members. More significant than the sheer expansion of numbers is the diversity of these new nations. The original United Nations was dominated by the United States and Western Europe. The only significant challenge to power and influence came from the Soviet bloc. Only India and China represented Asia, and the only black African members were Ethiopia and Liberia. Because of the eurocentric preoccupation with Nazi atrocities, the atrocities committed by Japan in the Asian war theater—which to this day are a source of deep bitterness in China, Indonesia, Korea, and other East Asian nations—contributed little to the impetus behind the Universal Declaration.[17] One can't help but think, however, that a more substantial Asian participation in the drafting process would have meant a greater consciousness of Japanese atrocities. This Asian participation might have, in turn, significantly modified the language of the Universal Declaration and perhaps contributed to a greater consensus about the meaning and the universality of human rights principles.

The rapid fall of European colonial empires in Asia and Africa after World War II dramatically altered the world's political landscape. In the 1950s and 1960s, proud new nations emerged throughout Asia, Africa, and South America. Nearly forty new African nations, more than a dozen Asian nations, and another dozen Arab nations in the Middle East have joined the United Nations since its founding. These new nations were led by a remarkable group of charismatic and articulate leaders. In 1954, twenty-nine of these leaders, including Abdul Nasser of Egypt, Ho Chi Minh of Vietnam, Nehru of India, Cho Enlai of China, and Marshall Tito of Yugoslavia, convened in the gracious setting of Bandung, Indonesia. They came together at the height of the Cold War in the now legendary "spirit of Bandung" to declare their collective independence from the influence of the United States and the Soviet Union, thereby founding the "non-aligned" movement.

The new nations of Africa and Asia, joined by many of their Latin American counterparts (often collectively referred to as the "Third World"), were to have a significant impact on the agenda of the United Nations. Recently freed from the yoke of colonialism, Third World nations were especially concerned about racism and the right to self-determination and, in particular, with the apartheid regimes in Southern Rhodesia and South Africa. Third World nations also used the United Nations as a forum to press their demands for economic justice. They argued that centuries of exploitation by colonial powers were responsible for poverty in the developing world. Because developed nations enriched themselves at the expense of Third World nations, it was argued, a "New International Economic Order" was required to create a more equitable distribution of the world's resources. In 1967, the membership of the Human Rights Commission expanded from twenty-one to thirty-two, and twenty seats were allocated to the Third World according to a strict regional formula. (When later membership was increased yet again to fifty-three, the regional allocation formula was retained.) With the Third World dominating the commission, the demand for economic justice became a kind of de facto human right—a collective right of developing countries to receive aid from rich countries. Not surprisingly, Western nations reacted harshly to the redistributive aims of the Third World and the attempt to shoehorn such aims into human rights.

In addition to pressing for the collective rights to economic assistance, developing countries also put forward a number of arguments that presaged those made by the Communist Party in response to Western criticism of China's human rights record. The developing nations argued, for example, that economic well being was a prerequisite for the realization of civil and political liberty—that is, economic development was necessary before political and civil rights could be honored. The battleground for this conflict became U.N. General Assembly Resolution 32/130, introduced by Third World nations in 1977. The final wording of the resolution reflected some of the concerns of the United States and other Western nations, but it still contained many elements of the Third World economic agenda, such as the following:

(b) [T]he full realization of civil and political rights without the enjoyment of economic, social, and cultural rights is impossible; the achievement of lasting progress in the implementation of human rights is dependent upon sound and effective national and international policies of economic and social development. . . .
(f) The realization of the new economic order is an essential element for the effective promotion of human rights and fundamental freedoms and should also be accorded priority.

ISLAMIC AND ASIAN CULTURAL CHALLENGES TO THE IDEA OF HUMAN RIGHTS

With the rise of the Third World, two significant culturally based challenges to universal human rights emerged from Islam and Asia. In 1990, the Organization of the Islamic Conference issued the Cairo Declaration on Human Rights in Islam. The Cairo Declaration contends that Islamic civilization is fundamentally incompatible with the Western idea of human rights. The declaration rejects universal human rights norms in a variety of areas, including the equality of women; freedom of religion; freedom of the press, assembly, and association; and the right to privacy.

Iran's former ambassador to the United Nations, Sa'id Raja'i Khorasani, starkly proclaimed a common Muslim nation scorn for universal human rights principles:

[C]onventions, declarations, and resolutions or decisions of international organizations, which were contrary to Islam, had no validity in the

Islamic republic of Iran. . . . The Universal Declaration of Human Rights, which represented secular understanding of the Judeo-Christian tradition, could not be implemented by Muslims and did not accord with the system of values recognized by the Islamic Republic of Iran; this country would therefore not hesitate to violate its provisions, since it had to choose between violating the divine law of the country and violating secular conventions.[18]

To be sure, some challenge the existence of a consensus among Muslims that their religion requires the rejection of international human rights norms. They argue that a range of Muslim attitudes on human rights exists and that religious and cultural arguments are used by Muslims in nations such as Iran and Saudi Arabia to maintain power, stifle legitimate challenges to authority, and subjugate women.[19] Others, however, maintain that there is a distinct Islamic perspective that is incompatible with Western ideas about human rights. According to this view, individuals have obligations to God, fellow humans, and nature, all of which are defined by Shariah (the code of law based on the Koran). Only when individuals meet these obligations do they enjoy certain rights and freedoms prescribed by Shariah. Moreover, male Muslims enjoy greater rights and freedoms than infidels and female Muslims. Whatever rights exist derive not from the fact that one is a human being, but rather from one's social status and one's fulfillment of obligations.[20]

The Asian view of human rights was characteristically delineated in the 1993 Bangkok Declaration.[21] In preparation for the World Conference on Human Rights in Vienna that same year, regional conferences were held for African states in Tunis; for Latin American and Caribbean states in San Jose, Costa Rica; and for Asian states in Bangkok. Each of these conferences produced their own declarations that placed some qualification on the concept of universality in human rights. It was the Bangkok Declaration, however, that aroused the most controversy.

The nations subscribing to the Bangkok Declaration included Myanmar, China, and Indonesia, countries whose human rights records have been sharply criticized by the United States and other Western countries. These nations affirmed "the interdependence and indivisibility of economic, social, cultural, civil, and political rights, and the need to give equal emphasis to all categories of human rights."[22] Not surprisingly, Asian nations, beleaguered by international pressures on human rights, also extolled "the principles of respect for national sovereignty and territorial integrity as well as non-interference in the internal affairs of states, and the non-use of human rights as an instrument of political pressure." To press the point further, the declaration sought to "discourage any attempt to use human rights as a conditionality for extending development assistance."

Underlying the principles espoused in the Bangkok Declaration was the fundamental belief that "while human rights are universal in nature, they must be considered in the context of a dynamic and evolving process of international norm-setting, bearing in mind the significance of national and regional particularities and various historical, cultural and religious values." This relativistic view of human rights was unacceptable to the United States and other Western nations, as well as to many NGOs attending the Vienna Conference. United States Secretary of State Warren Christopher declared in Vienna, "We cannot let cultural relativism become the last refuge of repression."[23]

The Third World Legacy in Human Rights: Institutional Reform and Politicization

Over time, the bitterness concerning collective economic rights subsided somewhat, as developed countries increased foreign aid to developing countries and the focus of Third World economic development shifted to structural adjustment, trade, and foreign investment. Certain concerns raised by the Third World, however, persisted as sources of conflict with developed nations—in particular, the priority of economic development over political rights, and the subordination of individual human rights to collective cultural and religious norms. Added to these issues was the widespread belief in Third World nations of the necessity of balancing individual rights against demands for political order and stability.[24] These controversies continue to be a source of bitter disagreement, even as the twenty-first century dawns.

One enduring legacy of the new nations was the strengthening of the powers of the Human Rights Commission. It was the Third World nations that in the late 1960s and early 1970s provided the impetus behind granting monitoring powers to the commission. Throughout the 1950s and most of the 1960s, the human rights activities of the United Nations were exclusively educational. Numerous U.N.-sponsored conferences were held throughout the world to facilitate discussion of and generate support for human rights ideals.[25] In 1967, however, the United Nations authorized the commission to review and report on human rights violations in particular countries. Composed by independent committees of experts, these reports provide a detailed, credible, and independent assessment of the country concerned,[26] although political maneuvering too often plays a large role in the list of countries selected for review.

HUMAN RIGHTS CONTROVERSIES IN THE CHINESE CONTEXT

The various complexities and controversies emerging from the first half-century of human rights history are mirrored, with all their virulence, in the debate over human rights in China. In November 1991, the Information Office of China's State Council issued a white paper defending China's human rights record.[27] The publication of the white paper was in itself a major step for China. It represented an implicit acknowledgment that, in the wake of the Tiananmen Square massacre, China needed to justify its human rights practices to the world. The nature of the justification itself, however, suggests little basis for hoping that the Chinese government would anytime soon stop abusing the human rights of its citizens.

From the white paper and other official pronouncements, three basic contentions can be discerned: (1) China must give priority to political stability and economic rights over political rights; (2) human rights fall within the purview of China's national sovereignty, and so foreigners should not try to influence human rights conditions within China; and (3) human rights must be interpreted and implemented in accordance with China's cultural values, which emphasize the group over the individual. Each of these contentions requires a response, because to say that multinational corporations, or any other actors for that matter, have a moral duty to promote and protect human rights doesn't make much sense if all attempts by foreigners to influence human rights conditions in China are illegitimate.

The white paper contends that "the right to subsistence is the most important of all human rights, without which the other rights are out of the question." As a result of the perceived historical link between China's poverty and its political instability, the Chinese government believes that it faces a stark choice between two kinds of human rights—economic and political/civil. Given the inevitability of this choice, the white paper argues that the "right to subsistence" must take priority over political and civil rights in a large, poor nation such as China. As one sympathetic Western reporter chimed in, "as a matter of priorities, many people would probably prefer a healthy baby to a meaningful vote."[28] The basic contention is that the curtailment of one type of human right (namely, political rights) is necessary to protect another, more important type of human right (namely, economic rights).

Assuming for the moment that the purportedly inverse relationship between the two kinds of rights is valid, one major problem with the position espoused in the white paper is that it sets no bounds on how much repression of political and civil rights is justified in the name of economic development. The white paper is a blank check on repression in the name of economic development, an account, incidentally, that the Chinese government has drawn on liberally and often.

Whether the particular type and amount of political repression practiced by the Chinese Communist Party contributes to the country's economic prosperity can be debated—unless, of course, you happen to be a Chinese citizen. It is, therefore, incorrect to presume that the position advocated in the white paper fairly represents the views of the Chinese people themselves. Time and again in China, ordinary citizens and political leaders who challenge the Communist Party's view are either jailed or purged from power. It was precisely for suggesting that the position espoused in the white paper is incorrect that Wei Jingsheng was sentenced to jail for fifteen years. His "big character" poster, hung on Beijing's "Democracy Wall" on December 5, 1978, had the temerity to argue that in addition to the four economic modernizations propounded by Deng Xiaoping, China needed a "Fifth Modernization," namely democracy.[29] Zhao Ziyang was deposed as the premier of China after Tiananmen for advocating political reform. Speaking at the Thirteenth Party Congress in 1987, Zhao declared that "without reform of the political structure, reform of the economic structure cannot succeed in the end."[30]

Today in China only a handful of people would dare to challenge the government's position. One of the very few who has done so is Wang Ruoshi. Mr. Wang was deposed as the deputy chief editor of the Communist Party newspaper *People's Daily* for his liberal views. Mr. Wang has observed that "the current leaders say stability takes precedence over everything, but what they really mean is the survival of their regime. China does need stability, but not the kind that protects corruption. Political reform is the best way to prevent instability."[31] As Mr. Wang's comments suggest, the position in the white paper is based on a false factual assumption. The putative connection between repression and economic prosperity is not borne out by the evidence. In general, economic prosperity and political freedom are mutually reinforcing rather than at cross-purposes.[32] Moreover, political freedom yields economic benefits even in very poor countries. Nobel Laureate Armatya Sen has observed that, rather than causing economic disasters, political and civil rights actually help to prevent them. Sen writes:

> Civil and political rights give people the opportunity not only to do things for themselves but also to draw attention forcefully to general needs and to demand appropriate action. Whether and how a government responds to needs and suffering may well depend on how much pressure is put on it, and the exercise of political rights (such as voting, criticizing, protesting, and so on) can make a real difference. . . . For example, one of the remarkable facts in the terrible history of famines in the world is that no substantial famine has ever occurred in any country with a democratic form of government and a relatively free press. This applies not only to the affluent countries of Europe and America, but also to poor but broadly democratic countries (such as India, Botswana, Zimbabwe).[33]

For an example of the connection Sen draws between the absence of political rights and famine, the Chinese government need only consider the more than 30 million people who died during Chairman Mao's ill-conceived Great Leap Forward when the fear of telling the truth about lagging agricultural production levels contributed greatly to the human tragedy.

A second argument that China raises to defend its human rights practices from international criticism is that human rights constitute a purely internal matter falling within the purview of state sovereignty. Thus, it is claimed, China's human rights record, even if it does not adhere to international norms, should be of concern only to China. According to the principle of national sovereignty enshrined in Article 2 of the U.N. Charter, a state has the right to exercise exclusive control over purely internal affairs, including the treatment of its own citizens. Other states have a corresponding duty under international law of noninterference in the internal affairs of a sovereign state. The white paper notes:

> China has firmly opposed any country making use of the issue of human rights to sell its own values, ideology, political standards and mode of development, and to any country interfering in the internal affairs of other countries on the pretext of human rights.
>
> Human rights are essentially matters within the domestic jurisdiction of a country. Respect for each country's sovereignty and non-interference in internal affairs are universally recognized principles of international law. . . .

The argument that the principle of non-interference in internal affairs does not apply to the issue of human rights is, in essence, a demand that is contrary to international law.

Communist Party officials have invoked nationalism to generate public sympathies over issues ranging from human rights and territorial controversies with Japan to relations with Taiwan. Before the founding of the People's Republic of China, China lived under foreign domination for nearly one hundred years. Sovereignty and national pride thus have great resonance for Chinese who believe that foreign powers still conspire to keep it from its rightful place in the world. Many Chinese, for example, viewed the reversion of Hong Kong from British to Chinese rule in July 1997 as an important milestone in the restoration of national pride. Respect should be shown to the emotions felt by Chinese citizens about foreign domination. As a matter of international law, however, whether foreign influence on China's human rights situation violates China's sovereignty depends on the particular role that is proposed for foreigners. Articles 2(7) and 39 of the U.N. Charter make clear, for example, that military intervention for human rights purposes would only be justified when a "threat to the peace, breach of the peace, or act of aggression" has taken place. Absent such conditions, it would be illegal as a matter of international law for a foreign nation to accomplish human rights objectives through military intervention.[34]

Attempts at influence that fall short of military intervention do not, however, violate the principle of state sovereignty. For example, trade sanctions—the suspension of purely voluntary commercial relations among states and private firms—do not, absent an existing economic treaty, violate international law.[35] Unless and until China becomes a member of the World Trade Organization, the United States and Western European countries have no legal duties to trade with China according to any particular schedule of tariffs and duties such as those they accord to other nations who are members of the World Trade Organization. Just as China has rights as a sovereign nation, so, too, do other sovereign nations have the right to trade or not trade with China in part on the basis of China's human rights record. Similarly, foreign business firms do not violate China's sovereignty when they attempt to conduct their operations in China so as to avoid participating in the government's human rights violations. Western consumers have the right to choose or decline to buy Chinese-manufactured goods. In sum, contrary to the position espoused in the white paper, as a matter of international law state and nonstate actors are legally entitled to take various sorts of actions to affect human rights conditions in China without violating the principles of state sovereignty.

If China were to become a member of the World Trade Organization, then it would be legally entitled to trade with the United States according to MFN status (increasingly, trade negotiators have preferred the term *Normal Trade Relations*.) Until China joins the WTO, however, and is thereby granted permanent MFN status, the United States as a sovereign nation has the legal right to trade or not trade with China on whatever terms it wishes.

Chinese officials also make a relativist argument that the principles contained in the Universal Declaration of Human Rights and other international human rights documents must be interpreted so as to take into account the varying circumstances of different nations, particularly in developing nations. The philosopher Bernard Williams has written that the aim of relativism is "to take views, outlooks, or beliefs that apparently conflict and treat them in such a way that they do not conflict: each of them turns out to be acceptable in its own place."[36] When these circumstances are taken into account, it is claimed, China's human rights practices are not found to conflict with international norms. As the white paper comments:

> Owing to tremendous differences in historical background, social system, cultural tradition and economic development, countries differ in their understanding and practice of human rights. From their different situations, they have taken different attitudes towards the relevant U.N. conventions. . . . Therefore a country's human rights situation should not be judged in total disregard of its history and national conditions, nor can it be evaluated according to a preconceived model or the conditions of another country or region.

Chinese officials argue that two factors in particular are relevant to judging China's human rights practices. The first is China's historical experience with political instability and poverty, which supposedly necessitates the precedence of economic rights over political rights. A second relevant factor is China's cultural tradition emphasizing the group over the individual. The claim is that a theory of rights founded on individualism is alien to Chinese culture. Attempts to force "Western" human rights values on China constitute a type of cultural imperialism. The relativist argument is thus an attack on the idea that human rights can be universally applicable to all cultures and societies.

Both Eastern and Western thinkers have made many valiant efforts to attempt to grapple with the impact of cultural diversity on the universality of human rights. Some, such as Professor Gong Xiangrui of Beijing University, have asserted the fundamental incompatibility of Chinese culture with human rights:

> In China it is the state that comes first, the collective second, and the individual the last. If any conflict should occur, the collective benefit (such as that of the family, the school, and the union) should be sacrificed for the state's interest: similarly, the individual's personal interest should give way to the interests of the collectives and the state. . . . If any conflict arises, the interests of the individual are subject to those of the collectives and the state. Putting the individual first is sometimes called individualism, and sometimes condemned as "bourgeois-liberalism."[37]

The case for the incompatibility of human rights with Chinese culture is even more long-standing than the founding of the People's Republic of China. In fact, the Chinese preference for group interests over the individual dates back to the second century B.C., when the Han Dynasty Emperor Wu banned the "hundred schools of thought" (i.e., the many philosophical schools contending for dominance at the time) and adopted the thought of Confucius as the official state ideology. Since that time, Confucianism has been an integral part of Chinese cultural values, and Asian values generally. For millennia, familiarity with the writings of Confucius has been the mark of an educated person and an important subject in the civil service examinations marking the traditional route to bureaucratic power in pre-communist China. Although there have been rivals to Confucian thinking that might be closer to espousing human rights values, these rivals have had only minor impacts on Asian values. Professor Yu Haocheng has written that the adoption of Confucianism as the state ideology has had "enormous negative repercussions on the historical development of thought" in China.[38]

A number of thoughtful Asian human rights scholars have wrestled with the significance of the Confucian emphasis on the duties and loyalty of the individual to the group. The problem they address is that if an Asian preference for the collective over individual rights is, in fact, grounded in Confucian thought, then emphasis on individual human rights may be rejected as being inconsistent with Asian culture. One approach to this problem is to suggest an underlying intellectual unity. Du Gangjian of the People's University of China and Song Gang of the

Chinese Academy of Social Science have argued that classical Confucian theory contains elements that are consonant with human rights values. In particular, they try to demonstrate that certain aspects of human rights—which they term "the ideology of human rights" (*ren quan zhu yi*), "tolerance" (*kuan rong zhu yi*), "resistance" (*di kang zhu yi*), and "neo-constitutionalism" (*xin xian zheng zhu yi*)—are in accord with classical tenets of Confucianism—namely, "benevolence" (*rem dao*), "tolerance" (*shu dao*), "justice" (*yi dao*), and "government" (*zheng dao*). Du Gangjian and Song Gang write that "Without advocating a completely Western form of democracy, we believe there is ample room within the traditional dictates of Chinese culture which embodies a strong commitment to modern human rights values. . . . [T]he modern concept of human rights is not alien to Chinese soil."[39]

Wang Gungwu, the former vice-chancellor of the University of Hong Kong, has written that an implied idea of rights lies in the Confucian ideas of hierarchy and reciprocity. According to Confucian thought, individuals at every hierarchy of society owe duties. The entitlement of the superior to the obedience of the subordinate is based on the superior doing what is in the best interests of the subordinate. Wang Gungwu sees in this reciprocity a kind of right belonging to the subordinate. He writes: "The subject's rights were expressed in terms of the rules of propriety due to him, and the ruler's rights in terms of the subject's loyalty which he could expect. . . . Propriety and loyalty were not simply duties; they were also, implicitly, rights in a given reciprocal relationship."[40]

Although such efforts to reconcile Chinese culture with the idea of human rights are well-intentioned and interesting exercises, ultimately they are doomed to fail. As Wang Gungwu concedes, the idea of rights has not, for various historical reasons, taken hold in China as it has in the West. Given the fundamental incompatibility between Chinese culture and human rights, the question that remains—as Margaret Ng has posed it—is whether "because it was historically, or even linguistically absent, the concept of rights is somehow inappropriate for China or the Chinese."[41] Ng writes that the validity and implementation of human rights values in Asia should not depend on the source of those values. After all, Ng observes, even in the West human rights ideas struggled to achieve acceptance and legitimacy. She writes:

> Writers of classical liberalism, in so far as they were original thinkers, were not reporting values prevalent in their society (they were if anything attacking contrary values), but rather proposing principles which they

believed should be recognized as having universal validity. Whether they should be accepted or rejected must depend on whether they are valid or invalid, not whether they originated from the West or the East.[42]

For Ng, the applicability of human rights to modern China is based on a highly pragmatic calculation. In China's mostly feudal past, human rights were irrelevant and unnecessary. The Confucian "princely man" looked after the common people as a matter of duty. The people did not need rights to defend their interests. In modern China, however, the Chinese people have as much need for the protections of human rights as do people in other cultures. Ng writes, "One may acknowledge that the concept of rights is generally 'alien' to the Chinese tradition in its *past and present state*. But this does not make out the case that rights are alien to Chinese society *by nature*. Nor does it establish that it is therefore legitimate to exclude Chinese society from the application of human rights."[43]

Ng's pragmatic account of the applicability of human rights to Chinese culture is in accord with the view of the Western human rights scholar Jack Donnelly. For Donnelly, as for Ng, it is a mistake to ask whether human rights values are universal values. Clearly, the individualism at the core of human rights is not a universal ideal, as even a cursory examination of traditional African, Asian, and Islamic cultures reveals.[44] Donnelly believes, as well, that human rights would be misplaced in many traditional societies where the individual has a "place in society and a range of personal and social relationships that provide material and nonmaterial support" that in the West is provided by individual human rights. However, for Donnelly and Ng human rights become relevant when these traditional societies are transformed by modernity in such a way that they cease to look after the human dignity of the individual. In particular, the power of the modern state to oppress and dominate the individual gives rise to the need for human rights. Donnelly writes, "Economic, social, and cultural changes in and disruptions of traditional communities have often removed the support and protection that would 'justify' or 'compensate for' the absence of individual human rights. . . . In such circumstances. . . . [T]he individual *needs* individual rights."[45]

The common thread running through the works of Ng and Donnelly emphasizes that human rights values, although not universally applicable to all societies (and particularly not to certain premodern traditional societies), nevertheless are relevant to modern societies in which the individual is vulnerable to oppression from the state. Of course, an alternative view of human rights is that they are indeed relevant in traditional societies, particularly for oppressed and disenfranchised members of such societies. In any event it is clear that modern China is not a traditional society in which Confucian values offer very much protection to the average citizen. China is governed by a highly organized modern state with the power to oppress the individual. In this context, human rights values, with their emphasis on the individual, are relevant for Chinese society. Human rights are needed to protect Chinese citizens from their own government.

Chinese officials would no doubt insist that, although China is no longer a traditional society, in the socialist state the interests of the individual are looked after by the state. As Professor Gong Xiangrui of Beijing University writes, "A popular saying is that under socialism the interests of the state, of the collective, and of the individual are in general harmony."[46] They are one and the same, according to Communist Party ideology, just as individual rights against the state are unnecessary in traditional society. As the Tiananmen massacre and subsequent political oppression in China have made clear, however, this identity of interest between the state and the individual has very little practical reality. As a consequence, human rights values are an effective, practical response to the need for citizens of China to protect their interests from attack by their own government.

The controversies about human rights that have arisen in the past fifty years and found reprise in the white paper are not going to result in a philosophical consensus anytime soon. In the case of controversies emanating from cultural differences, it is not even clear what such a consensus would look like or how it could be achieved.[47] My own view is that a consensus is impossible without severely watering down the idea of human rights, and that attempts to do so are ultimately futile. One must accept the fact that the human rights movement is a struggle to promote one vision of what it means to be human. It is a view of humanity that arose in the West, but, as Margaret Ng has argued, this vision is not necessarily limited in appeal to Western societies. It most certainly contradicts the vision of humanity embodied in other cultures, notwithstanding attempts to reconcile cultural differences and reach a consensus about the universality of human rights.

It is my belief that, relatively speaking, too much ink and energy have been spent on trying to achieve a consensus on human rights, and too little attention has been devoted, particularly among those who are convinced of the universal applicability of human rights, to sorting out what kinds of responsibilities human rights entail for various actors. I say this because I don't believe a consensus is possible or indeed desirable, particularly when the fundamental source of the human rights controversy is a true cultural conflict.

I agree with Professor Samuel Huntington when he observes that the human rights movement is an inherently divisive subject that is bound to cause a clash of cultures. Huntington writes, "Western efforts to propagate such ideas produce instead a reaction against 'human rights imperialism' and a reaffirmation of indigenous values, as can be seen in the support for religious fundamentalism by the younger generation in non-Western cultures. The very notion that there could be a 'universal civilization' is a western idea, directly at odds with the particularism of most Asian Societies and their emphasis on what distinguishes one people from another."[48] Where I part ways with Professor Huntington is in his thinking that it is wise in all cases to shy away from such conflicts. I believe that human rights and the values they embody are worth advocating, even at the risk of offending certain cultural sensitivities. In doing so I have no wish to be culturally insensitive. Quite the contrary; it is important to be sensitive to the values of others and to try to understand why certain cultures, in this case Chinese culture, might be at odds with the values espoused by the human rights movement. I simply refuse to accept culture as the ultimate arbiter of truth and justice, especially as that culture might be interpreted at any given moment in history by particular individuals occupying certain positions of power. To assess the legitimacy of attempts to influence other cultures, the means employed to this end must be evaluated on legal and moral grounds. Cultural imperialism is abhorrent, but so too are moral cowardice and indifference.

Conclusion

This chapter has argued that the Universal Declaration failed to result in any meaningful long-term consensus about human rights ideals or in an adequate institutional framework for protecting human rights. Given the fragility of the initial ideological consensus, and given the subsequent stresses posed to that weak consensus, that the institutional framework designed to enforce human rights remains rudimentary should not be altogether surprising. This assessment of the historical importance of the Universal Declaration is at odds with the view that its adoption constituted an authoritative consensus about the international normative universality of human rights, and that the second half of the twentieth century can be viewed as a steady march of progress toward the implementation of universally recognized ideals.

To a certain extent, the Universal Declaration has promoted respect for human rights. Many nations have adopted the language of the Universal Declaration in their constitutions, and court cases throughout the world have cited the authority of the Universal Declaration. But overall, progress in human rights since the declaration's institution would have to be counted as disappointing. As the Italian political theorist Norberto Bobbio has observed:

> I would advise anyone who wishes to carry out an unbiased examination of the development of human rights after the Second World War to carry out this sobering exercise: to read the Universal Declaration and look around. Such a person would be obliged to recognize that in spite of the enlightened advances of philosophers, the bold formulations of lawyers and the efforts of well-intentioned politicians, there is still a long way to go. Human history, in spite of its millennia, will appear to have just commenced given the enormity of the tasks ahead.[49]

In assessing the implications of the foregoing historical account for our analysis of corporate responsibility for human rights, a number of points warrant emphasis. First, the human rights controversies raging between the United States and China are part and parcel of a long and bitter legacy. There is no authoritative international consensus about the universality of human rights values, notwithstanding the noble language of the Universal Declaration and the adoption by many nations of the human rights covenants. One should make no mistake about the fact that the struggle on behalf of human rights represents a challenge to the legitimacy of certain forms of government and cultural norms. As Jack Donnelly has written, "The equal and inalienable rights of all people, simply because they are human—human rights—is a distinctive principle of social and political organization. Human rights are compatible with only a limited range of practices. They are not, and should not be, neutral with respect to political forms or cultural traditions."[50] Whether the Chinese people are better off adopting and implementing human rights values can be debated. Whether foreigners should be trying to bring human rights values to China may also be debated. But there is no debating the fact that human rights values can only be implemented in China if major political and cultural change occurs there.

The lack of an authoritative ideological consensus has been accompanied, not surprisingly, by the absence of authoritative institutions to monitor and enforce human rights. This institutional void has been filled somewhat by the emergence in the 1970s, 1980s, and 1990s of NGOs devoted to ferreting out and publicizing human rights abuses throughout the world.[51] These organizations have done an admirable job of putting human rights violations on the forefront of international affairs. They have been somewhat less successful in applying pressure on various countries to improve their human rights conditions. Despite the good work done by NGOs, as independent nonstate actors, they are only able to accomplish so much.

For human rights advocates, the limited powers of NGOs and the nascent character of international human rights institutions have been the source of great frustration. Increasingly, human rights advocates have turned, therefore, to the multinational corporation, seeking to enlist it as an engine for human rights progress. Although multinational corporations are indeed uniquely positioned to be a positive human rights force in countries in which they do business, they do not have sufficient power to act as a replacement for authoritative international institutions. A question thus arises as to how much of the work of human rights multinational corporations can reasonably be expected to carry out. On the basis of historical observation, we can offer some observations about the practical possibilities.

It seems obvious that businesspeople and the multinational corporations they run cannot be expected to accomplish dramatic results in matters that have generated and continue to generate so much international controversy. The principal participants in this controversy must continue to be national governments and international institutions. This doesn't mean that corporations should not be expected to do anything about human rights, even the civil and political rights that engender the greatest controversy. However, we can't expect businesspeople to act as statesmen and stateswomen might. They are not professionally equipped to do so, nor can they act with the political authority of elected representatives. It simply isn't very useful, as a practical matter, to ask multinational corporations to do the work of nation-states and international institutions. As Chapter 8 demonstrates, these practical realities are highly relevant to our assessment of the moral duties of corporations.

To say that the world has not yet realized the ideals of human rights is not to say we have not progressed toward this goal. The human rights movement should be looked at as an international moral struggle with vast political and cultural implications. Some hard-won progress has been made, but the moral struggle is ongoing. Multinational corporations can have a positive role to play in this struggle. They can even, in certain respects, lead. They cannot, however, shoulder the principal burden of what is essentially a grand political and cultural struggle between very different moral systems. Chapter 8 explores what moral duties we can reasonably expect of multinational corporations in promoting human rights.

CHAPTER EIGHT

✫

A Fair Share Theory
of Human Rights Responsibility

This chapter is highly theoretical. Building on the seminal philosophical contributions of others, but also introducing several novel concepts, the chapter constructs a broadly applicable "fair share" theory of moral responsibility for human rights. From this broad theory, a set of principles are derived that enable us to determine where to draw the line between human rights duties that corporations are morally required to carry out and actions that corporations have no moral duty to perform.

The fair share theory is founded on four premises:

1. Several kinds of actions can be carried out to help to protect and promote human rights.
2. Diverse categories of actors, including multinational corporations, international institutions, nation-states, NGOs, and individuals, share collective moral responsibility for human rights.
3. To achieve the most effective overall impact on human rights conditions, the burden of performing these actions should be fairly shared among the various moral responsible actors.
4. A fair allocation of human rights duties should take into account the relative ability of various actors to assume the associated burden, the relationship of each actor to the human rights victim, and the likelihood of an action being effective if performed by a particular actor.

When considered in this multi-duty, multi-actor moral context, the human rights duties of multinational corporations are limited, and they do not include actions that can more effectively be performed by other actors. If a corporation cannot make a positive impact by performing an action, then it makes little sense to say that it is morally required to do so. Multinational corporations should not be expected to undertake ineffectual actions that would needlessly jeopardize their commercial interests. Moreover, corporate responsibility for human rights does not extend to actions that can more effectively be undertaken by international institutions and nation-states.

As earlier chapters show, considerable disagreement exists among government officials, human rights advocates, and the business community about the human rights responsibilities of multinational corporations. How is one to decide which view is right and which is wrong? In this chapter, we do so by reasoning about the nature of human rights and the duties they create. We begin by reflecting on why corporations have moral duties to undertake any actions other than those that maximize profits for shareholders.

BASIS OF CORPORATE RESPONSIBILITY FOR HUMAN RIGHTS

The moral argument establishing corporate responsibility for social issues such as human rights can be constructed from many premises. One useful approach has come from applying the philosophical concept of the "social contract."[1] As the business ethicist Tom Donaldson writes in his groundbreaking book *The Ethics of International Business*, "all productive organizations . . . are viewed as engaging in an implied contract with society, not unlike that employed by Locke, Rousseau, and Hobbes in understanding the moral and political foundations of the state."[2]

The idea of the social contract is meant to signify the relationship of trust existing between corporations and the societies in which they operate. The very existence, legally speaking, of a corporation as a "fictitious person" and all of the special privileges allowed to it by law—not the least of which is the "corporate veil" of limited liability for shareholders—are made possible by society. The wealth amassed by a corporation is, therefore, at least in part attributable to society. As a consequence of the privileges and benefits society allows them to enjoy, corporations are accountable to society—that is, they owe a "contractual" duty to operate in a way that benefits society. Most successful business executives intuitively understand this responsibility. The social contract is a philosophical concept that attempts to provide a moral justification for this intuitive sense.

Corporations thus owe duties to the societies in which they operate. One category of such duties concerns human rights. As Donaldson observes, the human rights responsibility of a corporation is a special case of its general duty to exercise social responsibility: "The terms of the contract demand that [the corporation] honor rights as a condition of its justified existence." But what precisely does "honoring" human rights require? Which kinds of actions are required of corporations and which are not?

Social contract theory does not, in and of itself, suggest any rational basis for deciding among the visions of corporate responsibility presented by AmCham, HRW, and the Clinton administration. Donaldson has written that the extent of corporate social responsibility for human rights should depend on the particular human right at stake. For example, he suggests that corporations have greater duties with respect to free speech than they do with respect to the right to a fair trial. It is unclear, however, whether in the case of free speech rights, Donaldson would require firms to adopt the "proactive" role envisioned by HRW. Having different concerns than the present inquiry, Donaldson offers only a brief sketch of what he had in mind. He interprets the duty to help protect free speech and association as including "refraining from lobbying host governments for restrictions that would violate the right in question." This would not appear to be tantamount to the "proactive" HRW approach rejected in Chapter 6. However, Donaldson then goes on to suggest that this duty includes "perhaps even . . . protesting host government measures that do violate it," which would seem to cross the line into the proactive approach.

To decide among competing views of corporate human rights responsibilities, it is useful to move beyond a social contract analysis. Corporate human rights duties need to be considered within a broader theory of human rights that takes into account the human rights duties of noncorporate actors. From this general theory, the particular attributes of corporate human rights responsibility can then be derived. We begin this process by assembling some fundamental building blocks. In order, we will consider some of the distinctive qualities of human rights, the multiplicity of actions that may be undertaken in furtherance of human rights, and the variety of actors who might potentially have a duty to undertake such actions.

HUMAN RIGHTS AS MORAL RIGHTS

As do all rights, human rights imply duties. According to a classic legal definition, a *right* is a claim that the right holder may assert against someone else who is said to owe correlative duties to the right holder. Someone who holds a right possesses a claim that may be asserted against other persons. For example, Tom's right to physical safety implies that Mary has a duty not to punch Tom in the nose. The claim inherent in a right inherently, or by definition, implies the existence of correlative duties. Some rights are negative rights, requiring other actors to refrain from doing something. Tom's right to physical safety is such a right. It requires Mary to refrain, among other things, from punching him. Other rights are positive and impose duties on others to act in a certain way. If we say, for example, that every child has a right to decent health care and education, we are implying that some entity—presumably the state—has a duty to provide these things to every child. A quick perusal of the list of human rights in the Universal Declaration and the two principal human rights covenants reveals that they include both positive and negative rights.

With each right, including human rights, there exists a set of duties owed by others to the holder of the right.[3] Because human rights are special kinds of moral rights, the moral duties correlative to human rights have special characteristics. These are explored later in this chapter. First, however, another building block is needed—the distinction between legal and moral rights and duties.

Rights and their correlative duties may or may not be recognized by law. If a right is based on moral principles, the person holding the right has a moral right and the correlative duties are moral duties. In nations with well-developed legal systems, a substantial (but not perfect) overlap exists between legal and moral rights; moral rights are recognized as legal rights, and most legal rights are morally justified. However, a legal right might not be morally justifiable, even though it is legally valid in the strict technical sense that it is enforceable by a court of law.

Law is not always in harmony with morality. The legal rights of nineteenth-century slaveholders in the United States constitute a quintessential example of legally valid rights that lack moral justification. Under the fugitive slave statutes, slave owners could sue in federal courts for the return of their "property." Although the claim of a slave owner was legally valid and could be enforced in a court of law, this legal right had no moral validity.[4] Conversely, moral rights are not always recognized by the law. One may not have a legal right to do what one has a moral right to do. The American civil rights activist Rosa Parks acted on the basis of this distinction when, in a courageous act of civil disobedience, she refused to give up her seat on a bus to a white man in Montgomery, Alabama. Segregation laws required Ms. Parks to sit in the back of the bus, but she knew perfectly well that she had a moral right to sit where she pleased.

Human rights are moral rights. In certain nations, particular human rights may be recognized in law and enforced by the government. Thus, they may also be legally valid rights. For example, an American's right to free speech is, within certain limits, guaranteed by the First Amendment and, if necessary, it will be protected by the courts. However, even human rights that are legally protected exist, in Judith Jarvis Thomson's phrase, "prior to law."[5] They do not depend for their validity on being incorporated into law. Their justification is based on moral principles.

A variety of moral justifications have been proposed for the moral power of human rights. Maurice Cranston has observed that human rights belong to a person simply by virtue of that person's being human.[6] Alan Gewirth believes that human rights are necessary for a person to act as a moral agent.[7] R. J. Vincent has written that "human rights are what ought to be distributed to everybody whatever their circumstances."[8] For Jack Donnelly, human rights are necessary to protect individuals from the economic and social disruptions caused by the breakdown of traditional societies.[9] As Donnelly has written:

The human nature that is the source of human rights rests on a moral account of human possibility. It indicates what human beings might become rather than what they have been, or even what they "are," in some scientifically determinable sense. Human rights rest on an account of a life of dignity to which human beings are "by nature" suited and the kind of person worthy of and entitled to such a life. And if the rights specified by the underlying theory of human nature are implemented and enforced, they should help to bring into being the envisioned type of person. The effective implementation of human rights should thus result in a self-fulfilling moral prophecy.[10]

HUMAN RIGHTS AND INTERNATIONAL DUTIES

Human rights are special kinds of moral rights because they create duties throughout the international community. Because human rights concern matters of such fundamental importance, they imply correlative moral duties extending beyond national borders to various international actors. This extrajurisdictional reach is a distinguishing feature of human rights, separating them from other kinds of moral rights concerning matters of lesser importance.

The responsibility of foreigners is necessary to complete the meaning of human rights and to make possible their ultimate realization. Sometimes, a citizen's own government abuses that person's human rights. When this happens, the citizen must appeal outside of his or her country to other states and nonstate actors. In China, for example, the state itself abuses the political and civil rights of its citizens. In nations with independent judicial systems, a citizen can petition the judiciary to safeguard a right against government abuse. However, if, as in China, the judiciary has minimal independence, then the right holder must seek aid from others outside of his or her national borders. The involvement of foreigners is required to redress the violation of an individual's human rights by his or her own government.

This idea of international moral responsibility is part of the very essence of human rights. It dates back, as the last chapter discusses, to the founding of the human rights movement in the wake of Nazi atrocities in Germany. The human rights movement was internationalist from the outset, and any account of the meaning of human rights that does not include a role for foreigners in protecting those rights is nonsensical. Obviously, the internationalist aspect of human rights is fundamentally at odds with the notion of state sovereignty and the corresponding principle of noninterference by other states in the internal affairs of sovereign states. This irresolvable conflict has been one of the more controversial features of human rights.

Which Rights Qualify as Human Rights?

Not every moral right is sufficiently important to warrant international concern. International actors only owe duties regarding those moral rights that are of sufficient importance to be human rights. Henry Shue has written that the various duties correlated with rights can be put into one of three categories: (1) the duty to avoid depriving of rights; (2) the duty to protect rights from deprivation; and (3) the duty to aid one whose rights have been deprived.[11] Only in the case of human rights do the latter two duties extend beyond national borders. For example, a person who is owed a debt by another person also has a claim against his or her government to assist in collecting the debt. That person has the right to sue in a court to secure the claim. If the government does not help to recover the money, a citizen does not, however, have a claim against third parties (foreign or domestic) to help in collection. The right to recover money loaned to another, although a moral right that deserves legal enforcement, is simply not significant enough to be considered a human right worthy of international protection. (As a matter of law, of course, courts of one nation may offer a remedy to a creditor if there are sufficient contacts with the jurisdiction in which the court is located.) By contrast, when human rights, such as the right to be free from torture, are threatened, the duty to do something about it extends beyond national borders to foreign state and nonstate actors. Who these actors are and what these duties might consist of is considered later. For the moment, we focus on another difficult question suggested by a definition of human rights as important moral rights imposing correlative duties across international borders, to wit: Which rights are important enough to qualify as human rights?

As we saw in the last chapter, the list of human rights has been a controversial issue from the beginning of the modern human rights movement. Even the list in the Universal Declaration and the human rights covenants is not authoritative. There is great disagreement over whether the predominantly positive economic and social rights and the predominantly negative civil and political rights are equal in status, and whether some rights should take priority over other rights. The difficulty does not end there.

An ever-expanding myriad of international instruments has created what might be termed, depending on one's point of view, human rights "inflation" or "pluralism." The University of Minnesota Human Rights Internet Library lists more than 120 international declarations, treaties, protocols, principles, and conventions, as well as regional conventions, on diverse subjects ranging from genocide, self-determination, and torture to the rights of children, women, and minorities.[12] All of these various human rights instruments create implicit moral claims for a wide array of rights that often overlap and sometimes conflict with one another.

Given the plethora of human rights claims in existence, how can the emphasis, in the case of China, on a selective list of civil and political rights and the rights of workers be justified? One could argue that because civil and political rights are essential for the realization of economic rights, they command greater attention. Maurice Cranston takes an even more aggressive position on the question of which human rights command our attention. He argues that the positive rights to food, shelter, security, and education, all of which are enshrined in the core human rights documents, depend on adequate resources and thus cannot be guaranteed categorically and universally. Cranston even goes so far as to acerbically note that recognition of many economic rights in the Universal Declaration and the human rights covenants hinders the enforcement of the "correct" list of fundamental human rights that involve "moral urgency which is far removed from questions of holiday with pay."[13]

Such an exclusive approach to the list of human rights might offer the promise of a tidy justification for this book's focus on a particular set of human rights problems in China. I do not believe, however, that it is necessary to draw the circle of human rights so tightly. I am not prepared to exclude, for example, minority rights and women's rights, or even economic and social rights, as human rights worthy of international stature and attention. The power of the concept of human rights is not undermined by the large number of rights that are purported to qualify as human rights. On the contrary, the fact that people perceive power in labeling women's rights or minority rights as human rights is a testament to the power of the idea of human rights. This does not mean that every claim of the existence of a human right must be accepted, but the idea of human rights is not enriched by being portrayed as a club whose membership is fully subscribed.

In a similar spirit, the emphasis of this book on political and civil rights and the rights of workers is not intended to suggest that the human rights responsibilities of international actors is limited to those kinds of rights. The issues focused on here are the human rights concerns that most often arise for multinational corporations in the course of doing business in China and other developing nations. Having said that, I would also suggest that the responsibilities of multinational corporations regarding women's rights are a sorely neglected area meriting much greater attention from human rights advocates and scholars alike. Moreover, minority rights and the rights of indigenous peoples may be the most important human rights issues facing a very few multinational corporations and NGOs, such as the World Bank, that are engaged in development projects displacing tens of thousands of Tibetans, Mongolians, and the Uighers minorities in China's western territories.[14]

DIVERSITY OF ACTORS WITH HUMAN RIGHTS DUTIES

If human rights are moral duties involving matters of such importance that they impose various correlative duties on diverse actors across international borders, which actors have human rights duties? What kinds of duties do these actors have? As we shall see, there are diverse actors who have diverse duties. Moreover, to achieve the best overall result for human rights, it is useful to allocate these various duties among the various responsible actors in accordance with the fair share principle.

The responsibility for human rights begins with individuals. The phrase "crimes against humanity" often is used to describe the most heinous abuses of human rights. Labeling an action a *crime* signals its severity and the fundamental importance of human rights. To say that a crime is "against humanity," however, also implies that in some subtle but profound sense all individuals are victims of human rights abuses against any particular individual. This, in turn, implies that the ultimate responsibility to safeguard human rights belongs to all of us as individuals. As individuals, we have a responsibility to refrain from committing human rights abuses or from lending our support to those who commit abuses. We have a duty, for example, to refrain from buying products manufactured in sweatshop factories that abuse the human rights of workers. Although such human rights abuses may not rise to the level of being "criminal," they are deeply offensive to every person because they demean humanity itself. We ought to care about human rights violations to others wherever in the world these victims are, because we are all part of a human community.

Although moral responsibility for human rights belongs ultimately to individuals, it is most effectively discharged through collective enterprises. Acting collectively, individuals are able to accomplish more than they can alone. This is as true for human rights as it is for other kinds of endeavors. It is thus sensible to speak of the human rights responsibilities of various political, social, and economic institutions through which individuals conduct their collective affairs. International institutions, such as the United Nations, are intergovernmental organizations through which the nations of the world collectively act. Nation-states, in turn, represent the will and interests of their citizens.

The most powerful *private* institutions with the power to affect human rights are business corporations and the press. In recent history, NGOs such as HRW and Amnesty International have also become important channels for collective efforts to promote human rights. NGOs directly represent the collective will of a group of individuals, bypassing the nation-state system that has been the traditional route of participation in international affairs.

Multinational corporations are thus but one of several types of actors with human rights duties. The duties of any one actor cannot be understood in isolation. The duties of each actor depend on the duties of the other actors. All of these public, private, and nongovernmental actors have unique strengths and weaknesses. They all bear some responsibility for human rights. However, before we can determine precisely what responsibilities each actor has, the range of possible actions that can be carried out to promote and protect human rights must be considered.

DIVERSITY OF HUMAN RIGHTS DUTIES

There are various types of human rights duties and various means of accomplishing these duties.[15] The most fundamental duty is to refrain from violating or indirectly helping others to violate human rights. All actors, including corporations, have a duty to refrain from engaging in activities that have the effect of directly or indirectly violating the human rights of any person.

Two other human rights duties are preventing a deprivation of a right and coming to the aid of a victim who has been deprived of a right. The means appropriate to accomplishing these duties depend partly on the particular human right at issue. For example, some have argued that, in the case of the human right to subsistence, the rich nations of the world have a duty to transfer resources to poor nations.[16] In the case of civil and political rights and the rights of workers, various means are available to prevent or come to the aid of a human rights victim. We need to understand the nature of these means before we can determine whether a particular actor (e.g., a multinational corporation) has a moral duty to carry out any of them. By looking closely at the various means for preventing and redressing human rights violations, we can come to understand that certain kinds of actors are simply not able to effectively perform some of these duties. Thus, it is futile to assign them a moral duty to do so.

The most coercive means of enforcing human rights is the use of *force* against either individuals or states. Less extreme than force is the use of *economic sanctions*, "the deliberate, government-inspired withdrawal of customary trade or financial arrangements."[17] There are also other, less coercive and more persuasive, ways to do something about human rights violations by third parties. In certain instances, an actor is uniquely positioned between the right holder and the third party threatening the right. The responsible actor in such a position is capable of *upholding* a right by refusing to cooperate with the third party. Without the cooperation of the responsible actor, the third party would not be able to commit the human rights violation. In such a case, the responsible actor has a duty to uphold human rights by withholding participation in the human rights abuse. *Monitoring* consists of the observation, critical evaluation, and reporting of adherence to international human rights norms. *Criticism* involves speaking out against human rights abuses. It may include publicly rebuking a government for its poor human rights record. *Education* involves engagement, cultural exchange, and persuasion. Education can lead to changes in attitudes and practices.

These various means of accomplishing human rights duties can themselves be viewed as second-order human rights duties. We can, therefore, speak of the duty to use force, to impose sanctions, to uphold, to monitor, to criticize, and to educate. Each of these second-order duties can serve as a means of preventing human rights violations or coming to the aid of one whose rights have been violated.

RATIONALE FOR ALLOCATING HUMAN RIGHTS DUTIES

With so many human rights duties and so many potentially responsible actors, one might wonder why human rights are ever in jeopardy. If one actor fails to fulfill a human rights duty, many others can step in and fill the void. Despite this seeming embarrassment of riches, however, serious human rights abuses persist throughout the world without any effective international response. Although the Universal Declaration and the human rights covenants create a bold vision of human rights ideals, no enforcement regime is in place to ensure the achievement of any of these ideals. As a result, the task of transforming these ideals into reality is a haphazard and confusing affair. What one might call a "responsibility gap"[18] exists between the full range of actions and responsible actors necessary to effectuate human rights, and the often heroic but on the whole inadequate efforts of a small number of these actors. If the world is to make any progress toward achieving human rights ideals, it is necessary to draw more actors, including multinational corporations, into the struggle. To do so, however, a clear, limited, and fair set of duties must be established for corporations. Otherwise, human rights advocates will discourage corporate executives from taking on any human rights responsibilities at all.

Ironically, the very extensiveness of potentially responsible actors and potential means of fulfilling human rights duties contributes to the human rights "responsibility gap." The pioneering game theory economist Thomas Schelling has described a class of collective action problems in which "equilibria achieved by unconcerted or undisciplined actions are inefficient—the situations in which . . . some collective total could be made larger, by concerted . . . decisions."[19] The struggle to effectuate human rights is such a collective action problem. A strong but regrettably vague general sense exists that someone should do something. There is, however, little clarity about exactly who owes these duties and how these duties should be fulfilled. As a result, human rights efforts are sparse, uncoordinated, and ineffective.

To close the human rights "responsibility gap," particular types of human rights duties need to be allocated to particular types of actors according to a set of fairness principles. Allocating responsibility solves the collective action problem by providing the actors with a clear sense of extent and limitations of their moral duties. This increases the likelihood that corporations in particular will accept and discharge their human rights duties.

An allocation of human rights duties also would lead to greater overall effectiveness in promoting and protecting human rights. Every class of morally responsible actor has distinctive strengths and weaknesses and is able to perform different human rights duties more or less effectively. When different responsibilities are assigned to different kinds of actors, the system as a whole functions more effectively to promote and protect human rights.[20] A corollary benefit of such increased effectiveness is that the limited resources of the various responsible international actors are deployed most efficiently.

PRINCIPLES FOR A FAIR ALLOCATION OF HUMAN RIGHTS DUTIES

To distribute the burdens created by human rights duties fairly among various actors, and to enhance overall effectiveness in promoting and protecting human rights, human rights duties should be allocated according to three factors: relationship, effectiveness, and capacity.[21]

Different actors have different relationships with human rights victims and potential victims. The nature, duration, and physical proximity of such a relationship are important factors in determining how the relationship might affect an actor's human rights duties. The closer, longer, and more involved the relationship, the more that can reasonably be expected. In addition to the relationship with a potential victim, the relationship with a victim's country is also relevant. If the actor derives economic benefits from the relationship with that country, more should be expected.

A fair allocation of responsibility also takes into account the varying abilities of different actors to carry out different human rights duties. International institutions and nation-states, by virtue of the sheer numbers of individuals whom they represent, can most effectively use coercive means such as force or economic sanctions to redress the deprivation of human rights. An NGO might be more effective at educational and monitoring duties. Each actor has different strengths and weaknesses, and these should be taken into account when allocating human rights duties.

Inevitably, the enforcement and promotion of human rights involves costs of one sort or another. Corporations can lose profits if host countries retaliate against them for taking a strong human rights stand. Nation-states can jeopardize other military, political, and economic interests by stressing human rights. A fair allocation of human rights duties considers such costs and the capacity of various actors to absorb different costs.

When these three factors are taken into account, the duties that can be fairly allocated to some actors—for example, nation-states—are not only different from those assigned to other actors—for example, multinational firms—but they also may be, as a practical matter, more onerous as well. By taking into account the human rights duties of all responsible actors, we can develop a relevant context for understanding the extent and limits of corporate responsibility. Appendix C contains a thumbnail sketch of the relevant factors affecting the human rights duties of various actors.

APPLYING THE FAIR SHARE THEORY
TO THE MULTINATIONAL CORPORATION

Multinational corporations often have a direct relationship to human rights victims. Firms may be the employers of the victims or of their family members. Moreover, a firm may have extensive operations within the rights-violating nation, thereby establishing a physical closeness with the human rights victims even if no direct employer-employee relationship exists. Multinational corporations most certainly derive great benefits from operating in societies in which human rights are violated. For all of these reasons, there can be no doubt that multinational corporations should have important human rights duties.

The potential effectiveness of a multinational firm varies, depending on what kind of duty it is being asked to carry out. Multinational corporations are in a potent position to uphold human rights, particularly the labor rights of workers, because they can control and direct their own personnel actions and those of their business partners. Multinational corporations are not, however, particularly effective at general criticism of the human rights practices of their host governments. Discussion and debate about human rights evoke controversies with grand cultural and political implications. The vast majority of corporate executives simply aren't very good at understanding the many nuances of human rights controversies. As a result, they are unlikely to be effective as vocal critics of general human rights conditions in their host countries. For multinational corporations, actions speak louder than words. Executives of multinational corporations can make a more effective statement by upholding human rights in their operations than they can by making public speeches.

Another constraint on the multinational corporation's ability to criticize the human rights practices by their host governments is economic vulnerability. This is particularly true in China. Because so many firms are pursuing a limited number of business opportunities, the capacity of a multinational firm to withstand retaliation by the Chinese government is very limited in most cases. Even large multinational firms in industries such as aerospace, telecommunications, energy, and automobiles must fear losing out to European and Japanese competitors on multibillion-dollar joint-venture contracts. In many ways, the biggest companies are the most vulnerable of all to retaliation because they have expended many years and billions of dollars trying to establish a foothold in the Chinese market.

In certain rare instances, a firm may be so important to the economy of a particular nation that it has the power to influence the policies of the host government. For example, because Shell Oil generates 50% of the government's revenues, it has significant influence in Nigeria. As a result, in 1995 the company was criticized by many when it failed to use its power to prevent the politically motivated killings of nine environmental activists from the Ogoni region (including the writer Ken Saro-Wiwa), who were protesting Shell's proposed $3.6 billion gas development project in the Nigerian Delta.[22] In most instances, however (and certainly in a large and varied economy such as China's), multinational firms do not have that kind of influence over their host nations. No one company is so important to China that it has the ability to influence government policy on a broad scale.

By applying the relationship, effectiveness, and capacity criteria, a picture begins to emerge of corporate responsibility for human rights. To uphold human rights, an actor must be "present" in China. The kinds of contacts and interactions with Chinese society and government must exist that place the actor in a position to defend human rights against attacks by others by acting or refusing to act in a certain way. In China, multinational firms are so positioned, particularly as employers of Chinese citizens. Moreso than any other potentially responsible actors, multinational firms are in a unique position to uphold human rights because of the extensiveness and intensity of their interactions with employees in the places in which they do business. Lest anyone think that the fair share theory lets multinational corporations off easy, it needs to be emphasized that upholding human rights is by no means a trivial duty. A company that upholds human rights may potentially be headed for an economically costly confrontation with the Chinese government, something that Chrysler must have understood when, as described in Chapter 6, it had to make a decision about whether or not to fire Gao Feng.

As our analysis of human rights spin-off demonstrated in Chapter 4, multinational corporations are also in a unique position to educate, albeit indirectly and for self-interested reasons, their workers and business partners about values underpinning human rights. Multinational firms are not, however, particularly well positioned to exert economic pressure to enforce human rights. They do not have sufficient economic power to do so, and they are too vulnerable to economic retaliation. Such attempts to impose economic sanctions are best undertaken by international institutions or powerful individual nations that possess the requisite economic leverage. Moreover, multinational firms in China can only pursue limited human rights objectives. Although in rare cases a multinational firm may be able to exert economic pressure to achieve broad human rights objectives, in most cases, and certainly in the case of China, multinational firms do not have the clout to do so. Multinational firms are more effective if they uphold human rights on a case-by-case basis as opportunities present themselves.

CONCLUSION

For some, this view of corporate responsibility may be setting the moral bar too low. In fact, it might be argued that moral responsibility requires courage and vision. Indeed, one of the most moving images of the

Tiananmen massacre was that of a solitary Chinese citizen stubbornly blocking the path of a tank. There is no doubt that such acts of courage are the engines of moral betterment. Progress typically comes when people who are willing to go beyond the minimum act as leaders. This may especially be true in the case of corporate social responsibility, whereby many companies have endeavored to do more than the morally required minimum. So too in China, companies willing to lead by doing more than the minimum can have a significant positive impact on human rights conditions. To say that multinational firms do not have a duty to criticize the Chinese government is not to detract from or discourage leaders who might be courageous enough to speak out when they have a chance of making a difference. A framework of moral *duties*, however, is about a *minimum* standard that should be expected of all.

In the two final chapters of this book, the general precepts of the fair share theory are applied to address the moral and practical questions typically faced by multinational firms operating in China. The account of corporate responsibility that emerges is a mixed one. In many respects, multinational corporations remain on the human rights hot seat. They have moral responsibilities that pose threats to their commercial goals. In these cases, practical strategies are suggested for meeting these responsibilities with a minimum of risk to financial interests. Just as important as staking out the ground for which multinational corporations have responsibility is articulating the ground that is more appropriately the responsibility of other actors. Drawing this line sharply, fairly, and realistically is an important step toward effectively enlisting the aid of multinational corporations in the promotion and protection of human rights. Corporate executives and human rights advocates alike need to understand that when it comes to human rights, the world is entitled to expect multinational corporations to do their fair share—no more and no less.

☆

Solving the Sweatshop Problem: Prospects for Achieving Responsible Global Labor Conditions

In this chapter, the fair share theory is applied to shed light on the moral responsibility of multinational corporations for labor conditions in factories operated by their suppliers, subcontractors, and other business partners in China and other developing nations. We also consider some practical marketplace problems facing "good" firms that manufacture their products in legitimate factories but that must compete with firms employing sweatshop labor. Several initiatives by NGOs that attempt to address the problem of sweatshop labor are then evaluated. Finally, we consider whether it is appropriate and useful for the WTO to play a role in enforcing labor standards.

As we have seen, operators of labor-intensive manufacturing facilities face enormous competitive economic pressures to lower costs. The temptation is great to accomplish this by abusing the human rights of their employees—by, among other things, paying unconscionably low wages, cutting corners on environmental and safety policies, and compelling employees to work excessive overtime hours without extra pay. In what has been called a "race to the bottom," these factory operators compete with each other to win supply and subcontracting contracts with multinational corporations that market and sell products in Western countries.

Although it is tempting to heap the moral blame for human rights abuses exclusively on the factory operators, there is plenty of responsibility to go around. To be sure, the individuals who own and operate sweatshops deserve moral condemnation. A key tenet of the fair share theory, however, is the idea of collective responsibility for human rights. The factory operators are only able to run these sweatshops because the global economic environment tolerates and in certain respects fosters human rights abuses. In the case of Chinese sweatshops, the web of moral responsibility includes many actors besides the factory owners. Within China, the local and national governments share some of the responsibility because they turn a blind eye to illegal practices in sweatshops. They do so for a number of reasons: the competition for capital with other cheap labor locales in Asia and elsewhere; conflicts of interest involving government officials who have economic stakes in the sweatshops they are supposed to be regulating; and, in some cases, outright corruption and bribery. In the United States, Europe, and elsewhere, other actors share in the moral blame as well. Retail stores lend a hand to and profit from labor abuses by selling goods manufactured in sweatshops. Consumers who buy goods manufactured in sweatshops enjoy cheap products at the expense of abused laborers.

The web of moral responsibility includes many actors within and outside China who in some manner benefit from labor abuses in sweatshops. The multinational corporation is at the core of this web of responsibility. By setting up supply and subcontracting relationships with sweatshop factories in China, corporations derive significant economic benefits from human rights abuses. The corporation has the power, however, to affect the conditions in these factories. Next, we consider what moral responsibilities accompany this power and how it might most effectively be harnessed to improve human rights conditions. As we will see, though, even when multinational corporations possess significant power, their human rights efforts are most effective when carried out in partnership with the entire community of responsible actors. Although the multinational corporation is the at the center of the web of responsibility, no solution to the problem of human rights abuses can ultimately be successful unless it extends to include every morally responsible actor—from factory operators in developing countries to consumers in Western shopping malls and department stores.

POWER AND RESPONSIBILITY: *RESPONDEAT SUPERIOR*

Foreign corporations do not directly control labor conditions in factories operated by their subcontractors, suppliers, and other business partners. However, they can apply economic pressure on these partners. They can, in fact, refuse to do business with partners whose operations don't meet certain standards. Do corporations have a moral duty to use their economic clout in this way? The three accounts of corporate responsibility we consider in Chapter 6 each answered this question in a somewhat different manner, as summarized in Question 1 of Table 6.1.

The fair share principles would require multinational corporations to ensure that their business partners do not violate the human rights of factory workers. Any firm seeking to minimize production costs in China, or any other developing nation, has a moral duty to do so without directly or indirectly violating the human rights of Chinese workers. Such firms are morally obliged to uphold human rights by refusing to do business with partners that fail to adhere to minimal standards. Indeed, if there were no way to establish these business relationships in China without the use of sweatshop labor, then a firm would have a duty to manufacture their products elsewhere.

Foreign firms in China cannot, moreover, turn a blind eye to the operations of their business partners. They have a duty to monitor the operations of their business partners. Unannounced check-ups may be required to ensure compliance, but more fundamental than the method of oversight is the nature of the responsibility. Quite simply, multinational corporations are morally responsible for the way their suppliers and subcontractors treat their workers. The applicable moral standard is similar to the legal doctrine of *respondeat superior*, according to which a principal is "vicariously liable" or responsible for the acts of its agent conducted in the course of the agency relationship. The classic example of this is the responsibility of employers for the acts of employees. Moreover, ignorance is no excuse. Firms must do whatever is required to become aware of what conditions are like in the factories of their suppliers and subcontractors, and thereby be able to assure themselves and others that their business partners don't mistreat those workers to provide a cheaper source of supply.

The moral responsibility for conditions in sweatshops derives from the unique and prominent role of the multinational corporation in the protection and enforcement of human rights. Of all the potentially responsible actors, the multinational firm by far has the most extensive contacts with Chinese citizens. It profits from the labor these workers do for the business partners of the firm. Moreover, through their direct operations and their contractual relations with suppliers and other business partners, multinational firms are able to uphold human rights in a unique way: They can effectively uphold human rights by choosing and carefully monitoring those with whom they do business. It is their moral duty to do so.

One of the first efforts to create a code of behavior for subcontractors and suppliers was Levi Strauss's "Business Partner Terms of Engagement" (Appendix D). Adopted in 1992, these sourcing guidelines established standards in the areas of worker health and safety, employment practices, ethics, the environment, and human rights. Levi Strauss devoted thousands of hours of management time and significant financial resources to formulate and implement these guidelines. The company undertook a major corporate effort to communicate the purposes and requirements of the new policy to their own executives and to their suppliers and contractors. Within the first year of adopting the policy, the company sent audit teams to inspect seven hundred contractors in sixty countries. Seventy percent of the contractors were found to be in compliance. However, one-fourth of the factories required changes in facilities and practices. Five percent were dropped completely as business partners.[1]

THREE COMPETITIVE PROBLEMS FOR "GOOD" FIRMS

As the Levi Strauss program illustrates, creating, implementing, and monitoring a code of behavior for suppliers and subcontractors is an expensive process that consumes significant amounts of valuable management time. Moreover, the requirement that factories must adhere to the standards of the code increases production costs, thereby putting companies with such codes at a competitive disadvantage to other companies. The resulting practical economic problems faced by "good" firms that adopt labor codes might be broadly grouped into three areas: economies of scale, consumer preferences and moral signaling, and moral free-riders.

Economies of Scale

Companies adopting labor codes of conduct for their business partners face adverse economies of scale. The endeavor takes up a considerable amount of time. It adds an entire layer of managerial concerns to the production process. The time and financial resources required to set up and run a truly effective program make it an especially onerous burden for small and medium-sized companies. Large companies such as Reebok, Liz Claiborne, and Mattel are able to absorb these costs better than small companies, but even for them it is a large undertaking. All of these companies, moreover, have to go it alone. Although they can do a certain amount of moral "benchmarking" by looking at the programs of leading companies, each of these companies must, in certain respects, invent the wheel for itself. The direct financial costs and time-consuming managerial distractions impose significant economic disincentives for both small and large firms considering the adoption of a labor code, particularly in light of the absence of any corresponding economic benefit that can be expected to result from implementing a code.

Consumer Preferences and Moral Signaling

Most companies that implement strong ethics codes cannot, for a number of reasons, recoup the resulting cost increases from consumers. The most important reason is that many consumers just don't care. One study conducted by researchers at Marymount University in Virginia found that 84 percent of U.S. consumers would be willing to pay an additional $1 on a $20 clothing item if they knew it had been made in a factory that was not a sweatshop.[2] Although encouraging, this finding is of little comfort to companies that incur the added costs of a labor code. Perhaps, when asked, consumers avow that they would pay an extra dollar for a guilt-free article of clothing. But this does not mean that people will go out of their way to find out which items are manufactured by "good" companies. Observing the way people actually behave is the only reliable way to test consumer preferences for products manufactured in legitimate factories. In the shopping aisles at K-Mart, Brooks Brothers, and Neiman-Marcus, not too many people are wondering about the social consequences of their purchases for Chinese workers. At the moment, the marketplace reveals little evidence to support the inferences of hypothetical studies such as that conducted by Marymount.

For some branded products such as Levi jeans or Nike shoes, companies that adopt strong labor codes have a profit cushion to compete successfully with higher prices against unbranded products manufactured in sweatshops. However, brands cost money to develop and maintain. Branded products are in competition with unbranded products, and consumers are willing to pay only so much extra for branded athletic apparel. Moreover, very few companies have been adept at marketing brands whose value depends to any appreciable degree on the social responsibility of the product. Those companies that have been successful in attaching value to the socially responsible nature of their products have been able to do so primarily in regard to environmental and animal-testing concerns. One is hard pressed to think of any brand that consumers value even partially because of the manufacturer's adherence to good human rights practices.

Even if putative consumer preferences for legitimately manufactured articles did result in socially responsible purchasing behavior, a deeper economic problem faces the "good" firm—there is no way for it to signal that it is a "good" firm. When a consumer walks into the store and looks at the $21 shirt and the $20 shirt, even if she prefers to pay the $21 for a shirt made by a "good" firm, she won't buy it if she can't tell which is which. If all she is able to see is the price, then she will view the shirt manufactured in a sweatshop and the shirt manufactured by a "good" firm as essentially the same. All other things being equal as far as she can tell, she will buy the cheaper shirt.

Moral Free-Riders

Another major practical problem confronting the "good" firm in the marketplace is that its competition won't necessarily be so "good." Firms that have no scruples about using sweatshop labor will exploit the consumer preference and signaling problems faced by their "good" competitors. Even if there is a critical mass of "good" firms that creates a "good" image for an industry, there will always be an enormous temptation for moral free-riders to take advantage of this by continuing to sell sweatshop goods at prices that "good" firms can't meet because of the extra costs associated with enforcing a code. Consumers simply don't have a way to express any latent preferences they may have for branded or unbranded products manufactured by "good" firms in factories that honor the human rights of their workers. Until this kind of information is readily available to consumers, the moral free-riders will continue to pose a formidable threat to "good" companies in the marketplace.

VOLUNTARY SOLUTIONS: STANDARDIZED AUDITING,
INDUSTRY-WIDE CODES, AND PRODUCT LABELING

A number of NGOs have embarked on initiatives attempting to deal with global sweatshop issues. These initiatives also have attempted to address, with varying success, the practical marketplace penalties faced by firms with good human rights practices. In January 1998, the Council on Economic Priorities launched a program called Social Accountability 8000 (SA8000). This program is modeled after the International Organization for Standardization 9000 (ISO9000) worldwide standard for quality assurance and the ISO14000 standard for environmental management.

Following the example of the ISO standards, SA8000 endeavors to create a standardized, global system enabling companies to monitor and control the labor practices of their suppliers and subcontractors.

SA8000 is training a network of independent firms that will conduct social audits of factories in nine areas—child labor, forced labor, health and safety, freedom of association, discrimination, disciplinary practices, working hours, management oversight, and compensation. The SA8000 standards are derived from a number of existing human rights instruments, including the Universal Declaration of Human Rights and the U.N. Convention on the Rights of the Child.

The SA8000 initiative has the potential to address a number of the practical competitive problems that "good" firms face in the marketplace. By attempting to develop a worldwide network of social auditing firms, SA8000 could create a cost-effective way for firms to implement an effective factory monitoring system, thereby eliminating the economy of scale problems each company faces when attempting to set up such a system alone. Perhaps the most potentially significant marketplace impact of SA8000, however, is its Certification Mark. Companies whose plants are certified as being in compliance with SA8000 will be entitled to place the SA8000 Certification Mark on their products. If it becomes known and accepted among consumers, the Certification Mark has the potential to solve the problem "good" firms face in signaling their goodness to consumers. For the first time, consumers will be given information enabling them to reveal their latent preferences for products that are manufactured with respect for the human rights of workers. Of course, the ultimate test of these preferences will be in the marketplace, where we can observe whether consumers are willing to pay more for SA8000-certified products than for uncertified products.

SA8000 is an ambitious program whose success depends on the development of a critical mass of acceptance among consumers and manufacturers. By the summer of 1999, three international auditing organizations had been accredited to conduct audits. Audits had been performed in China, Italy, the United States, Vietnam, and Brazil. Together the sales of companies committed to the SA8000 program totaled more than $75 billion. These companies included France's Pomodes, Italy's Coop Italia, Dutch WE Europe, and Germany's Otto Versand.[3] Tom DeLuca, vice president for imports at Toys 'R Us, has stated that eventually all of its five thousand suppliers will be required to obtain certification under SA8000.[4]

An alternative approach to sweatshop reform has been pioneered by a group calling itself the Fair Labor Association (FLA). The FLA, formerly called the Apparel Industry Partnership, is a nonprofit entity whose membership is made up of apparel and footwear companies—including L.L. Bean, Nike, and Reebok—and human rights groups. It also has participation from labor and religious organizations, as well as the National Consumers League. The FLA's Workplace Code of Conduct covers essentially the same nine areas as SA8000, but the standards are worded slightly differently. The FLA also has a monitoring and a certification program entitling companies in compliance with the standards to use a compliance mark. Unlike SA8000, there is no requirement for external monitoring. However, the FLA provides partial reimbursement to participating companies that use external monitors.

The industry-wide approach of FLA is notable because, along with the certification mark, it represents a promising way for companies to address the signaling and moral free-rider problems described earlier. By trying to enlist as participants a critical mass of companies in the footwear and apparel industry and by offering an industry-specific compliance mark, the FLA would provide information enabling consumers to identify products manufactured by "good" companies. The FLA thus offers companies a means of signaling their "goodness" to consumers and thereby distinguishing their products in the marketplace from products manufactured in sweatshops.

Another effort to bring accountability to corporate human rights practices is the "U.S. Business Principles for Human Rights of Workers in China" (Appendix E). Administered by a coalition of industry and NGO groups, this China-specific program has been endorsed by Levi Strauss, Mattel, Reebok, and other companies that together employ more than one hundred thousand workers in China, mostly women.[5] In the summer of 1999, a group of apparel industry manufacturers initiated yet another voluntary human rights labor code and compliance mark—the Worldwide Responsible Apparel Production Certification Program.

TOWARD A COMPLETE HUMAN RIGHTS PARTNERSHIP: DEVELOPING
CONSUMER AWARENESS AND CONCERN FOR HUMAN RIGHTS

The aforementioned voluntary codes are creative and important initiatives in the struggle against sweatshop labor conditions in developing countries. However, they fail to address some critical issues in that struggle. First, it should be noted that the various programs are in a somewhat competitive position to one another. With three separate compliance marks, four different sets of standards, and several different monitoring systems, the possibility exists for consumer confusion. Moreover, these are not the only such certification programs being launched. In the United States and Europe, a growing number of trade groups and nonprofit organizations are setting up similar programs.[6] If such social accountability programs and marks proliferate, consumers are apt to be very confused about which are reliable indicators of compliance with human rights principles. This suggests that a need will emerge for a universal, global standard. Such a universal standard could evolve from one of the programs in existence, but ultimately an intergovernmental solution may be required to settle the confusion.

Even more problematic than the issue of unsettled standards, however, is a deeper fault in these approaches. They are all excessively focused on issues of compliance and not devoted enough to educational and promotional activities that would encourage consumer awareness and concern for human rights issues. The reasons for this focus on compliance are understandable. For many human rights advocates in NGOs, it has been a long and hard-fought struggle to publicize human rights abuses and convince multinational corporations to adopt labor codes of conduct. Indeed, many other companies are still unconvinced of the merits of joining rigorous and transparent voluntary human rights certification programs. NGOs need to learn, however, that the stick is only so useful in promoting good human rights behavior and that it is also necessary to use the carrot. The carrot, in this case, consists of creating a monetary marketplace value for the certification trademark. This, in turn, means creating consumer awareness of human rights issues and preference for goods manufactured in compliance with human rights standards.

Compliance with a human rights code of conduct costs money. Although good ethics sometimes means good business, this is not always true. It certainly is not true if compliance with human rights programs increases production costs without creating some kind of a marketing benefit. The use of a human rights compliance certification mark is a step in the right direction, because it holds forth the possibility for "good" firms to distinguish themselves from firms that still use sweatshops. Unless the use of the mark is accompanied by a substantial public campaign to inform consumers of the virtues of "good" companies, however, the mark will not level the marketplace playing field between "good" companies that spend money on human rights compliance and sweatshop companies that are able to sell a cheaper product. To make programs such as FLA and SA8000 truly effective, consumers must be educated about human rights issues. It is a mistake to assume that the majority of consumers care or are even aware of human rights issues, notwithstanding the findings of surveys such as the Marymount study described earlier.

A real danger exists that human rights advocates will push multinational corporations far ahead of what consumers really care about. This is not only potentially costly for business, it also poses a threat to the cause of human rights. It will take a global collective effort to safeguard human rights. "Good" companies can't do it on their own. Consumers are a very big part of the web of moral responsibility for human rights. Ultimately, it is consumers who wear the shoes and clothes manufactured in sweatshops. It simply won't do to pressure corporations into caring more about human rights than consumers do. What is needed is a real partnership between companies and consumers, based on a very simple moral compact. Companies must agree to manufacture products in compliance with human rights codes, and consumers must agree to place a monetary value on such compliance. Both sides of the compact are necessary to safeguard human rights. We need both "good" companies and "good" consumers.

THE WORLD TRADE ORGANIZATION: AN INTERGOVERNMENTAL SOLUTION TO THE SWEATSHOP PROBLEM?

Product-labeling programs such as those described above rely on voluntary participation by manufacturers and consumer acceptance. As we have seen, there are significant limits on what such voluntary programs can accomplish due to a number of factors, including the marketplace disadvantages suffered by "good" companies trying to compete with moral free-riders that manufacture competing products in sweatshops. Moreover, companies employing sweatshop labor are not the only moral free-riders. Some consumers can be moral free-riders by buying products that are not labeled as being in compliance with human rights standards, thereby leaving the costs of improving labor conditions in sweatshops to be borne solely by those who pay for labeled products. Compounding the problems with voluntary solutions are the dynamics of competition for foreign capital among developing nations, which create incentives for governments to relax enforcement of their own labor laws.

The inherent limitations of voluntary private solutions in addressing sweatshop conditions have led some to call for the enforcement of labor standards through the WTO. According to such proposals, violations of internationally recognized labor standards would become grounds for the imposition of trade sanctions by the WTO. This suggestion has engendered significant controversy and bitterness between developed and developing nations, echoing many of the historical human rights controversies described in Chapter 7. Indeed, when at the Seattle WTO meeting held in December 1999, U.S. President Bill Clinton called on the WTO to consider placing workers' rights on the negotiating agenda, the outcry from third world nations was so great that it caused the meeting to collapse. The Seattle meeting was not the first time that labor issues jeopardized WTO negotiations. Indeed, in 1994, the issue threatened to prevent the WTO from coming into existence fifty years after it was initially conceived.

Although the Bretton Woods conference in 1944 was devoted primarily to monetary and banking issues, the conference participants recognized the need for a trade institution to complement the work of the International Monetary Fund and World Bank. Four years later in Havana, a draft charter was completed for the proposed International Trade Organization. Largely because of the unwillingness of the U.S. Congress to approve the new organization, however, the International Trade Organization never came into existence.[7] In April 1994, in Marrakesh, Morocco, the signing of the Uruguay Round treaty of the GATT fulfilled the vision of the Bretton Woods conferees by creating the WTO. The creation of the WTO required a last-minute compromise that narrowly averted disruption of the signing of the treaty. U.S. Trade Representative Mickey Kantor and European Union representative Sir Leon Brittan threatened to delay the signing unless the WTO was empowered to consider labor rights. Developing nations in Latin America, Africa, and Asia vehemently opposed this last-minute proposal, attacking it as a protectionist measure designed to deprive developing countries of their comparative advantage in unskilled, low-wage labor.

The compromise provided that labor rights would be mentioned in the closing statement of the GATT, but substantive discussion about the controversial suggestion to include labor rights on the WTO agenda was postponed until after the Marrakesh meetings. The crux of this controversy is whether labor rules, such as those governing the minimum wage, child labor, factory safety, and the right to form independent unions, are trade issues that should be discussed in and governed by the WTO, or whether they are purely domestic matters wholly within the sphere of sovereign nations. As a result of a similarly acrimonious disagreement about environmental rules, the new WTO has a standing committee on the environment. However, largely because of pressure from developing nations, the WTO has resisted pressures to form an analogous committee for labor rights.

The international community long has been involved in the public discussion of minimum labor standards. Founded in 1919, the International Labor Organization (ILO) now has more than 170 members. The governance structure of the ILO includes participation from groups representing both workers and employers. The ILO has adopted more than 170 conventions dealing with diverse labor issues, including the right to organize and bargain collectively, forced labor, migrant workers, hours of work, minimum working age, radiation protection, and exposure to benzene.

Not every member nation has ratified every ILO convention. Nevertheless, the former director-general of the ILO, Michel Hansenne, has claimed that "a well-developed normative framework for determining on the basis of international agreement what constitutes fair or decent labor practices already exists in the ILO." The success of the ILO has come mostly through cooperative and consultative procedures. The ILO relies, in Mr. Hansenne's words, "on moral effect, on the force of public opinion, on pressure from other governments and the social partners to secure compliance."[8] Since 1980, the ILO has made more than one thousand determinations of treaty violations that have led to changes in national policies.[9]

Despite its many and notable successes, however, the ILO is essentially a voluntary system that lacks the authority to enforce labor standards against the most egregious nations who choose not to cooperate with the ILO. Recognizing these limitations in November 1994, then Director-General Hansenne recommended finding a way to embody the ILO's work in the WTO, which, by virtue of its power over trade, would possess far greater leverage to enforce minimum labor standards.

Predictably, Hansenne's recommendation was roundly criticized by representatives of developing countries. Not surprisingly, many of the loudest critics came from nations with the worst abuses of workers' rights. But some of the harshest objections came from the business community in developed nations. By contrast, political support for the idea of linking trade with labor rights has come primarily from labor unions in developed economies.

The controversy over international labor standard boils down to two sets of questions. First, there is the economic question of who benefits and who loses from universal adherence to a set of minimal labor standards. Conventional wisdom is that workers in developed nations would gain, that workers in developing nations would lose, and that business interests and consumers would lose. However, this calculus depends on what exactly is meant by minimal labor standards. If it means creating new and higher labor standards, such as an international minimum wage and uniform working conditions throughout the world, then this calculus pretty well sums up the likely winners and losers. However, if only the minimum standards already embodied in the ILO conventions are enforced through the WTO, then universal adherence to those standards would likely have a very different result. In this case, for reasons explained below, both developing countries and business interests would gain, and workers in developed nations are unlikely to achieve any comparative advantage vis-à-vis workers in developing nations.

Another issue entirely distinct from the question of whom minimal labor standards benefit and harm is the question of whether the WTO should enforce adherence to such standards through trading sanctions. This depends on whether such a system can be fairly administered and thereby win the political support and trust of both developed and developing nations. Before turning to that issue, however, let us consider in some greater detail what universal adherence to minimal labor standards would really mean for the four groups with the most at stake—workers in developed nations, workers in developing nations, the business community, and consumers.

Misconceived Sources of Support for International Labor Standards: Fear of Wage Erosion and Job Losses in Developed Countries

Developing countries often accuse more advanced nations, particularly the United States, of disguising protectionist economic intentions behind the façade of principle. This accusation is not without justification in the case of labor rights, where humanitarian and economic concerns are often difficult to disentangle. In a speech delivered in April 1994, former U.S. Labor Secretary Robert B. Reich essentially affirmed that economic self-interest (i.e., the protection of U.S. workers from foreign competition) underpinned the U.S. position on labor rights. "As low-standard producers exploit their edge," Reich proclaimed, "producers in high-standard countries will be forced to respond by cutting wages and benefits and worsening working conditions in a destructive race for the bottom. The solution, according to this line of reasoning, and the best hope for hard-pressed low-wage workers in America, is to take labor costs out of competition by establishing international labor standards." Moreover, Reich confirmed the worst fears of developing nations by advocating "a menu of potential responses to labor standard abuses, varying in both the nature and severity of their effects." According to Reich, this "menu" includes general trade sanctions, sector-specific restrictions, the loss of preferential trade status, and ineligibility for international grant and loan programs.[10]

It is understandable that the United States and the European Union would seek to protect (or at least be perceived to protect) their workers from the impact of seemingly unlimited world labor supply at wages and working conditions that appear to have no bottom. However, the unfortunate reality for many unskilled American workers is that universal adherence to minimal international labor standards would not appreciably affect their job prospects. The minimum wage levels and working conditions of unskilled labor in the United States and Europe are simply too high to expect that adherence to minimum standards in developing countries would cause jobs to miraculously wash back ashore. Even if they adhere to minimum labor standards, developing nations will continue to have a huge comparative advantage in labor-intensive manufacturing.

In the United States, manufacturing employment peaked at approximately 19.3 million workers in 1989, and by 1999 it declined to around 18.4 million, despite an almost decade-long economic expansion.[11] The companies that are still manufacturing in the United States have made substantial investments in computers and assembly-line robots. There are, as a consequence, fewer but better jobs in manufacturing. Moreover, many of these jobs call for specialized technical skills. It is a cruel chimera of false hope to dangle a WTO labor standard as the salvation for American and European workers. Those who have lost or are in danger of losing their jobs to overseas competition need training in new skills, not protectionism, to cope with the disruptive forces of globalization. For American and European workers, there is no turning back the clock on globalization. Survival requires investments in education and skills. Sadly, those who are not afforded such opportunities will suffer one of the most bitter pills of globalization—poverty in the midst of plenty.

MISCONCEIVED SOURCES OF OPPOSITION TO INTERNATIONAL LABOR STANDARDS: THE EXIGENCIES OF DEVELOPMENT

Although developing nations denounce the promotion of economic protectionism behind a façade of moral concern for human rights, in the case of labor rights, leaders of developing countries might do some soul-searching of their own. Their harsh rhetorical accusations of protectionism and the waving of the sovereignty flag may mask their own hidden agenda—the expansion of exports and attraction of foreign direct investment without sufficient regard for the social costs to domestic workers.

Exports and foreign direct investment have become critical to the development plans of newly emerging economies. Until the 1980s, the Third World pursued import substitution policies and erected high tariff barriers to protect infant industries. Since the mid-1980s, however, at the insistence of key lenders, such as the International Monetary Fund and the World Bank, developing countries have adopted "structural adjustment" programs, consisting of trade liberalization, internal investment, and privatization, all geared toward expansion of the economy by increasing exports based on comparative advantages. Unfortunately for many nations with poor educational systems and meager resources, this comparative advantage consists mostly of cheap, unskilled labor. Export-led growth is expected to occur by allowing domestic and international capital access to the labor pool in the most unfettered, unregulated manner. In many cases, therefore, "structural adjustment" has come at the expense of the rights of low-skilled workers.[12]

In some countries, past flawed economic policies have led to an especially pressing need to increase exports. Indonesia, for example, beset with a massive and mounting national debt, has been all too willing to allow the exploitation of workers to attract capital and promote exports. Because of these pressures, Indonesia has opposed, often by brutal military force, the creation of independent trade unions within its borders. Violations of the official minimum wage are common. There may be a lot of sanctimonious talk about national sovereignty and the vast improvement low-wage jobs make in the lives of desperate workers, but the reality is that with bond payments spiraling out of control, there is not much of an incentive to look out for the human rights of workers.[13]

The competition for foreign direct investment also is becoming increasingly intense as developing nations vie for shares of a slow-growing pie of foreign capital. China now receives almost one-fourth of the flow of foreign direct investment to developing countries. In the future, as it seeks to meet the massive energy, transportation, and communication infrastructure needs required to sustain its continued economic development, China will continue to soak up investment capital that might otherwise go to neighboring Asian nations such as Indonesia, Thailand, and Malaysia, which also need capital to continue their own economic development.

This competition for investment capital creates downward pressure on labor standards. Dani Rodrik has conducted a cross-country study finding that lax labor standards were highly correlated with lower labor costs, even after accounting for productivity variables. Rodrik concluded that "comparative advantage in labor intensive goods . . . was associated with indicators of labor standards in the expected manner: the more relaxed the standard, the larger the revealed comparative advantage in labor intensive goods." Although Rodrik did not find a perfect correlation between relaxed labor standards and foreign investment, the correlation was strong enough to support the view that developing countries have an extremely pressing economic incentive to relax labor standards to a point lower than the local laws and generally accepted international standards would allow.[14]

Given the harsh realities of the foreign capital flows described by Rodrik, leaders of developing nations understandably regard international labor standards as a threat to their development aims. Instead of instinctively lashing out against them, however, developing nations may come to see that universal adherence to a set of minimal standards can yield increased economic and social benefits for their citizens. A growing but limited world market exists for goods produced by cheap labor. Less developed nations must compete against each other for their share of this world market. Without international labor standards, this competition has turned ugly as developing nations vie to attract investment capital by offering the cheapest and most exploited workforce. If a basic set of labor standards is followed by all developing nations, however, the competition for foreign capital will be a much healthier process that will create more overall welfare among workers in developing countries. In this way, the forces of global capital flows and free trade can be channeled into more positive social outcomes, as more of the benefits of foreign direct investment are captured by the host nations rather than the investing firms and consumers in rich nations. As the labor leader Jay Mazur has written, "The demand for enforceable labor rights in global trading accords . . . is not an effort to build walls against the global economy. It is an effort to build rules into it, and a floor under it, to lift wages up rather than drive them down."[15]

Embracing the concept of international labor standards holds another benefit for developing countries. Without such a standard, important trading partners such as the United States and the European Union can force developing countries into concessions on labor issues by threatening the kind of unilateral economic sanctions suggested by former Labor Secretary Reich. The United States, for example, has successfully employed section 301 of the Trade and Tariff Act of 1974 for a variety of purposes against numerous trading partners.[16] By participating cooperatively in the development of an acceptable set of minimum labor standards according to which they are willing to compete, developing nations can better defend themselves from unilateral interpretation and enforcement of potentially protectionist labor standards by developing nations.

How should the business community regard the question of universal adherence to minimum labor standards? With the free movement of investment capital across national borders, even minimal labor standards would raise the production costs of many international manufacturing operations. A short-sighted approach would thus regard enforcement of labor standards as against the interests of business. Typical of such a view was the reaction of the president of the U.S. Council for International Business, who declared that "U.S. business is unified in opposing the use of trade sanctions to enforce workers' rights. . . . Let's drop that idea and we'll go on from there."[17]

It does not, however, make sense for business firms to continue to oppose international labor standards; on the contrary, such standards would have the beneficial effect of leveling the competitive playing field for all firms. Multinational firms are under increasing pressure from NGOs and other human rights advocates to produce goods without violating the basic rights of their factory workers in developing countries. As a result of these sorts of pressures and because of their own ethical values, many multinational firms in diverse industries are adopting voluntary ethical codes of conduct to govern their operations in developing countries. Others are joining in voluntary cooperative systems such as the FLA and SA8000. As we have seen, however, these voluntary programs render "good" firms vulnerable to competition from moral free-rider firms that continue to manufacture in sweatshops. "Good" firms should, as a consequence, applaud rather than oppose efforts to achieve universal adherence to minimal labor standards by developing countries. Such universal adherence is superior to voluntary programs because it puts all firms on an equal competitive basis by reducing the competitive threat from moral free-riders.

WESTERN CONSUMERS: THE DECIDING VOTE
ON GLOBAL HUMAN RIGHTS STANDARDS

Ultimately, the success of the various initiatives to curtail human rights abuses in China and other developing countries depends on the degree to which consumers in Western Europe and the United States begin to incorporate into purchasing decisions a consciousness about how and by whom imports are manufactured. Consumers must be willing to pay a little more for toys, clothes, household items, and other products whose declining prices we have grown accustomed to enjoying.

There are, as we have seen, efficiencies to be gained from coordinated efforts to monitor and prevent human rights abuses in manufacturing facilities located in China and other developing nations. Such efforts level the competitive playing field between "good" companies and companies that take advantage of sweatshop labor. Smaller "good" companies can take advantage of collective monitoring capacities that they would not have the resources to construct themselves. Despite these efficiencies, however, there are some net costs associated with the enforcement of human rights in manufacturing operations. No sleight of hand will make it possible to fashion out of thin air a way of paying for the human rights benefits that will accrue to Chinese workers. Monitoring and enforcing minimal labor standards will impose costs on manufacturing. Unless and until Western consumers are willing to absorb some of this cost in the form of higher prices, then it is grossly unrealistic to expect multinational corporations to solve the problem of labor abuses by adopting human rights codes of conduct.

For human rights advocates, the focus should no longer be exclusively on multinational corporations. The next big campaign should be to garner more widespread consumer support for tackling human rights abuses. At the moment, awareness of and concern for the human rights implications of products is limited mostly to student activists who are demanding that licensed collegiate apparel conform with minimal labor standards.[18] To make a real impact on human rights practices in China and elsewhere, the rest of us have to follow the moral leadership of these students and begin to think about how the clothes on our backs are made.

CONCLUSION

Those who stand to lose the most from the implementation of minimal international labor standards are the firms that would exploit voluntary efforts by continuing to manufacture products in sweatshops. Both private voluntary efforts such as SA8000 and the FLA and voluntary intergovernmental systems such as the ILO give moral free-riders the opportunity to exploit and undermine the good intentions and efforts of others. Therefore, much is to be gained by enforcing a labor clause through the WTO. Only with the threat of economic sanctions can the powerful negative forces in the global economy that give rise to sweatshops be counterbalanced and the problem of moral free-riders be ameliorated.

Developing countries would do well to support such efforts and to work cooperatively with each other to ensure that the labor standards that are enforced through the WTO do not rob them of their existing comparative advantages in unskilled labor, while at the same time protecting the economic and social interests of their workers. Multinational corporations should also welcome the enforcement of labor standards through the WTO, because it will create a level economic playing field for socially responsible firms.

Some free trade "purists" argue that the WTO is not an appropriate venue for enforcing what they deem to be nontrade social issues. According to this view, no real consensus exists about labor standards, and attempts to shoehorn such concerns into the world trading system infringe on the sovereignty of developing nations.[19] I would argue two points in response to this point of view. First, as the work of the ILO has demonstrated, more consensus exists about labor rights than about other kinds of human rights. Moreover, I am not advocating the imposition through the WTO of any set of standards that would not create a net benefit for workers in developing nations. Indeed, significant progress in the struggle against sweatshop labor can be achieved only if the national and local labor laws already on the books are enforced. This will occur, however, only if developing nations act collectively instead of competitively on the issue of labor law enforcement.

A second point to be made is that, with the conclusion of the Uruguay Round of the GATT talks in Marrakesh, the nations of the world have already expanded the scope of proper trade negotiation subjects beyond simple tariff reductions. The principle that the manner in which products are manufactured has important fairness implications for free trade has already won acceptance. GATT rules have long permitted members whose domestic industries have suffered "material injury" to impose countervailing duties on goods that have been subsidized by the government of the exporting country. Other examples in GATT abound to illustrate that the international trading system is a carefully negotiated regime balancing the ideal of free trade with the reality that certain practices allow nations to unfairly capture the benefits of free trade. In the 1990s, the definition of what is a proper trade-related issue expanded considerably. For example, the Uruguay Round GATT treaty provides that economic sanctions can be imposed against countries that fail to adequately protect "trade related intellectual property."[20] Environmental matters are also being linked to free trade. Many governments have come to realize that unless all countries compete according to a certain set of minimal standards in manufacturing products, free trade will never mean fair trade. Eventually labor standards will be seen in the same light.

Over time, developing countries and multinational firms might both learn to welcome the labor standards initiatives at the WTO. It would, as has been argued, behoove both groups to stop fighting a short-sighted and self-defeating ideological battle of words and work to establish a WTO labor provision that protects workers without being protectionist. Such a provision would serve both humanitarian and efficiency aims. However, the truth will always remain that unless Western consumers are willing to bear the associated costs of such a provision, there can be no satisfactory solution to the issue of global labor standards.

Unfortunately, in the twenty-first century, the issue of international labor standards promises to continue to be a contentious one. Developing nations will continue to view it as a threat to their development rather than a means to enhance the welfare of their citizens. Western political and labor leaders will continue to dangle international standards as a quick fix to the challenges of globalization. As the twenty-first century begins, the neglected state of the human rights of workers is yet another reminder of how far the world is from embracing and realizing the noble sentiments expressed in the Universal Declaration of Human Rights more than half a century ago.

CHAPTER TEN

✯

Human Rights in the Office Suite: How to Succeed in Business in an Authoritarian Nation without Compromising Moral Integrity

Article 19. Everyone has the right to freedom of opinion and expression; this right includes freedom to hold opinions without interference and to seek, receive and impart information and ideas through any media and regardless of frontiers.

Article 20. Everyone has the right to freedom of peaceful assembly and association. No one may be compelled to belong to an association.

Article 21. Everyone has the right to take part in the government of his country, directly or through freely chosen representatives. Everyone has the right to equal access to public service in his country. The will of the people shall be the basis of the authority of government; this will shall be expressed in periodic and genuine elections which shall be by universal and equal suffrage and shall be held by secret vote or by equivalent free voting procedures.

—Universal Declaration of Human Rights, December 10, 1948

Some of the most challenging decisions facing multinational executives in China stem from the government's serious and pervasive violations of civil and political rights. There are thousands of prisoners of conscience in China. These brave men and women have been put in jail for expressing their political beliefs or practicing their religion in an unauthorized venue. They are in jail for having the temerity to criticize the Communist Party or to call for democracy in China.

A multitude of examples can be culled from to get the flavor of political repression in China. In May 1999, the Guilin Intermediate People's Court in Guanxi Province sentenced twenty-nine-year-old Li Zhiyou to three years in prison for "inciting to overthrow state power." His crime? He posted leaflets about the banned China Democratic Party (CDP). That same month, the writer Liu Xianli was given four years in prison for trying to publish a book about political dissidents in China. The previous year, a leading figure of the CDP was convicted of subversion and sentenced to thirteen years in prison. In April 1999, Zhang Youju, also a member of the CDP, was sentenced to four years in prison for posting signs calling for a reassessment of the Tiananmen protests.[1]

The precise number and conditions of prisoners of conscience in China are difficult to determine, in part because basic information about prisoners is inaccessible to international humanitarian organizations such as the International Committee of the Red Cross. Amnesty International estimates that thousands of people arrested during the Tiananmen massacre remain in prison. The U.S. State Department more cautiously estimates the number to be "hundreds—perhaps thousands," adding, however, that "former detainees have credibly reported that officials used cattle prods, electrodes, prolonged periods of solitary confinement."[2] In January 1995, a Chinese Ministry of Justice official claimed that a total of 2,678 prisoners convicted of "counter-revolutionary" offenses were in jail.[3] Amnesty International, however, called this number "only a fraction of the real number of political prisoners. It excludes many thousands of people who are jailed for political reasons but convicted of other offenses, or held under various forms of administrative detention without charge or trial, or detained for long periods for investigations pending trial."[3] The U.S. State Department has reported that more than 230,000 Chinese citizens have been sentenced for up to three years, through administrative procedures without a trial, in reeducation-through-labor camps.[4]

Executives of multinational corporations obviously would prefer not to grapple with these types of human rights issues. It is one thing to take responsibility for sweatshop issues concerning pay, health and safety, and forced labor. It is another thing entirely to confront the Chinese government about civil and political repression. The difference is that a company can tackle the labor rights issues without incurring the wrath of the government. Grappling with political and civil rights, however, has the potential to pit multinational corporations against the Communist Party, which is a very risky thing for any company that is trying to establish a sustainable business in China. As much as multinational executives would like to ignore the issue, however, it is not possible to do so. Political and civil repression in China is too serious and too pervasive to avoid. Sooner or later, the harsh realities of doing business in an authoritarian country find their way into the office suite.

There are two ways in which political and civil repression can insinuate itself onto the agenda of even the most studiously apolitical corporate executive in China. One is through hiring, firing, and promotion decisions. As the Chrysler–Gao Feng incident described in Chapter 6 illustrates, Chinese officials may pressure foreign executives to fire a political or religious dissident. When this happens, the foreign executive faces a moral and business crisis. When asked how he would handle the Gao Feng scenario, one executive with many years of business experience in China replied as follows: "The first thing I would do is to tell my secretary to hold my calls, and then I would close my door to think, because this would be a very serious situation, which, if not handled properly, could have serious repercussions for my company. I would take this very seriously."[5]

A second way in which multinational executives are called on to grapple with civil and political rights in China stems from the pressure by NGOs urging them to speak out and to use their influence on government officials. As we saw in Chapter 6, the NGO HRW espoused such a view of corporate responsibility when it urged that

> senior management should raise concerns about respect for human rights with appropriate Chinese officials including the detention, arrest or conviction of people whose only "offense" is the nonviolent expression of their political views. . . . Often U.S. companies are well-placed to use their influence in the course of their dealings with central, provincial, and local authorities. Concern can be expressed discreetly and in a non-provocative manner, *and can be framed not as a criticism but as a problem threatening the expansion of a mutually beneficial business relationship* [emphasis added].[6]

For corporate executives, the suggestion that they should become involved in the Chinese political situation is threatening and confusing. The potential for a serious misstep is very high, and the economic consequences could be disastrous. Chinese government officials do not like hearing criticism from their own citizens; they certainly do not want to hear political criticism from foreign business executives. Moreover, talking about human rights is not easy for international leaders, and it is especially hard for multinational executives with little training in the subject. The subject of human rights involves grand historical, cultural, and geopolitical issues. The chances are very high that a corporate executive who speaks out about human rights will say something that is going to upset Chinese officials. For all of these reasons, most business executives avoid taking public stances on human rights like the plague. As one Shanghai-based executive admitted, "Let's face it. This is an authoritarian state, and words are easily misinterpreted."[7]

When it comes to human rights in China, avoidance is not really an option for multinational executives. Managers would be wise to prepare to deal effectively with the sticky situations in which they are likely to find themselves. They need to think out in advance both the nature of their moral responsibilities and the practical alternatives available to minimize the negative impacts of their actions. In this chapter, the fair share theory developed in Chapter 8 is used to clarify what moral duties are owed and not owed by multinational corporations in regard to political and civil repression in China. This chapter also offers some practical advice about how to minimize the potential negative economic repercussions that could potentially result from honoring a human rights duty.

Upholding the Rights of Dissidents Who Work for Foreign Companies

As we saw in Chapter 6, neither the AmCham code of conduct nor the Clinton principles ventured to address the moral responsibilities of a multinational corporation that is asked by the Chinese government to fire a dissident who happens also to be an employee. The HRW proposal was, however, quite explicit in arguing that corporate executives should refuse to do so (see question 2 in Table 6.1).

Chrysler faced a difficult business situation when a representative of its joint venture partner reportedly suggested that it fire Gao Feng for attempting to practice his religion in an unauthorized venue. Refusing to do so would surely have made Chrysler's joint venture partner and the Chinese government angry, thereby jeopardizing existing and potential business contracts in China. A lot of money was at stake and, therefore, Chrysler had a very difficult and complex business matter to resolve. From a moral perspective, however, the decision was pretty obvious and straightforward on the basis of the facts as reported in the press. The Chinese government needed Chrysler's cooperation to violate Gao's rights. Chrysler was thus in a unique position to uphold Gao's rights. By refusing to fire Gao and by standing up to the Chinese government, Chrysler could have helped to protect

Gao's rights. In failing to do so, Chrysler breached its moral duty to uphold Gao's rights and, in fact, became complicit in the violation of his rights.

As the Gao Feng case poignantly illustrates, a multinational firm's duty to uphold human rights can seriously threaten its commercial prospects in China. The potential risk to profits does not, however, change the firm's responsibility to uphold human rights by witholding its complicity and participation in a human rights violation. If the risk of losing out on China business from upholding human rights seems high for multinational firms, it should be put in perspective. The allocation of human rights duties was made with an eye toward a fair allocation of the burdens of enforcing human rights. The point was not to eliminate all costs for morally responsible agents, but rather to distribute those costs fairly and with a view toward creating a system that overall protects human rights in the most effective and efficient manner.

Upholding human rights by refusing to fire an employee for his or her political or religious expression is one task that a multinational corporation is uniquely positioned to accomplish. A multinational corporation must be prepared to bear the associated cost of that duty, *even if it means being forced to withdraw from business in China*. To do otherwise would undermine the positive human rights spin-off that multinational corporations generate in China. Failure to uphold human rights in a Gao Feng–type scenario is tantamount to aiding and abetting a human rights abuse. It would be a poor lesson in democracy and human rights for corporations to help the Chinese government to violate the human rights of their workers. Such complicity would constitute a loud and profound statement that contradicts and undermines everything multinational corporations are formally and informally teaching their workers about speaking out, taking responsibility, and asserting their independence.

A corporation that becomes complicit in human rights abuses should not be doing business in China at all. Because the financial penalty for adhering to human rights principles is potentially so devastating, it behooves multinational managers to learn how to uphold human rights with a minimum of risk to their commercial interests. This is not easy to do, but corporations can take some practical steps to accomplish this delicate task.

As we have seen, moral responsibility for human rights is not merely a matter of convenience. The multinational executive must be prepared to uphold the human rights of a firm's employees even if it means putting the firm's commercial interests at risk or ceasing operations in China altogether. With such high moral and financial stakes pitted against one another, a head-in-the-sand approach is not advisable for corporate executives who might suddenly find themselves in the middle of a potentially career-threatening human rights scenario. However, upholding the human rights of employees does not require a corporate executive to adopt a confrontational style with the Chinese government. In fact, a creative manager can take a number of steps to minimize the risks posed to a firm's commercial interests.

Four factors are crucial to handling such situations in a morally and practically satisfactory manner:

1. Get your head out of the sand and *be morally prepared*. It is better to anticipate human rights dilemmas in advance than to hope you will never have to confront such issues.
2. Use your knowledge of Chinese society creatively. China's unique political, economic, and cultural circumstances require you to *be resourceful and flexible in applying moral principles in practice*.
3. *Assert control over the human resources function.* There are many good business reasons to do this anyway. In this way, personnel decisions about dissidents can be cast in a professional rather than political light.
4. Seek safety in numbers. *Find opportunities for collective action with other companies* through trade associations and chambers of commerce. Encourage these organizations to talk about human rights issues rather than to pretend such issues do not exist.

First, multinational corporations need to *be morally prepared*. Being caught flat-footed, as Chrysler was in the Gao Feng scenario, is a huge mistake. It is extremely important for a company operating in China to think through in advance how it will handle such situations. Indeed, for a company to do business in China without a human rights policy that is formulated with the participation of the top levels of management borders on the reckless. Ideally, the output of this process should be incorporated into a provision in the company's code of conduct. Alarmingly, however, very few multinational corporations are prepared to address issues arising from the violation of the civil or political rights of their employees. According to a study conducted by the International

Labor Organization, for example, only 15 percent of the codes of conduct adopted by multinational corporations contain a reference to freedom of association.[8]

The rationale for including a provision about the human rights of political and religious dissidents in a corporate code of conduct is to enable a corporation to clarify the principles that it stands for before those principles are tested in a crisis. Corporate principles define the core beliefs of a corporation. Unless a corporation knows what its principles are and what it stands for, it will be unable to respond to the bewildering array of demands that are placed on it in the context of operations in developing societies. With a strong set of core principles, however, a company is equipped to act decisively when moments of moral crisis arise.

When a company enters the Chinese market, it must make a variety of decisions. It must decide, among other things, how it will finance an investment, whether it will take on a joint venture partner or proceed through a wholly-owned subsidiary, as well as how and to whom it will market its product. Added to this mix of indispensible strategic questions is an equally indispensible moral question: What are our company's values and what do we stand for? Corporations operating in China must learn to think of moral principle not as an afterthought, but rather as Confucius did when he compared virtue to the North Star "which the multitudinous stars pay homage to while it stays in its place."

Multinational executives also can minimize the negative commercial impact of upholding human rights by *being creative and flexible in applying principles in practice.*[9] The success of multinational firms in upholding human rights depends vitally on the resourcefulness of individual business executives. This is especially true in the case of China, where an understanding of historical and cultural factors is so essential to doing business. As we have seen, the AmCham and Clinton principles both went out of their way to avoid treating China as a special case. This, however, seems to deny the obvious. China *is* special in certain respects, and an executive who has been in China long enough to understand Chinese culture should try to put that knowledge to work in implementing a strong human rights policy. One executive who faced a situation analogous to the Gao Feng scenario (involving a request by a government official to help to enforce the one-family–one-child policy by firing a pregnant woman) emphasized the importance of allowing the government officials to maintain "face." He resolved the situation artfully by making sure that the government was compensated (i.e., assuaged by a concession in another unrelated matter) for the firm's refusal to punish the worker in question.[10]

The area that probably requires the most creativity to reconcile moral principles with local conditions in China concerns the right of workers to organize independent unions and engage in collective bargaining. China outlaws independent trade unions and requires workers to accept representation by affiliates of the Communist Party–controlled All China Confederation of Trade Unions. The government has attempted to stamp out all independent union activity. In 1998, Li Qingxi was sentenced to a year of reeducation-through-labor for calling for independent trade unions. Tan Li, a founder of the independent China Labor Alliance, has been arrested in Guangzhou. Zhou Shanguang has been sentenced to ten years in prison for "illegally providing intelligence to a foreign organization." His crime consisted of speaking with a Radio Free Asia reporter about a demonstration by eighty farmers who were protesting excessive taxes.[11]

According to official government statistics reported in 1996, 4.54 million workers (75 percent of the total number) in enterprises with foreign investment were members of unions belonging to the All China Confederation of Trade Unions. Foreign companies dealing with worker representatives obviously cannot guarantee the rights of workers to organize independent trade unions. Therefore, to continue to do business in China without compromising the moral principle involved, corporate executives must find an alternative means of ensuring that workers' concerns are adequately taken into account. They need, in other words, to find ways of giving workers effectively the same rights that they would have if they were able to organize independent trade unions. The SA8000 standards offer an interesting approach to this problem, providing that "the company shall, in those situations in which the right to freedom of association and collective bargaining are restricted under law, facilitate parallel means of independent and free association and bargaining for all such personnel."[12] In China, such moral creativity is essential if corporations are to honor the free-association rights of workers.

A third, and perhaps the most important, practical step that a multinational corporation can take to protect its commercial interests as it meets its human rights responsibilities is to *assert control over the human resources function*. In China, the human resources office is an important battlefield in the struggle for human rights. Political control over dissidents often is exercised through hiring and firing actions, work assignments, and decisions about promotions and raises. In Chinese SOEs, there is virtually no professionalism in human resource management. Human resource officers within SOEs are trained in Communist Party propaganda. As we observed in Chapter 4, they accept the fact that personnel decisions must to a large degree be dominated by issues of political correctness.

By establishing and asserting control over a professional human resources function in its foreign operations, a multinational firm can defuse potential human rights issues well before they ignite. By treating personnel issues as professional issues requiring professional responses, multinational executives can create a layer of discretion and protection in the event that they are asked to fire a political or religious dissident. By not sharing hiring and firing decisions as a general matter with foreign governments and joint venture partners, multinational corporations can from the outset of their operations de-emphasize the importance of political correctness as a factor in personnel decisions.

This admonition to gain control over the human resources function is complementary to other trends already taking place. As we saw in Chapter 4, control over personnel decisions is critical for multinational corporations who need to establish meritocratic principles in their hiring and promotion practices as part of their strategy of developing local management talent. However, the trend toward retaining managerial control has even broader roots. When foreign companies first began to conduct operations in China in the 1980s, the government required them to do so with a joint venture partner. Even apart from the legal requirement to do so, multinational corporations were eager to seek out local partners, believing that such allies would be useful in understanding and exploiting the then-unfamiliar Chinese markets. Experience has taught foreign companies that picking a useful joint venture partner in China was a dicey hit-or-miss proposition. Partners were as likely to be impediments to successful penetration of Chinese markets as they were to be assets. For example, when Otis Elevator first entered the Chinese market, it took on as partner a company under the control of the municipality of Tianjin. Very soon after commencing operations, Otis Elevator executives realized that its choice of partner was thwarting its expansion efforts through other regions in China.[13]

In the 1990s, many multinational corporations have advanced rapidly along the learning curve, and they are now more confident in their ability to conduct business in China without a joint venture partner. Foreign companies have lobbied the government to change China's foreign investment laws. As a result, multinational corporations are now allowed to conduct operations through wholly owned subsidiaries.[14] Multinational corporations are realizing that it makes good business sense to establish maximum managerial control over their China operations. Shrewd managers establish relationships with a whole network of business partners, but ultimately they seek to retain as much control as possible over their operations. The most crucial decision-making function a multinational corporation needs to retain to be successful is control of human resources decisions. Daniel Rosen reports that, "freedom to recruit and dismiss workers and freedom to set their salary and bonus levels . . . were at the top of the list for foreign managers. . . . [C]ontrol over appointing the . . . director of human resources is critical."[15] It makes good business sense for multinational firms to assert control over the human resources function. It can also help multinational executives to meet their human rights responsibilities without needlessly sacrificing their economic interests, by turning potentially thorny political questions into professional management issues.

A fourth crucial element of a successful human rights strategy is to *seek out opportunities for collective action with other companies.* Political and civil repression is serious and pervasive in China. At the same time, the commercial importance of China as an emerging market is unprecedented. To address these unique circumstances, multinational corporations would be wise to pool their collective experiences and clout to formulate a strategy for meeting the challenges of doing business in a repressive environment. Shanghai, Beijing, and Hong Kong each have large and active chambers of commerce that provide forums for foreign corporations to pool their resources and address issues of common concern to multinational corporations doing business in China. These organizations generally have avoided the issue of political and civil repression. Their attitude seems to be that if we do not discuss the political situation, it will not have an impact on our business. There may also be a sense that the very act of placing the human rights issue on the chamber's agenda will create problems with the Chinese government. However, in many issues, particularly in the area of developing principles for human resource management, the chambers of commerce can provide leadership and support to corporate executives striving to manage their way through the special challenges of operating in China. A great many knowledgeable and talented managers who have long-standing experience in China and knowledge of local culture are members of these chambers of commerce. These managers need to demonstrate some moral leadership. The first step in such leadership is to find "safe" and discreet ways for business executives to frankly discuss options for dealing with various situations—such as the Chrysler–Gao Feng scenario—that require a foreign enterprise to formulate a strategy for managing the moral and practical challenges emanating from political and civil repression in China. The chambers of commerce are shortchanging their members if they do not provide guidance, leadership, and opportunities for collective action on this crucial aspect of operating a business in China.

MORAL RESPONSIBILITY FOR GENERAL HUMAN RIGHTS ABUSES UNRELATED TO CORPORATE OPERATIONS

The activities of multinational firms directly affect only a very tiny percentage of the human rights abuses in China. Foreign employers account for a minuscule percentage of jobs. The overwhelming majority of human rights violations in China occur outside of the purview of foreign companies. As a consequence, multinational corporations can have only a very limited impact on the overall human rights situation in China by honoring and upholding human rights in their business dealings. This raises a question about whether multinational companies should do more. Should they raise concerns with Chinese officials about human rights matters that are unrelated to the firm's operations? (See question 3 in Table 6.1.)

As noted above, advocacy groups such as HRW have urged firms to in "good faith" undertake "proactive" measures with respect to the general human rights situation in China. However, business executives have been reluctant to do so for fear of alienating Chinese government officials. NGOs such as HRW have done a superb job of uncovering and publicizing human rights abuses in China and elsewhere in the world. HRW itself is one of the leading human rights NGOs in the world. Its effort to engage the corporate community in human rights work, however, was unsuccessful. HRW issued its proposal without any meaningful consultation with the business community. As a consequence, the HRW proposal was out of touch with the reality of operating a multinational corporation in China, and not surprisingly, it failed to garner much support from business leaders.

So what kind of duties would HRW's "proactive" measures require of multinational firms? When a firm acts proactively in the HRW sense, it is assuming duties with respect to human rights violations to which the firm itself has no connection. Unlike the manufacturing supplier issues discussed in Chapter 9 and the Gao Feng scenario discussed above, the duties to honor or uphold human rights are not at issue in the HRW proposal. In asking firms to express concern "discreetly" and in a "non-threatening manner" about human rights conditions "as a problem threatening the expansion of a mutually beneficial business relationship," HRW is essentially asking multinational firms to threaten economic sanctions in the hopes of influencing general human rights conditions in China.

One obvious problem with HRW's suggested approach is that, as a negotiating strategy, issuing a half-cocked threat is unlikely to accomplish anything. A threat must be credible to be effective. A vague threat, even politely posed, will serve very little purpose. There are, however, more serious problems with the suggestion that multinational firms use economic leverage to accomplish broad human rights goals. Under the fair share principles set forth in Chapter 8, it is international institutions and nation-states that are best suited, and therefore who have the duty, to use economic pressure to help enforce human rights. Why is this allocation of duties fair and effective? Why shouldn't multinational firms attempt to use their economic leverage to bring about a general improvement in human rights? In short, the answer is that, in China at least, multinational firms cannot use economic pressure effectively to achieve human rights results outside the purview of their operations. Because they are not able to do so, they have no duty to do so. Certain companies in other countries may have greater economic leverage with the national government. Such leverage could, in turn, engender responsibility for general human rights conditions unrelated to a company's business operations. For example, some have suggested that the Shell Oil company, because of its dominant role in the Nigerian economy, could and should have done more to prevent the 1995 execution of environmentalist Ken Sao-Wiwa and other activists.[16] In China, however, no one firm or group of firms has this kind of influence, and economic threats to the Chinese government would be extremely unlikely to result in any positive human rights result.

The power of multinational corporations to achieve improvements in general human rights conditions is also constrained by a number of other factors, including the limited knowledge and expertise of business executives about complex political and social issues such as human rights. Business firms are organized to produce goods and services, not to accomplish political and social objectives. Human rights, in particular, constitute an unfamiliar subject for most business executives. As a general rule, business executives are not trained to pursue general political and social objectives, and they are not particularly effective at doing so. Although multinational firms may have many dealings with government officials, such contacts are not normally about the management of broad and complex issues, such as human rights, that are unrelated to business operations. Where multinational firms do attempt to influence local political conditions, it is usually to ensure a compliant environment for their business operations. As we have seen, broad historical controversies underlie the dialogue between China and the West about China's human rights record. The charged and complex nature of these controversies make them especially difficult for businesspeople to be involved in at a leadership level. For all of these reasons, broad pronouncements on general human rights conditions in a particular country are best undertaken by international institutions or (less ideally) by individual nations.

Another factor influencing the potential effectiveness of multinational firms to proactively address general human rights conditions is the competitive leverage of the Chinese government. Put simply, firms that confront the Chinese government about human rights are likely to lose their China business. European, Japanese, and U.S. firms are competing fiercely for market share. Under such circumstances, even if it wanted to, a firm could not effectively pressure the Chinese government on human rights. If the Chinese government is unhappy enough with the message being delivered by one multinational firm, it can and will simply give its business to a less audacious company. Moreover, because of these competitive conditions, businesses with operations in China have a very limited capacity to withstand the retaliation of the Chinese government. The swift result of undertaking proactive human rights efforts is likely to be the complete loss of a foothold in the Chinese market. As we saw in Chapter 9, multinational firms already face this risk because of their duties to honor and enforce human rights when the human rights of their employees are at stake. It is asking too much, however, that they should take on additional risks when they can accomplish little by doing so.

Even a rich and powerful nation such as the United States can exert only a limited influence on the Chinese government. It should not be too surprising that a multinational corporation would have little, if any, influence on the human rights policies of the Chinese government. This does not mean that multinational executives can never effectively address human rights violations that are unrelated to their business operations. In certain rare instances, a discreet communication or "quiet diplomacy" can have a positive impact. However, such efforts are more likely to be successful when they seek narrow objectives such as the release of particular prisoners and when they are persuasive rather than subtly threatening in tone. The American chemical industry executive (and former chairman of the

American Chamber of Commerce in Hong Kong) John Kamm has helped in this way to obtain the release of scores of political prisoners from Chinese prisons. He has been able to do so without harming his business interests. Kamm is fond of quoting the old Chinese proverb, "your best friend is a critic,"[17] and he believes that more foreign business executives can do similar human rights work. Kamm, however, has been doing business in China for more than two decades. He is fluent in Mandarin, thoroughly knowledgeable about Chinese society and culture, and he can draw on a wealth of old contacts. Not many foreign business executives possess the kind of deep-rooted experience that would enable them to assume such a quasi-diplomatic role on human rights.

Although executives in multinational firms do not have a duty to speak out about general human rights conditions in China, it is not appropriate for executives to kowtow to Chinese leaders by parroting the government's human rights propaganda. If a multinational executive is not going to criticize human rights conditions in China, then it is better that he or she remain silent on the subject. When I say that multinational executives are unsuited by training to speak out about general human rights conditions, I am referring not only to how they can get in trouble with the Chinese government by being critical. I am also referring to craven and ill-informed attempts to take a position conspicuously supporting the Chinese government.[18] This kind of behavior only serves to fuel the outrage of critics such as *New York Times* columnist A. M. Rosenthal, who was moved (correctly, I believe) to write that such executives "just don't give a damn" about human rights.[19] The world has the right to expect more of multinational executives. Throughout this book, I have tried to distinguish between what we should and should not reasonably expect of multinational firms. If that reasonable expectation does not, as I have argued, include acting as a powerful voice for human rights, then at the very least we have a reasonable expectation that multinational executives should not blithely undermine human rights ideals in a crass effort to win business contracts. Despite the generally positive role that business can play in the future of human rights and democracy in China, business executives who defend China's human rights practices continue to be part of the problem rather than the solution.

CONCLUSION

The application of the fair share principles has resulted in the adoption of some elements of the HRW proposal, but it also has led to the rejection of other HRW proposals in favor of the position adopted by AmCham (Table 10.1).

For executives running a business in China, the fair share theory answers some difficult moral and practical questions. Multinational corporations must accept their fair share of human rights duties, but if asked to go beyond their fair share, executives can in good conscience decline to assume further responsibilities. This fair share includes honoring human rights by maintaining humane working conditions in their own operations and by requiring their business partners to do the same. The fair share principles also require corporate executives to uphold human rights by resisting pressures from the Chinese government to use personnel decisions as a means of punishing workers for their political or religious beliefs. However, the fair share theory puts a clear outer boundary on corporate human rights responsibility. Executives operating in China need not concern themselves with human rights violations that have no connection to the firm's operations. They have no duty to address the general human rights situation in China. If they are asked to assume such duties, corporate executives can in good conscience decline to do so.

For human rights activists, the fair share theory can serve as a road map for more effective advocacy. After the Clinton administration reversed its position on MFN renewal in 1994, human rights advocates turned to multinational firms to pick up the slack. This initiative was misguided for two reasons. It overstated the duties of multinational firms in a way that undermined the effectiveness of moral persuasion—

Table 10.1 Summary Comparison of AmCham, HRW, Clinton Codes, and Fair Share Theory

	AmCham	HRW	Clinton	Fair Share Theory
Refuse to do business with business partners with unsafe and inhumane working conditions?	Yes	Yes, plus— includes unannounced check-ups	No—only "encourages" them not to follow such practices	Yes, plus— should ensure compliance
Refuse to fire employees because of their political views?	Not addressed	Yes	Not addressed	Yes
Proactively raise human rights issues with Chinese government?	Not addressed	Yes	Not addressed	No

that is, because HRW was asking corporations to take on unreasonable duties, many corporations felt too comfortable denying responsibility for human rights altogether. The HRW initiative also was tactically inept because it irritated and alienated an important potential human rights resource. Moreover, underlying the attitude of many human rights NGOs seems to be a belief that most multinational corporations should be regarded as enemies rather than potential allies in the struggle for human rights.

A better policy for human rights activists would be to expect no more and no less than a fair share from multinational firms but to work harder at making sure that companies adhere to those reasonable expectations. Instead of quixotically asking firms to take on an expansive human rights agenda, human rights advocates should step up monitoring and publicity efforts. When multinational firms are not doing their fair share, human rights advocates should publicize such shortcomings, as HRW did very effectively in the case of Chrysler and Gao Feng. However, when firms do their fair share, human rights advocates should not be grudging in parceling out praise and encouragement. Human rights advocates must, in other words, practice their own form of "constructive engagement" with multinational firms based on reasonable human rights responsibilities that do not unnecessarily threaten the commercial prospects in China. This involves occasionally listening to the perspectives of business executives instead of always preaching at them. Conversely, multinational executives must learn to look at human rights advocates as an important resource. Workers in human rights NGOs have a deep-rooted knowledge of and commitment to human rights that can be very useful to multinational executives operating in a repressive nation such as China. Business executives and human rights advocates need one another, and they should try to find more ways to cooperate.

Human rights advocates will no doubt observe that adherence by multinational firms to the minimal standard set forth in the fair share theory will not by itself bring about a dramatic improvement in human rights in China. Indeed, the role proposed for multinational firms will have only a modest impact. Nevertheless, this is all that can reasonably be asked of multinational firms acting essentially alone on the front lines of the human rights struggle. Ultimately, greater progress can only occur from internal developments in China. If we are to expect more from external influences, then it must come from international institutions, which are able to muster the collective will and resources of many nations. Such institutions possess authority and prestige. They are able to withstand retaliation. As a consequence of these factors, it is international institutions, among the potential foreign actors, that have the greatest potential influence on general human rights conditions in China. None of the other potentially responsible foreign actors (i.e., individual nations, multinational firms, NGOs, the press, or individuals) can be as effective in promoting human rights in China.

Until a strong international human rights institution with enforcement powers is created, human rights will continue to be in severe jeopardy throughout the world. Such an institution is a remote utopian vision at this point in history. The general mistrust of international institutions is still too great among both developing and economically advanced nations. Human rights, in particular, remains a subject that engenders as much controversy as consensus. Those who struggle to advance the cause of human rights—and I count myself among them—need to be realistic about this state of affairs and continue to pursue the long-term goal of building an international consensus for human rights values and institutions. In the meantime, human rights advocates should resist the temptation to ask multinational firms to single-handedly accomplish what can only be achieved by many actors working together.

☆

American Chamber of Commerce in Hong Kong Business Principles (August 1994)

It is fundamental to the philosophy of the American Chamber of Commerce in Hong Kong that good ethics and good business are synonymous. AmCham believes that American business plays an important role as a catalyst for positive social change by promoting human welfare and the principles of free enterprise. AmCham recognizes that American companies already set the highest standards for ethical business practices. We encourage members to communicate information about their existing programs and practices relative to good corporate citizenship in the markets in which they operate.

AmCham endorses the following business principles and encourages member companies to embrace them in all their operations in the context of existing statements of corporate values of individual companies. We adopt these principles as a foundation for dialogue and action by business leaders.

(1) We shall abide by the laws of the United States and the countries where we operate.

(2) We shall aspire to be good corporate citizens, seeking opportunities to make positive contributions to the cultural, social, education, scientific and artistic life of the communities in which we operate.

(3) We shall uphold the dignity of the worker and set positive examples for their remuneration, treatment, health and safety. To that end we shall refuse to do business with firms which employ forced labor, or treat their workers in inhumane or unsafe ways.

(4) We shall endeavor to promote the highest possible standards of training and education for our employees. Training objectives derive from raising issues such as promoting self-confidence, independent and innovative thinking, self-improvement, and problem solving through teamwork.

(5) We shall engage environmentally responsible business practices in our operations and be proactive in promoting the value of such behavior in the communities in which we operate.

(6) We shall be vocal in support of improved market access and intellectual property rights protection in the countries in which we operate.

(7) We shall uphold high standards of professional and business ethics and incorporate these values into our employee training programs.

✫

Clinton Administration Model
Business Principles (April 1995)

Recognizing the positive role of U.S. business in upholding and promoting adherence to universal standards of human rights, the Administration encourages all businesses to adopt and implement voluntary codes of conduct for doing business around the world that cover at least the following areas:

(1) Provision of a safe and healthy workplace.
(2) Fair employment practices, including avoidance of child and forced labor and avoidance of discrimination based on race, gender, national origin or religious beliefs; and respect for the right of association and the right to organize and bargain collectively.
(3) Responsible environmental protection and environmental practices.
(4) Compliance with U.S. and local laws promoting good business practices, including laws prohibiting illicit payments and ensuring fair competition.
(5) Maintenance, through leadership at all levels, of a corporate culture that respects free expression consistent with legitimate business concerns, and does not condone political coercion in the workplace; that encourages good corporate citizenship and makes a positive contribution to the communities in which the company operates; and where ethical conduct is recognized, valued and exemplified by all employees.

In adopting voluntary codes of conduct that reflect these principles, U.S. companies should serve as models, encouraging similar behavior by their partners, suppliers, and subcontractors.

Adoption of codes of conduct reflecting these principles is voluntary. Companies are encouraged to develop their own codes of conduct appropriate to their particular circumstances. Many companies already apply statements or codes that incorporate these principles. Companies should find appropriate means to inform their shareholders and the public of actions undertaken in connection with these principles. Nothing in the principles is intended to require a company to act in violation of host country or U.S. law. This statement of principles is not intended for legislation.

✭

Criteria for Allocating Human Rights Responsibilities: Summary Notes

Agent	Relationship	Effectiveness	Capacity
International institutions	Through member states; geographically distant	Capable of coordinating and directing the actions of many nations	Marshals the resources of many nations
Foreign nations	No direct political or social ties; frequently geographically distant	Varies according to the resources of nations	Varies; potential for suffering damaging retaliation is high when acting alone
Multinational firms	May be employer of human rights victim	Varies according to relative economic importance in nation; significant presence through activities	Varies; in many cases, vulnerable to retaliation
Nongovernmental organizations	No direct relationship	Very effective at monitoring	Limited resources
Press	No direct relationship	Highly effective at publicizing facts, one aspect of monitoring	Limited resources; for the most part, independent, but subject to intimidation
Individuals	Varies	Little, acting alone	Little, acting alone

☆

Levi Strauss & Co.'s "Business Partner Terms of Engagement"

Our concerns include the practices of individual business partners as well as the political and social issues in those countries where we might consider sourcing.

This defines Terms of Engagement which addresses issues that are substantially controllable by our individual business partners. We have defined business partners as contractors and suppliers who provide labor and/or material (including fabric, sundries, chemicals and/or stones) utilized in the manufacture and finishing of our products.

Employment Practices
We will only do business with partners whose workers are in all cases present voluntarily, not put at risk of physical harm, fairly compensated, allowed the right of free association and not exploited in any way. In addition, the following specific guidelines will be followed.

Wages and Benefits
We will only do business with partners who provide wages and benefits that comply with any applicable law or match the prevailing local manufacturing or finishing industry practices. We will also favor business partners who share our commitment to contribute to the betterment of community conditions.

Working Hours
While permitting flexibility in scheduling, we will identify prevailing local work hours and seek business partners who do not exceed them except for appropriately compensated overtime. While we favor partners who utilize less than 60-hour work weeks, we will not use contractors who, on a regularly scheduled basis, require in excess of a 60-hour week. Employees should be allowed one day off in seven days.

Child Labor

Use of child labor is not permissible. "Child" is defined as less than 14 years of age or younger than the compulsory age to be in school. We will not utilize partners who use child labor in any of their facilities. We support the development of legitimate workplace apprenticeship programs for the educational benefit of younger people.

Prison Labor/Forced Labor

We will not knowingly utilize prison or forced labor in contracting or subcontracting relationships in the manufacture of our products. We will not knowingly utilize or purchase materials from a business partner utilizing prison or forced labor.

Discrimination

While we recognize and respect cultural differences, we believe that workers should be employed on the basis of their ability to do the job, rather than on the basis of personal characteristics or beliefs. We will favor business partners who share this value.

Disciplinary Practices

We will not utilize business partners who use corporate punishment or other forms of mental or physical coercion.

☆

U.S. Business Principles for Human Rights of Workers in China (May 1999)

As companies doing business in China, we seek to hear and respond to the concerns of workers making our products. We want to ensure that our business practices in China respect basic labor standards defined by the International Labor Organization, and basic human rights defined by the United Nations Universal Declaration of Human Rights and encoded in the International Covenants on Economic, Social and Cultural Rights, and Civil and Political Rights, signed by the Chinese government, as well as in China's national laws. To this end, we agree to implement and to promote the following principles in the People's Republic of China:

(1) No goods or products produced within our company-owned facilities or those of our suppliers shall be manufactured by bonded labor, forced labor, within prison camps or as part of reform-through-labor or reeducation-through-labor programs.

(2) Our facilities and suppliers shall provide wages that meet workers' basic needs, and fair and decent working hours, at a minimum adhering to the wage and hour guidelines provided by China's national labor laws and policies.

(3) Our facilities and suppliers shall prohibit the use of corporal punishment, as well as any physical, sexual or verbal abuse or harassment of workers.

(4) Our facilities and suppliers shall use production methods that do not negatively affect the occupational safety and health of workers.

(5) Our facilities and suppliers shall not seek police or military intervention to prevent workers from exercising their rights.

(6) We shall undertake to promote the following freedoms among our employees and the employees of our suppliers: freedom of association and assembly, including the rights to form unions and to bargain collectively; freedom of expression; and freedom from arbitrary arrest or detention.

(7) Employees working in our facilities and those of our suppliers shall not face discrimination in hiring, remuneration or promotion based on age, gender, marital status, pregnancy, ethnicity or region of origin.

(8) Employees working in our facilities and those of our suppliers shall not face discrimination in hiring, remuneration or promotion based on labor, political or religious activity, or on involvement in demonstrations, past records of arrests or internal exile for peaceful protest, or membership in organizations committed to non-violent social or political change.

(9) Our facilities and suppliers shall use environmentally responsible methods of production that have minimum adverse impact on land, air and water quality.

(10) Our facilities and suppliers shall prohibit child labor, at a minimum complying with guidelines on minimum age for employment within China's national labor laws.

(11) We will work cooperatively with human rights organizations both to ensure that our enterprises and suppliers are respecting these principles, and more broadly to promote respect for these principles in China. We will issue an annual statement to the Human Rights for Workers in China Working Group detailing our efforts to uphold these principles and to promote these basic freedoms.

NOTES

✮

CHAPTER ONE. FROM THE SWEATSHOP TO THE OFFICE SUITE:
CHANGING PERCEPTIONS OF WESTERN BUSINESS IN CHINA

1. See Diane Orentlicher and T. Gelatt, "Public Law, Private Actors: The Impact of Human Rights on Business Investors in China," *Northwestern Journal of International Law and Business* 66 (1993): 14.
2. A. M. Rosenthal, "Meeting At Tiananmen," *New York Times*, 4 June 1999.
3. For a harrowing account of sweatshops in China, see Anita Chan, "Workers' Rights Are Human Rights," *China Rights Forum* (Summer 1997), also available at http://www.igc.apc.org/hric/crf/english/97summer/e4.html.
4. Motorola, *Introduction to Effective "I Recommend,"* company document.
5. Glenn Gienko, interview by author, Schaumburg, Ill., 22 September 1999.
6. Material for this section was drawn from a series of interviews conducted by the author in Shanghai, China, during the summers of 1997 and 1998.
7. David Youtz, interview by author, New York, 15 August 1999.
8. "Tom," interview by author, Tianjin, China, 24 June 1998.
9. "Ling," interview by author, Tianjin, China, 24 June 1998.

CHAPTER TWO. THE TWO FACES OF GLOBALIZATION:
HOW THE STRATEGIC IMPERATIVES OF GLOBAL CAPITALISM
UNLEASH BOTH POSITIVE AND NEGATIVE FORCES

1. World Bank, *China Engaged: Integration with the Global Economy* (Washington, D.C.: World Bank, 1997).

2. See United States–China Business Council, "Foreign and U.S. Direct Investment in China 1979–97," available at http://www.uschina.org/bas/invest.html.
3. See World Bank, *Clear Water, Blue Skies* (Washington, D.C.: World Bank, 1997).
4. See Hugo Restall, "Is China Headed for a Crash?" *Asian Wall Street Journal*, 2 September 1999.
5. International Monetary Fund, *World Economic Outlook: Globalization, Opportunities, and Challenges* (Washington, D.C.: International Monetary Fund, 1997).
6. Callum Henderson, *China on the Brink: Myths and Realities of the World's Largest Market* (New York: McGraw-Hill, 1999), 15–16.
7. Nicholas R. Lardy, *China in the World Economy* (Washington, D.C.: Institute for International Economics, 1994), 29–33. See also World Bank, *China Foreign Trade Reform: Meeting the Challenge of the 1990s* (Washington, D.C.: World Bank, 1993).
8. Lardy, *China in the World Economy*, 72.
9. Teresa Shuk-ching Poon, "Dependent Development: The Subcontracting Networks in the Tiger Economies," *Human Resource Management Journal* 6, no. 4 (1996): 38–49.
10. Ibid.
11. Ibid.
12. Ibid.
13. Han Dongfang, interview by author, Hong Kong, 11 May 1997. For an overview of the activities of Asian investment throughout the region, see George T. Haley, Chin Tiong Tan, and Usha C. V. Haley, *New Asian Emperors: The Overseas Chinese, Their Strategies and Competitive Advantages* (Boston: Butterworth–Heinemann, 1998).
14. Michael Porter, "Global Strategy: Winning in the World-Wide Marketplace," in *The Portable MBA in Strategy*, ed. L. Fahey and R. M. Randall (New York: Wiley, 1994).
15. See Joseph Badaracco and Allen Webb, *AT&T Consumer Products*, Harvard Business School Case no. 392-108 (1992).
16. Steven Greenhouse, "Student Critics Push Attacks on an Association Meant to Prevent Sweatshops," *New York Times*, 25 April 1999, p. A18. For information about the human rights efforts of college licensing administrators, see http://ur.rutgers.edu/news/ACLA.
17. Ron Woodward, "Normal Trade with China—'Sooner' Rather than Later," 5 May 1998, available at http://www.boeing.com/news/speeches/current/woodard05-05.html.

18. Conghua Li, *China: The Consumer Revolution* (New York: Wiley, 1998), 4.
19. Unilever, *Sending Wall's to China*, company document, available at www.unique.unilever.com/inside.view/brandstand/walls.brand.html.
20. Cris Prystay, "Investors Must Be Prepared for the Long Haul," *Asian Business* 32, no. 8 (August 1996): 28–32.
21. Ibid.
22. Unilever, *Sending Wall's to China*.
23. Anonymous, interview by author, Beijing, 15 June 1988.
24. Motorola, *Motorola in China*, company document, 1998.
25. Prystay, "Investors Must Be Prepared."
26. Jurgen Hambrecht, untitled speech, 27 March 1998, available at http://www.basf-sea.com.sg/hambrecht_speech.html.
27. Ira Cohen, interview by author, Beijing, 10 June 1998.
28. See John Gray, *False Dawn: The Delusions of Global Capitalism* (New York: The New Press, 1998).
29. See Thomas L. Friedman, *The Lexus and the Olive Tree: Understanding Globalization* (New York: Farrar, Straus Giroux, 1999).
30. Max Weber, *Economy and Society*, ed. Guenther Roth and Claus Wittich (Berkeley, Calif.: University of California Press, 1979).

CHAPTER THREE. DOING GOOD WHILE DOING WELL:
A THEORY OF HUMAN RIGHTS SPIN-OFF

1. William Jefferson Clinton, "U.S.-China Relations in the 21st Century," 11 June 1998, in *The China Reader: The Reform Era*, ed. Orville Schell and David Shambaugh (New York: Vintage, 1999).
2. Anonymous, interview by author, Beijing, 15 June 1988.
3. See generally Patricia H. Werhane, *Adam Smith and His Legacy for Modern Capitalism* (New York: Oxford University Press, 1991).
4. See James Stewart, *Den of Thieves* (New York: Simon & Schuster, 1992), 261.
5. Han Donfeng, interview by author, Hong Kong, 11 May 1997.
6. Anonymous, interview by author, Shanghai, 23 May 1998.
7. Deborah L. Spar, "The Spotlight and the Bottom Line: How Multinational Firms Export Human Rights," *Foreign Affairs* (1998).

8. Larry Diamond, *Developing Democracy: Toward Consolidation* (Baltimore: Johns Hopkins University Press, 1999), 3.
9. Fareed Zakaria, "The Rise of Illiberal Democracy," *Foreign Affairs* 76, no. 6 (1997), 22–43.
10. Larry Diamond, *Developing Democracy*, 4–5.
11. William H. Meyer, "Human Rights and MNCs: Theory Versus Quantitative Analysis," *Human Rights Quarterly* 18 (1996): 368.
12. Jacki Smith, Melissa Bolyard, and Anna Ippolito, "Human Rights and the Global Economy: A Response to Meyer," *Human Rights Quarterly* 21 (1999): 207; see also the response by William H. Meyer, "Confirming, Infirming, and 'Falsifying' Theories of Human Rights: Reflections on Smith, Bolyard, and Ippolito through the Lens of Lakatos," in the same issue, p. 220.
13. Quoted in Lewis A. Coser, *Masters of Sociological Thought. Ideas in Historical and Social Context*, 2d ed. (Fort Worth, Tex.: Harcourt, Brace, Jovanovich, 1977), 224.
14. See Max Weber, *The Protestant Ethic and the Spirit of Capitalism* (New York: Scribner, 1958).
15. See Adam Przeworski, *Sustainable Democracy* (Cambridge: Cambridge University Press, 1995), 7.

CHAPTER FOUR. HUMAN RIGHTS SPIN-OFF IN ACTION

1. American Chamber of Commerce in Shanghai, Manufacturers' Business Council, 1997 Salary Survey.
2. Daniel H. Rosen, *Behind the Open Door: Foreign Enterprises in the Chinese Marketplace* (Washington, D.C.: Institute for International Economics, 1999).
3. See, for example, Nicholas D. Kristoff, "Riddle of China: Repression as Standard of Living Soars," *New York Times*, 7 September 1993, p. 7.
4. Seymour Martin Lipset, "Some Social Requisites of Democracy: Economic Development and Political Legitimacy," *American Political Science Review* 53 (1959): 69–105.
5. Przeworski, *Sustainable Democracy*, 62–63.
6. Robert J. Barro, *Determinants of Economic Growth: A Cross-Country Empirical Study* (Cambridge: MIT Press, 1997), 52.
7. World Bank, *Meeting the Challenge of Chinese Enterprise Reform* (Washington, D.C.: World Bank, 1995).

8. Anonymous, interview by author, Shanghai, 20 May 1998.

9. Anonymous, interview by author, Shanghai, 20 May 1997.

10. "Lilly," interview by author, Shanghai, 25 May 1998.

11. Ibid.

12. "Dong," interview by author, Shanghai, 16 October 1998. All other references to comments by Dong are taken from this interview.

13. "Chen," interview by author, Shanghai, 16 October 1998. All other references to comments by Chen are taken from this interview.

14. "Louisa," interview by author, Shanghai, 18 October 1998. All other references to comments by Louisa are taken from this interview.

15. Rosen, *Behind the Open Door*, 102. For a more extensive discussion of personnel practices in Chinese SOEs, see John Child, *Management in China during the Age of Reform* (New York: Cambridge University Press, 1996).

16. Anonymous, interview by author, Hong Kong, 10 May 1999; anonymous, interview by author, Beijing, 10 June 1999.

17. Ira Cohen, interview by author, Beijing, 20 May 1999.

18. Anonymous, interview by author, Beijing, 11 June 1998.

19. For a detailed study of reform in China's state sector, see Edward S. Steinfeld, *Forging Reform in China: The Fate of State-Owned Industry* (Cambridge: Cambridge University Press, 1998).

20. Doug Guthrie, *Dragon in a Three Piece Suit: The Emergence of Capitalism in China* (Princeton, N.J.: Princeton University Press, 1999), 194.

21. In rural areas, private ownership of enterprises is also increasing. However, the demographic trends and dynamics of that phenomenon are in many respects different from those in urban areas, particularly because of the dynamism of enterprises owned and operated by towns and villages. See Jean Oi, *Rural China Takes Off: Institutional Foundations of Economic Reform* (Berkeley, Calif.: University of California Press, 1999), especially pages 62–65. See also Andrew G. Walder, ed., *Zouping in Transition: The Process of Reform in Rural North China* (Cambridge, Mass.: Harvard University Press, 1998).

22. Elizabeth Rosenthal, "Capitalists to Be Granted Official Status in Communist China," *New York Times*, 15 March 1999, p. A9.

23. Ibid.

24. See generally Geert Hofstede, *Cultures and Organizations: Software of the Mind* (New York: McGraw Hill, 1984).

25. Anonymous, interview by author, Hong Kong, 10 May 1998.

26. Anonymous, interview by author, Shanghai, 20 May 1998.
27. Anonymous, interview by author, Shanghai, 20 May 1998.
28. BASF in China, company brochure, undated.
29. Anonymous, interview by author, Hong Kong, 10 May 1998.
30. Anonymous, interview by author, Tianjin, 24 June 1998.
31. Jean-Michel Dumont, interview by author, Shanghai, 25 May 1998.
32. "Milly," interview by author, Shanghai, 28 October 1998.
33. Anonymous, interview by author, Beijing, 15 June 1998.
34. Anonymous, interview by author, Hong Kong, 10 May 1998.
35. Chao C. Chen, Xiao-Ping Chen, and James R. Meindl, "How Can Cooperation Be Fostered? The Cultural Effects of Individualism-Collectivism," *Academy of Management Review* 23, no. 2 (1998): 285–304; see also Xiao-Ping Chen and Chao C. Chen, "On the Intricacy of Chinese Guanxi," paper presented at the ASCIA Academy of Management, Hong Kong, 1998.
36. Anonymous, interview by author, Shanghai, 23 May 1998.
37. Duncan Garood, interview by author, Shanghai, 22 May 1998.
38. Robert D. Putnam, *Making Democracy Work: Civic Traditions in Modern Italy* (Princeton, N.J.: Princeton University Press, 1993).
39. Anonymous, interview by author, Tianjin, June 24, 1998.
40. Jean-Michel Dumont, interview by author, Shanghai, 25 May 1998.
41. See John Pomfret, "Frank Debate Surges on Internet Sites in China," *International Herald Tribune*, 24 June 1999, p. 4.
42. Anonymous, interview by author, Shanghai, 20 May 1998.
43. See Przeworski, *Sustainable Democracy*, 53–64.
44. Quoted in Gordon White, "The Dynamics of Civil Society in Post-Mao China," in *The Individual and the State in China*, ed. Brian Hook (Cambridge: Cambridge University Press, 1996), 205.
45. White, "Dynamics of Civil Society," 210 and 215.
46. White, "Dynamics of Civil Society," 219.
47. See Trish Saywell, "On the Edge," *Far Eastern Economic Review*, 25 February 1999.
48. Ken Grant, interview by author, Hong Kong, 7 May 1999.
49. "Sophie," interview by author, Shanghai, 20 May 1998.
50. Anonymous, interview by author, Hong Kong, 10 May 1998.
51. Hofstede, *Cultures and Organizations*, 182.
52. Larry Diamond, *Developing Democracy*, 188, 217.
53. Jonathan D. Spence, *To Change China: Western Advisors in China 1620–1960* (New York: Penguin, 1977).
54. Anonymous, interview by author, Shanghai, 20 May 1998.

1. For a ground-zero perspective on this point of view, see James R. Lilley and Wendell L. Willkie II, *Beyond MFN: Trade with China and American Interests* (Washington: D.C.: American Enterprise Institute Press, 1994).
2. For a critical and comprehensive review of the engagement efforts of various nations, see "From Principle to Pragmatism: Can Dialogue Improve China's Human Rights Situation?" *Human Rights in China*, 23 June 1998. Available at www.igc.apc.org/hric.
3. For an excellent and highly readable account of the Tiananmen disturbances, see Orville Schell, *Mandate of Heaven* (New York: Simon & Schuster, 1994). This section draws heavily from Schell's account.
4. See, for example, Zhao Ziyang, "Advance along the Road of Socialism with Chinese Characteristics," in *The China Reader: The Reform Era*, ed. Orville Shell and David Shambaugh (New York: Vintage, 1999).
5. Melinda Liu, *Beijing Spring* (Hong Kong: Asia 2000 Ltd., 1989), 32.
6. Liu, *Beijing Spring*, 36.
7. *The Truth About the Beijing Turmoil*, Chinese government publication (Beijing, 1989).
8. Ann Kent, *Between Freedom and Subsistence: China and Human Rights* (Hong Kong: Oxford University Press, 1993), 190.
9. Kent, *Between Freedom and Subsistence*, 197.
10. For an alternative historical interpretation of China as being open to foreign influences, see Joanna Waley-Cohen, *The Sextants of Beijing: Global Currents in Chinese History* (New York: W. W. Norton, 1999).
11. See John Jackson, *The World Trading System: Law and Policy of International Economic Relations*, 2d ed. (Cambridge, Mass.: MIT Press, 1997).
12. Executive Order 12850, 28 May 1993.
13. For a critique of the manner in which Most Favored Nation trading status was used as a tool to pressure China on human rights, see Michael A. Santoro, "The Pressure on China Needs Flexibility and Focus," *International Herald Tribune*, 11 March 1994, p. 6.
14. See Michael A. Santoro, "China Rights: Euros See No Evil . . ." *Asian Wall Street Journal*, 31 May 1994, p. 8.

15. William Jefferson Clinton, "China and the National Interest," address to Voice of America, 24 October 1997; reprinted in *The China Reader: The Reform Era*, ed. Orville Shell and David Shambaugh (New York: Vintage, 1999).

16. David Shambaugh, "The United States and China: Cooperation or Confrontation?" in *The China Reader: The Reform Era*, ed. Orville Shell and David Shambaugh (New York: Vintage, 1999).

17. See Andreas Lowenfeld, "Economic Sanctions: A Look Back and a Look Ahead," *Michigan Law Review* 88 (1990): 1930; and by the same author, "Economic Sanctions and U.S. Trade: Book Review," *American Journal of International Law* 86 (1992): 234–237. By the end of the twentieth century, the use of economic sanctions had fallen out of favor as a policy tool. See, for example, Richard N. Haas, "Sanctioning Madness," *Foreign Affairs* (November/December 1997); see generally, Gary Clyde Hufbauer, Jeffrey J. Schott, and Kimberly Ann Elliot, *Economic Sanctions Reconsidered: History and Current Policy* (Washington, D.C.: Institute for International Economics, 1990).

18. Lucien Pye, "What China Wants," *New York Times*, 26 November 1996, p. A21.

19. See James R. Sasser, "Engaging China," address to the Asia Society, Washington, D.C., 4 March 1997; Stanley O. Roth, "China Relations and the China Policy Act of 1997," remarks before the Senate Committee on Foreign Relations, Washington, D.C., 17 September 1997; Stuart Eizenstat, "Normal Trade with China," remarks before the House Ways and Means Subcommittee on Trade, Washington, D.C., 17 June 1997; and William Jefferson Clinton, "China and the National Interest," address to Voice of America, 24 October 1997.

20. Seth Faison, "Followers of Chinese Sect Defend Its Spiritual Goals," *New York Times*, 30 July 1999, p. A4.

21. U.S. Department of State, *China Country Report on Human Rights Practices for 1998*, 26 February 1999.

22. See, for example, William Kristol and Robert Kagan, "Call Off the Engagement," *The Weekly Standard*, 24 May 1999.

23. Robert J. Art and Kenneth N. Waltz, "Technology, Strategy and the Uses of Force," in *The Use of Force*, ed. Robert J. Art and Kenneth N. Waltz (Lanham, Md.: University Press of America, 1983), 6. Realism, the doctrine from which this belief stems, has classical roots dating back to Thucydides. However, the contemporary influence of realism originates with the post–World War II

writings of Hans Morgenthau, Henry Kissinger, and George Kennan, among others, and continues in the writings of "neo-realists" such as Kenneth Waltz. See generally Jack Donnelly, "Twentieth Century Realism," in *Traditions of International Ethics*, ed. Terry Nardin and David R. Mapel (Cambridge: Cambridge University Press, 1992).

24. Brewer Stone, interview by author, Hong Kong, 16 September 1999.
25. Michael Posner, "Beyond Linkage and Engagement: A New Approach to U.S.-China Policy," May 1998, available at http://www.lchr.org.
26. Barbara Crossette, "China Outflanks U.S. to Avoid Scrutiny of Its Human Rights," *New York Times*, 24 April 1996, p. A2.
27. Ibid.
28. See Santoro, "China Rights."
29. "Amnesty Raps U.N. over Human Rights," *Boston Globe*, 27 April 1996, p. 4.
30. Patrick Tyler, *A Great Wall: Six Presidents and China* (New York: Century Foundation, 1999), 390; see also James Mann, *About Face: A History of America's Curious Relationship with China, From Nixon to Clinton* (New York: Knopf, 1998).
31. "China: Yin and Yang," *Wall Street Journal*, 7 June 1999.
32. Andrew J. Nathan, "Influencing Human Rights in China," in *Beyond MFN: Trade with China and American Interests*, ed. James R. Lilley and Wendell L. Willkie (Washington, D.C.: American Enterprise Institute, 1994).

CHAPTER SIX. HUMAN RIGHTS ON THE FACTORY FLOOR:
WHEN PRINCIPLES COLLIDE WITH PROFITS

1. Quoted in Chan, "Workers' Rights are Human Rights," *China Rights Forum* (Summer 1997), available at http://www.igc.apc.org/hric/crf/english/97summer/e6.html.
2. Han Dongfang, interview by author, Hong Kong, 8 May 1997.
3. Dorothy J. Solinger, "Human Rights Issues in China's Internal Migration: Insights from Comparisons with Germany and Japan," in *The East Asian Challenge for Human Rights*, ed. Joanne R. Bauer and Daniel A. Bell (Cambridge: Cambridge University Press, 1999).
4. Ibid.
5. Mary Gallagher, "An Unequal Battle: Why Labor Laws &

Regulations Fail to Protect Workers," *China Rights Forum* (Summer 1997), available at http://www.igc.apc.org/hric/crf/english/97summer/e6.html.

6. Chan, "Workers' Rights are Human Rights."
7. Quoted in Robert A. Senser, "High-Priced Shoes, Low-Cost Labor," *America*, 28 October 1998. For a report on the status of working women in China, see Human Rights in China, et al., "Report on Implementation of CEDWA," December 1998, available at http://www.igc.apc.org/hric/reports/cedaw.html.
8. See, for example, sources cited in Solinger, note 3.
9. Seth Faison, "Followers of Chinese Sect Defend Its Spiritual Goals," *New York Times*, 30 July 1999, p. A4.
10. For a detailed discussion of personnel practices in state-owned companies, see John Child, *Management in China during the Age of Reform* (Cambridge: Cambridge University Press, 1994), especially pp. 157–183.
11. See Human Rights Watch, *World Report: China and Tibet* (New York: Human Rights Watch, 1996).
12. Chrysler has since merged with Germany's Daimler Benz and is now known as DaimlerChrysler.
13. See U.S. Department of State, *China Country Report on Human Rights Practices for 1998*, 26 February 1999.
14. Steven Mufson, "For U.S. Firms in China, A Struggle over Rights and Roles," *Washington Post*, 25 August 1994.
15. Gao's freedom was apparently short-lived once the publicity surrounding his case subsided. John Kamm reports that a few months after his reinstatement at Chrysler, Gao was arrested again and, without benefit of a legal proceeding, sent to a reeducation-through-labor camp. According to Kamm, Gao Feng was again released in 1998 after the highly publicized visit of a interdenominational group of clergy appointed by President Clinton to investigate religious freedom in China. (John Kamm, interviews by author, 10 July 1996; 12 September 1999.)
16. For a fuller account of the considerations behind Levi Strauss's decision, see Jane Palley Katz, "Levi Strauss & Co.: Global Sourcing (A)," in Lynn Sharp Paine, *Cases in Leadership, Ethics and Organizational Integrity* (Chicago: Irwin, 1997), 346–376.
17. Levi Strauss, "Talking Points on Conducting Business in China," company document, 8 April 1998, available at http://www.levistrauss.com/press/archives/arch_1998/04_08_98.html.
18. Edward A. Gargan, "U.S. Companies in China Resist Role of Policeman on Rights," *International Herald Tribune*, 25 May 1994.

19. George Grahan, "U.S. Code for Business Abroad 'Disappointing,'" *Financial Times*, 28 May 1995.
20. Mufson, "U.S. Firms in China."
21. Ibid.
22. Ibid.
23. Human Rights Watch, *A Working Paper: Corporate Measures on Behalf of Basic Human Rights in China*, May 1994.
24. Eduardo Lachica, "Reebok's Code for China Conduct Wins Few Fans among U.S. Firms," *Asian Wall Street Journal*, 25 May 1994.
25. Mike Jendrzejczyk, interview by author, 19 June 1996.
26. See Gary Clyde Hufbauer, Jeffrey J. Schott, and Kimberly Ann Elliot, *Economic Sanctions Reconsidered: History and Current Policy* (Washington, D.C.: Institute for International Economics, 1990), 221–248.
27. Steven Mufson, "The Beijing Duck: What U.S. Firms in China Don't Do for Human Rights," *Washington Post*, 9 April 1995.
28. Amy Gutmann and Dennis Thomson, eds., *Ethics and Politics: Cases and Comments*, 3d ed. (Chicago: Nelson-Hall, 1997), xii.

CHAPTER SEVEN. HUMAN RIGHTS IN THE LATTER HALF OF THE TWENTIETH CENTURY: IDEOLOGICAL AND INSTITUTIONAL FRAGMENTATION

1. The historical accounts in this and the next section are drawn from Howard Tolley, *The U.N. Commission on Human Rights* (Boulder, Colo.: Westview, 1987); see also Johannes Morsink, *The Universal Declaration of Human Rights: Origins, Drafting and Intent* (Philadelphia: University of Pennsylvania Press, 1999).
2. Up-to-date information on the ongoing effort to create an International Criminal Court can be found at http://www.iccnow.org.
3. Quoted in Tolley, *U.N. Commission*, 8.
4. Ibid.
5. See http://www.umn.edu/humanrts for a list of signatories and ratifications of the human rights covenants.
6. Ibid.
7. Louis Henkin, "U.S. Ratification of Human Rights Conventions: The Ghost of Senator Bricker," *The American Journal of International Law* 89 (1995): 341.
8. Henry Kissinger, "Reflections on Containment," *Foreign Affairs* 73 (1994).

9. Jack Donnelly, *International Human Rights* (Boulder, Colo.: Westview, 1993), 100–101.

10. Lisa L. Martin, *Coercive Cooperation: Explaining Multilateral Economic Sanctions* (Princeton, N.J.: Princeton University Press, 1992).

11. See generally Stephen B. Cohen, "Conditioning U.S. Security Assistance on Human Rights Practices," *American Journal of International Law* 76 (1982): 246–279.

12. Donnelly, *International Human Rights*, 105–117.

13. Jeane Kirkpatrick, "Dictatorships and Double Standards," *Commentary* 68 (November 1989).

14. Hufbauer, Schott, and Elliot, *Economic Sanctions Reconsidered*.

15. Quoted in ibid., 336.

16. Michael Richardson, "Jakarta under Scrutiny: Labor Practices Threaten Trade Stores," *International Herald Tribune*, 13 May 1994, p. 1.

17. For a harrowing account of Japanese atrocities in China, see Iris Chang, *The Rape of Nanking: The Forgotten Holocaust of World War II* (New York: Basic Books, 1997).

18. Quoted in Ann Elizabeth Mayer, "Universal versus Islamic Human Rights: A Clash of Cultures or a Clash with a Construct," *Michigan Journal of International Law* 15 (1994): 307–404.

19. Ibid.

20. Abdul Aziz Said, "Human Rights in Islamic Perspectives," in *Human Rights in Cultural and Ideological Perspectives*, ed. Pollis Adamantia and Peter Schwab (New York: Praeger, 1980).

21. For two interesting collections of essays debating Western and Asian perspectives on human rights, see Michael C. Davis, ed., *Human Rights and Chinese Values* (Hong Kong: Oxford University Press, 1995), and Joanne R. Bauer and Daniel A. Bell, *The East Asian Challenge for Human Rights* (New York: Cambridge University Press, 1999).

22. Michael C. Davis, "Chinese Perspectives on Human Rights," in *Human Rights and Chinese Values*, ed. Michael C. Davis (Hong Kong: Oxford University Press, 1995).

23. "Vienna Declaration and Programme of Action Set Goals for 21st Century," *UN Chronicle* (September 1993): 54.

24. Eddison J. M. Zvobgo, "A Third World View," in *Human Rights and American Foreign Policy*, ed. Donald P. Kommers and Gilburt D. Loescher (South Bend, Ind.: University of Notre Dame Press, 1979).

25. Tolley, *U.N. Commission*.

26. See generally Ann Kent, *China, the United Nations and Human*

Rights: The Limits of Compliance (Philadelphia: University of Pennsylvania Press, 1999).

27. State Council of The People's Republic of China white paper, *Human Rights in China* (November 1991).

28. Nicholas D. Kristoff, "The Riddle of China: Repression as Standard of Living Soars," *New York Times*, 7 September 1993, p. 1.

29. Wei Jingsheng, "The Fifth Modernization: Democracy," reprinted in Wei Jingsheng, *The Courage to Stand Alone* (New York: Penguin, 1997).

30. Zhao Zhiyang, "Advance along the Road of Socialism with Chinese Characteristics," reprinted in *The China Reader: The Reform Era*, ed. Orville Schell and David Shambaugh (New York: Vintage, 1999), 57.

31. Quoted in Erik Eckholm, "Communist China at 50: It's Stability vs. Reform," *New York Times*, 1 October 1999, p. 1.

32. See generally Robert J. Barro, *Determinants of Economic Growth: A Cross-Country Empirical Study* (Cambridge, Mass.: MIT Press, 1997).

33. Armatya Sen, "Human Rights and Economic Achievements," in *The East Asian Challenge for Human Rights*, ed. Joanne Bauer and Daniel A. Bell (New York: Cambridge University Press, 1999). See also Jack Donnelly, "Human Rights and Asian Values: A Defense of 'Western Universalism,'" in the same volume.

34. The white paper concurs that "the international community should interfere with and stop acts that endanger world peace and security, such as gross human rights violations caused by colonialism, racism, foreign aggression and occupation, as well as apartheid, racial discrimination, genocide, slave trade and serious violation of human rights by international terrorist organizations." This language mirrors the language in Articles 2(7) and 39 of the U.N. Charter. China has in fact voted in favor of U.N. investigations into human rights violations in Afghanistan and Chile. China's U.N. representatives also have spoken out against human rights violations in Israel, South Africa, and Vietnam. See Andrew Nathan, "Influencing Human Rights in China," in *Beyond MFN: Trade with China and American Interests*, ed. James R. Lilley and Wendell L. Willkie (Washington, D.C.: American Enterprise Institute, 1994).

35. See generally Andreas Lowenfeld, "Economic Sanctions: A Look Back and a Look Ahead," *Michigan Law Review* 88 (1990): 1930.

36. Bernard Williams, *Ethics and the Limits of Philosophy* (Cambridge, Mass.: Harvard University Press, 1985), 156.

37. Quoted in Margaret Ng, "Are Rights Culture Bound?" in *Human Rights and Chinese Values*, ed. Michael C. Davis (Hong Kong: Oxford University Press, 1995), 64.

38. Quoted in Du Gangjian and Song Gang, "Relating Human Rights to Chinese Culture: The Four Paths of the Confucian Analects and the Four Principles of a New Theory of Benevolence," in *Human Rights and Chinese Values*, ed. Michael C. Davis (Hong Kong: Oxford University Press, 1995), 36.

39. Gangjian and Gang, "Relating Human Rights"; see also Joseph Chan, "A Confucian Perspective on Human Rights for Contemporary China," in *The East Asian Challenge for Human Rights*, ed. Joanne Bauer and Daniel A. Bell (New York: Cambridge University Press, 1999).

40. Wang Gungwu, *The Chineseness of China* (Hong Kong: Oxford University Press, 1991).

41. Ng, "Are Rights Culture Bound?" 65. See also Margaret Ng, "Why Asia Needs Democracy: A View from Hong Kong," in *Democracy in East Asia*, ed. Larry Diamond and Marc F. Plattner (Baltimore: Johns Hopkins University Press, 1998).

42. Ibid.

43. Ibid., 67

44. Jack Donnelly, *Universal Human Rights in Theory and in Practice* (Ithaca, N.Y.: Cornell University Press, 1989), 49–60.

45. Ibid., 59–60.

46. Quoted in Ng, "Are Rights Culture Bound?" 64.

47. For interesting reflections by two distinguished philosophers on what it would mean to reach a consensus about human rights, compare John Rawls, "The Law of Peoples," in *On Human Rights: The Oxford Amnesty Lectures 1993*, ed. Stephen Shute and Susan Hurley (New York: Basic Books, 1993), with Charles Taylor "Conditions of an Unforced Consensus on Human Rights," in *The East Asian Challenge for Human Rights*, ed. Joanne Bauer and Daniel A. Bell (New York: Cambridge University Press, 1999).

48. Samuel Huntington, "The Clash of Civilizations," *Foreign Affairs* 72 (1993/1994): 40–41.

49. Noberto Bobbio, *The Age of Rights* (Cambridge: Polity Press, 1996).

50. Jack Donnelly, "Human Rights and Asian Values," 68.

51. See generally William Korey, *NGOs and the Universal Declaration: A Curious Grapevine* (New York: St. Martin's Press, 1999).

1. Thomas Donaldson and Thomas W. Dunfee, "Toward a Unified Conception of Business Ethics: Integrative Social Contracts Theory," *Academy of Management Review* 19, no. 2 (1994). For alternative approaches to the basis for corporate social responsibility, see Robert C. Solomon, *It's Good Business: Ethics and Free Enterprise for the New Millenium* (Lanham, Md.: Rowman & Littlefield, 1998); and Norman Bowie, *Business Ethics: A Kantian Perspective* (Oxford: Blackwell, 1999).
2. Thomas Donaldson, *The Ethics of International Business* (Oxford: Oxford University Press, 1989). See also Thomas Donaldson and Thomas W. Dunfee, *Ties That Bind: A Social Contracts Approach to Business Ethics* (Boston: Havard Business School Press, 1999); compare Richard T. De George, *Competing with Integrity in International Business* (New York: Oxford University Press, 1993), and Manuel Velasquez, "International Business, Morality, and the Common Good," *Business Ethics Quarterly* 2 (1992): 27–40.
3. See Joel Feinberg, *Social Philosophy* (Englewood Cliffs, N.J.: Prentice-Hall, 1976).
4. See Robert M. Cover, *Justice Accused* (New Haven, Conn.: Yale University Press, 1975), 199–229.
5. Judith Jarvis Thomson, *The Realm of Rights* (Cambridge, Mass.: Harvard University Press, 1990).
6. Maurice Cranston, *What Are Human Rights?* (New York: Taplinger, 1973).
7. Alan Gewirth, *Essays on Justifications and Applications* (Chicago: University of Chicago Press, 1982).
8. R. J. Vincent, *Human Rights and International Relations* (Cambridge: Cambridge University Press, 1986).
9. Jack Donnelly, *Universal Human Rights in Theory and Practice* (Ithaca, N.Y.: Cornell University Press, 1989).
10. Ibid., 22.
11. See Henry Shue, *Basic Rights: Subsistence, Affluence and U.S. Foreign Policy* (Princeton, N.J.: Princeton University Press, 1980).
12. See "Human Rights Treaties and Other Instruments," in the University of Minnesota Human Rights Library, available at http://www.umn.edu/humanrts/treaties.htm.
13. Cranston, *What Are Human Rights?*, 73.

14. Paul Lewis, "U.S. May Try to Stop Loan Seen as Bad for Tibetans," *New York Times*, 30 May 1999.
15. Compare with Shue, *Basic Rights*.
16. Shue, *Basic Rights*; see also Charles Beitz, *Political Theory and International Relations* (Princeton, N.J.: Princeton University Press, 1979).
17. Hufbauer, Schott, and Elliot, *Economic Sanctions Reconsidered*, 2.
18. See generally Lynn Sharp Paine, "Regulating the International Trade in Hazardous Pesticides: Closing the Accountability Gap," in *Ethical Theory and Business*, ed. Tom L. Beauchamp and Norman E. Bowie, 4th ed. (Englewood Cliffs, N.J.: Prentice-Hall, 1993), 547–556.
19. Thomas C. Schelling, *Micromotives and Macrobehavior* (New York: W. W. Norton, 1978), 225.
20. See generally David Luban, *Lawyers and Justice: An Ethical Study* (Princeton, N.J.: Princeton University Press, 1988).
21. Compare with James W. Nickel, *Making Sense of Human Rights: Philosophical Reflections on the Universal Declaration of Human Rights* (Berkeley, Calif.: University of California Press, 1987).
22. Paul Lewis, "Rights Groups Say Shell Oil Is to Blame," *New York Times*, 11 November 1995.

CHAPTER NINE. SOLVING THE SWEATSHOP PROBLEM: PROSPECTS FOR ACHIEVING RESPONSIBLE GLOBAL LABOR CONDITIONS

1. Jane Palley Katz, "Levi Strauss Global Sourcing Guidelines (A)," in *Cases in Leadership, Ethics, and Organizational Integrity*, ed. Lynn Sharp Paine (Chicago: Irwin, 1997), 346–376.
2. See Louisa Wah, "Treading the Sacred Ground," *Management Review* (July/August 1998).
3. Alice Martin Tepper, "Keeping an Eye on Sweatshops—Via Audits," letter to the editor, *Business Week*, 27 May 1999.
4. Aaron Bernstein, "Sweatshop Police," *Newsweek*, 20 October 1997.
5. "New Code of Conduct Meant Especially for China," *Human Rights for Workers* 4, no. 11 (2 June 1999).
6. For a useful summary of worker-oriented code of conduct efforts in Europe and the United States, see International Labor Organization, Working Party on the Social Dimensions of the Liberalization of International Trade, "Overview of global developments and office activities concerning codes of conduct, social

labeling and other private sector initiatives addressing labor issues," November 1998; for a summary of developments in global ethics codes on a broad spectrum of corporate responsibility issues, see Ronald E. Berenbeim, *Global Corporate Ethics Practices: A Developing Consensus* (New York: Conference Board, 1999); for an assessment of efforts in child labor, see Judith G. Oakley, "Child Labor, Sweatshops, and the Corporate Social Responsibility of MNCs," *Global Outlook* 11, no. 1 (1999).

7. See John Jackson, *The World Trading System*, 2d ed. (Cambridge, Mass.: MIT Press, 1997).

8. Michel Hansenne, "Trade and Labor Standards: Can Common Rules Be Agreed?" Presented at the 464th Wilton Park Conference, Steyning, West Sussex, 6 March 1996, available at http://www.ilo.org/public/english/bureau/dgo/speeches/hansenne/1996/wilton.htm.

9. Jack Donnelly, *International Human Rights* (Boulder, Colo.: Westview, 1993), 67–68; for a description of the International Labor Organization's work in China, see Ann Kent, *China, the United Nations, and Human Rights* (Philadelphia: University of Pennsylvania Press, 1999), 117–145.

10. "Reich Urges Development of Policy by U.S. on Global Labor Standards," *BNA International Business & Finance Daily*, 28 April 1994.

11. Glenn Somerville, "Factory Sector Missing Out on Jobs Bounty," *Reuters*, 4 June 1999.

12. See generally James Thuo Gathii, "Empowering the Weak while Protecting the Powerful: A Critique of Good Governance Proposals" (doctoral dissertation, Harvard Law School, 1999).

13. See Sidney Jones, "It Is Still Too Early Either to Punish or Reward Indonesia," *International Herald Tribune*, 14 February 1994, p. 6.

14. Dani Rodrik, *Has Globalization Gone Too Far?* (Washington, D.C.: Institute for International Economics, 1997); for a useful review of the economic literature on the issue of international labor standards, see Eddy Lee, "Globalization and Labour Standards: A Review of Issues," *International Labour Review* 136, no. 2 (1997).

15. Jay Mazur, "Globalization's Dark Side," *Foreign Affairs* 79, no. 1 (2000).

16. See Jagdish Bhagwati and Hugh T. Patrick, eds., *Aggressive Unilateralism* (Ann Arbor, Mich.: University of Michigan Press, 1990).

17. "U.S. Government, Labor Isolated in Backing Worker Standards in World Trade," *BNA Daily Labor Report*, 16 November 1994.
18. See Martin Van Der Werf, "Harvard, Notre Dame, and U. of California to Form Stricter Anti-Sweatshop Bloc," *Chronicle of Higher Education*, 4 May 1999.
19. See generally Jagdish N. Bhagwati and Robert E. Hudec, eds., *Fair Trade and Harmonization: Prerequisites for Free Trade?* 2 vols. (Cambridge, Mass.: MIT Press, 1996); and Paul Krugman, "What Should Trade Negotiators Negotiate About?" *Journal of Economic Literature* 35 (March 1997).
20. See Michael A. Santoro and Lynn Sharp Paine, "Pfizer: Protecting Intellectual Property in a Global Marketplace," in *Manager in the International Economy*, ed. Raymond Vernon, Louis T. Wells, and Subramanian Rangan (Englewood Cliffs, N.J.: Prentice-Hall, 1996).

CHAPTER TEN. HUMAN RIGHTS IN THE OFFICE SUITE:
HOW TO SUCCEED IN BUSINESS IN AN AUTHORITARIAN NATION WITHOUT
COMPROMISING MORAL INTEGRITY

1. Associated Press, "China Dissident Jailed for Leaflets," 9 June 1999.
2. U.S. Department of State, *Country Reports on Human Rights Practices for 1995* (Washington, D.C., 1996).
3. Amnesty International, *China: No One Is Safe* (New York, 1996), 14.
4. U.S. Department of State, *China Country Report on Human Rights Practices for 1998*, 26 February 1999.
5. Anonymous, interview by author, New York, 3 March 1999.
6. Human Rights Watch, "A Working Paper: Corporate Measures on Behalf of a Basic Human Rights in China," May 1994.
7. Anonymous, interview by author, Shanghai, 10 May 1997.
8. International Labor Organization, "Overview of Global Developments and Office Activities Concerning Codes of Conduct, Social Labeling and Other Private Sector Initiatives Addressing Labour Issues," November 1998, available at http://www.ilo.org/public/english/20gb/docs/gb273/sdl-1.htm. For an example of a general statement of principles suitable for adoption by a corporate board of directors, see "The Rutgers Principles on Human Rights," reprinted in *Management Research from Rutgers* 37 (Winter 2000).

9. On the use of creativity in ethical decision-making, see Lynn Sharp Paine, "Moral Thinking in Management: An Essential Capability," *Business Ethics Quarterly* 6, no. 4 (October 1996): 477–492.

10. Anonymous, interview by author, Shanghai, 11 May 1997. See generally Thomas Donaldson and Thomas W. Dunfee, *Ties That Bind: A Social Contracts Approach to Business Ethics* (Boston: Harvard Business School Press, 1999), 213–233.

11. U.S. Department of State, *China Country Report*.

12. Social Accountability 8000, standard IV.4.2, available at http://www.cepaa.org/sa8000.htm.

13. See *Otis Elevator Company (A): China Strategy*, Harvard Business School, Case No. 396-098.

14. See China Ministry of Foreign Trade and Economic Cooperation, "Basic Policies Governing China's Foreign Trade and Cooperation," available at http://www.moftec.com/official/html/about_moftec/basic_policies.html.

15. Daniel H. Rosen, *Behind the Open Door: Foreign Enterprises in the Chinese Marketplace* (Washington, D.C.: Institute for International Economics, 1999).

16. See generally William E. Newburry and Thomas Gladwin, "Shell and Nigerian Oil," in *Ethical Issues in Business: A Philosophical Approach*, ed. Thomas Donaldson and Patricia H. Werhane, 6th ed. (Upper Saddle River, N.J.: Prentice-Hall, 1999).

17. John Kamm, interview by author, San Francisco, Calif., 21 August 1999.

18. For some egregious examples of such corporate kowtowing, see Seth Faison, "China Fetes Capitalists, but the Air is Tense," *New York Times*, 29 September 1999.

19. A. M. Rosenthal, "St. Joseph's Murder," *New York Times*, 1 October 1999.

INDEX

★

Page references followed by *f* and *t* indicate figures and tables, respectively.
References followed by *n* indicate notes.

oners of conscience in, 180; Public
Safety Bureau, 104; rule over Hong
Kong, 133; SA8000 audits, 165; as
strategic partner, 89–90; subcontracting
system, 18–21; urban employment in,
54–55, 55f–56f; urban unemployment
in, 66; urban/rural employment in, 54f;
worker protections, 37; working conditions in, 45; World Trade Organization
membership, 86–87, 91, 134
China Democratic Party, 180
China Ministry of Foreign Trade and
Economic Cooperation, 225n14
China State Council Information Office
white paper, 130–34, 219n34
China Statistical Yearbook, 15f, 54f
Chinese Communist Party, 103; criticism of,
179–80; ideology of, 138; membership
in, 43, 48–49, 51; power of, 52–53; social
control by, 61; threat to, 65; and
Tiananmen Square protests, 75–78;
training programs, 52
Chinese culture, 9, 69
Cho Enlai, 126
Christopher, Warren, 80, 83, 129
Chrysler, 103–4, 216n12; and Gao Feng,
106, 157, 181–83
Chun Do Hwan, 123
civil rights, 39–40; corporate responsibility for abuses of, 102–5
Clinton, William Jefferson, 72, 169, 209n1,
214n15, 214n19; trip to China (1998), 4–5
Clinton Administration: China policy, 74,
79–81, 82–85, 91; Model Business
Principles (April 1995), 105, 106t,
109–11, 185, 193, 193t, 199–200
Coca-Cola, 25, 27
codes of conduct, 111; "Business Partner
Terms of Engagement" (Levi Strauss),
162; industry-wide, 164–66; problems for
firms that adopt, 162–64; references to
freedom of association in, 185; voluntary,
102; Workplace Code of Conduct, 166
Cohen, Ira, 28, 52, 209n27, 211n17
Cohen, Stephen B., 218n11
Cold War, 115, 120–22
collective action, 188
collective responsibility for human
rights, 159
collectivism, 62, 68
College Students Autonomous
Federation, 65

commercial diplomacy, 92
Committee for Asian Women, 100–101
communication, 57
communications professionals, 63
communism: Soviet, 121. *See also* Chinese
Communist Party
compensation: average expatriate packages, 27. *See also* wages
competition: for foreign direct investment,
173; global, 24; hypercompetition, 27;
for investment capital, 174
Comprehensive Anti-Apartheid Act, 110
comprehensive engagement, 34; as accidental human rights policy, 82–93;
comparison with economic sanctions,
73, 74t; vs constructive engagement,
84; effects of, 72; endgame, 65–67; evaluation of, 85–88
comprehensive engagement plus, 88–94;
initiatives of, 94
Confucianism, 57, 59, 135–36; "princely
man," 137
Confucius, 185
Conghua Li, 26, 209n18
conscience, prisoners of, 180
constructive engagement, 84, 194
consumer activism, 25
consumer awareness, 166–68
consumer market, 25–27
consumers: preferences of, 163–64;
Western, 23–25
containment, 124
contracts, social, 144
Coop Italia, 165
cooperation, 61–62
corporate education, 28
corporate executives, 179–95
corporate responsibility: for civil and
political rights abuses, 102–5; HRW
view of, 181; for human rights, 105–10,
144–50
corporate self-interest, enlightened, 109
corporations. *See* multinational corporations
cost-minimization strategy, 16–17; comparison with market-building strategy,
29–30, 31t; global, 17–25; as ideal,
30–32; moral and public policy issues
raised by, 29–30
Council on Economic Priorities, 164–65
Cover, Robert M., 221n4
Cranston, Maurice, 147, 149, 221n6,13
crimes against humanity, 151

criticism, 59–60, 153
Crossette, Barbara, 215n26–27
Cultural Revolution, 58, 77–78
culture: Chinese, 9, 69; International
Covenant on Economic, Social, and
Cultural Rights, 92, 101, 120; Islamic
and Asian challenges to human rights,
127–29; patterns of behavior among
workers, 9; transforming, 9
Czechoslovakia, 124

Daimler Benz, 106, 216n12
DaimlerChrysler, 216n12
dang an (dossier), 51
Davis, Michael D., 218n21–22
De George, Richard T., 221n2
DeLuca, Tom, 165
democracy, 39; "Goddess of Democracy,"
75; illiberal, 39; liberal, 39; prosperity
and, 41–47; sustainable, 42
Democracy Wall (Beijing), 131
democratization, 68; contributions from
foreign companies, 48
Deng Xiaoping, 13, 44, 76, 78, 114
Department of Civil Affairs (China), 66
developed countries: fear of wage erosion
and job losses in, 171–72
developing countries: structural adjustment, 173
development, 150; exigencies of, 172–75;
positive changes brought by, 46
di kang zhu yi (resistance), 136
Diamond, Larry, 39, 68, 210n8,10, 212n52
diplomacy: commercial, 92; quiet, 191
disciplinary practices: "Business Partner
Terms of Engagement" (Levi Strauss
& Co.), 203; firing decisions, 103, 181
discrimination: "Business Partner Terms
of Engagement" (Levi Strauss & Co.),
203; hiring decisions, 181
disinterestedness, 111
dissidents, 179–95; jailing of, 87; job
actions against, 103; release of, 82;
rights of, 182–83; who work for foreign companies, 182–83
diversity of human rights duties, 152–53
Dominican Republic, 122
Donaldson, Thomas, 144–45, 221n1–2
Donnelly, Jack, 122, 137, 140, 147, 214n23,
218n9, 218n12, 219n33, 220n44–45,50,
221n9–10, 223n9
Du Gangjian, 135, 136, 220n38–39

DuBois, W. E. B., 118
Duke University, 25
Dumont, Jean-Michel, 63, 212n31,40
Dunfee, Thomas W., 221n1
duties, 146; categories of, 148; human
rights, 151–53; international, 147–48;
moral, 158; rationale for allocating,
153–54
duty-free exports, 125

East Germany, 124
Eastern Europe, 82
Eaton, Robert J., 104
Eckholm, Erik, 219n31
ecological concerns, 14
e-commerce, 61
economic development, 46
economic incentives, 96–102
economic justice, 126
economic prosperity, 41–47
economic protectionism, 125
economic sanctions, 152–53; comparison
with comprehensive engagement, 73,
74t; under Reagan, 124
economic survival, 20–23
economies of scale, 162–63
economy, global, 20–23
Edelman, 63
education, 153; corporate, 28; exchange
programs, 7–8
Eizenstat, Stuart, 83, 214n19
El Salvador, 123
elite, technological and white collar, 10–12
Elliot, Kimberly Ann, 214n17, 217n26,
218n14–15, 222n17
employee benefits: average expatriate
packages, 27; "Business Partner Terms
of Engagement" (Levi Strauss & Co.),
202; at Motorola's Tinajin facility, 5–6.
See also wages
employees. *See* workers
employers: Chinese bosses, 59; criticism
of, 59–60; responsibility for acts of
employees, 161
employment: in foreign-invested enterprises, 67–68; manufacturing, 172;
urban, 54–55, 55f–56f; urban/rural,
54f; in U.S., 172. *See also* unemployment
Enderle, Georges, 225n9
engagement: "Business Partner Terms of
Engagement" (Levi Strauss & Co.),

globalization, 13–32; meaning of, 30
"Goddess of Democracy," 75
Gong Xiangrui, 135, 138
Gorbachev, Mikhail, 76
government (*zheng dao*), 136
Grahan, George, 217n19
Grant, Ken, 68, 212n48
Gray, John, 30, 209n28
Great Britain, 77, 116, 118
Great Leap Forward, 5, 64, 77, 132
Greenhouse, Steven, 208n16
gross domestic product: growth, 15–16, 15f; per capita, 42
growth: gross domestic product, 15–16, 15f; impediments to, 13–15
Guangdong, China, 98
Guangdong International Trust and Investment Corporation, 15
Guangdong Provincial Labor Union, 100–101
Guangdong Zhaoxing City Zhaojie Co., 96–97
Guangzhou, China, 14, 46
guanxi, 53, 62, 106
Guanxi Province, China, 180
Guatemala, 122–23
Guilin Intermediate People's Court (Guanxi Province), 180
Guthrie, Doug, 53, 211n20
Gutmann, Amy, 111–12, 217n28

Haas, Richard N., 214n17
Haiti, 117, 122
Haixi Province, China, 150
Haley, George T., 208n13
Haley, Usha C. V., 208n13
Hambrecht, Jurgen, 28, 209n26
Han Dongfang, 37, 98, 208n13, 209n5, 215n2
Hansenne, Michel, 170, 223n8
Harvard University, 8
health, 14
Henderson, Callum, 208n6
Henkin, Louis, 120, 217n7
Hewlett-Packard, 36, 106
high-tech values, 4–7
hiring decisions, 181
Ho Chi Minh, 126
Hofstede, Geert, 57, 68, 211n24, 212n51
homeworkers, 19
Hong Kong, 18–20, 133, 188
honoring human rights, 145

Hou Dejian, 76
household incomes, annual, 26
HRW. *See* Human Rights Watch (HRW)
Hu Yaobang, 75
Hubei Province, China, 100
Hudec, Robert E., 224n19
Hufbauer, Gary Clyde, 214n17, 217n26, 218n14–15, 222n17
human health, 14
human resources development, 28; control of, 186–187; firing decisions, 103, 181; hiring decisions, 181; professional managers, 52; promotions, 43, 47–56, 181
human rights, 10, 114–42, 148–50; claims, 22; Cold War and, 120–22; commercial impact of upholding, 185; complexities concerning, 115; concern for, 166–68; controversies, 115, 130–39; covenants, 119–20, 217n5–6; cultural challenges to, 127–29; development of concern for, 166–68; foreign companies and, 48, 67–70; foreign direct investment and, 40; foreign policy and, 72–94; global standards, 175–76; honoring, 145; ideology of (*ren quan zhu yi*), 136; as interest, 84; intermediate variables and, 41–43; market building as global force promoting, 28–29; military intervention for purposes of, 133; as moral rights, 145–47; most important issues, 150; multilateral approach to, 91–92; Muslim view of, 128; partnership development, 166–68; practices in China, 85–86, 88–93; principles of, 111, 140; proactive approach to, 108, 190–91; profit maximization and, 95–113; pursuit of, 122; relativistic view of, 129; responsibility for, 105–10, 143–78, 189–93, 201; source of, 147; strategy in China, 183–89; Third World legacy in, 129–30; upholding, 182–83; values of, 33, 84, 137–38
human rights (term), 115–16
human rights abuses, 98; as criminal, 151; global economic incentives for, 96–102; unrelated to corporate operations, 189–93; of workers, 22, 96–102
human rights duties: actors with, 151–52; diversity of, 152–53; fair allocation of, 154–55; international, 147–48
Human Rights for Workers, 222n5
Human Rights in China, 213n2

Protestant ethic, 42
Prystay, Cris, 209n20–21,25
Przeworski, Adam, 47, 210n15,5, 212n43
Public Law 93-189. *See* Foreign Assistance Act of 1961
public policy: human rights policy, 73, 82–93; issues raised by cost-minimization strategy, 29–30; manipulation of, 122–25. *See also specific policies*
Putnam, Robert D., 63, 212n38
Pye, Lucien, 83, 214n18

Qinghai Province, China, 150
quiet diplomacy, 191

Radio Free Asia, 186
Rawls, John, 220n47
Reagan administration, 122–24
realism, 214n23
Red Cross, 180
Reebok, 162, 166
Reich, Robert B., 171–72, 223n10
relativism, 134
rem dao (benevolence), 136
ren quan zhu yi (ideology of human rights), 136
Republican Party, 121
resistance (*di kang zhu yi*), 136
respondeat superior, 160–62
responsibility: for acts of employees, 161; collective, 159; corporate, 102–10, 144–50, 181; for general human rights abuses unrelated to corporate operations, 189–93; HRW view of, 181; for human rights, 105–10, 143–78, 189–93, 201; moral, 189–93; power and, 160–62. *See also* moral responsibility
responsibility gap, 153–54; closing, 159–78
Restall, Hugo, 208n4
Richardson, Michael, 218n16
rights, 145; of children, 165; civil, 39–40, 102–5; in Confucianism, 136; democratic, 41–47; of dissidents who work for foreign companies, 182–83; of indigenous peoples, 150; legal, 101, 146–47, 160–62; minority, 150; moral, 145–47; political, 40, 102–5; to subsistence, 130–31; trade, 133; upholding, 153; women's, 150; workers', 10. *See also* human rights

Rodrik, Dani, 174, 223n14
Roman Catholicism, 42
Romania, 124
Roosevelt, Eleanor, 118
Rosen, Daniel H., 46, 51, 188, 210n2, 211n15, 225n15
Rosenthal, A. M., 2–3, 192, 207n2, 225n19
Rosenthal, Elizabeth, 211n22–23
Roth, Stanley O., 83, 214n19
Rutgers University, 25
Rwanda, 117

Said, Abdul Aziz, 218n20
salaries, 27. *See also* wages
Samsung, 27–28
Santoro, Michael A., 213n13–14, 215n28, 224n20
Sao-Wiwa, Ken, 190
Sasser, James R., 83, 214n19
Saudi Arabia, 128
Saywell, Trish, 212n47
Schell, Orville, 66, 213n3
Schelling, Thomas C., 154, 222n19
Schott, Jeffrey J., 214n17, 217n26, 218n14–15, 222n17
self-interest: economic, 171; enlightened corporate, 109; human rights spin-off, 33–43
Sen, Armatya, 132, 219n33
Senser, Robert A., 216n7
sexual harassment, 59
Shambaugh, David, 81, 214n16
Shanghai, China: average daily wages, 17; average monthly wages, 45; chamber of commerce, 188; pollution in, 14; vacancy rates, 16; wage increases for local managers in, 46
Shanghai Manufacturers' Business Council, 45
Shariah, 128
Shattuck, John, 80
Shell Oil, 156, 190
Shenzhen, China, 99
shu dao (tolerance), 136
Shue, Henry, 148, 221n11, 222n15–16
Singapore, 18, 23
Smith, Adam, 35
Smith, Jacki, 210n12
Social Accountability 8000 (SA8000), 164–65, 175–77, 186, 225n12; Certification Mark, 165
social contract, 144

Kong, 20; in Southeast Asia, 20; urban, 66
Unilever, 26–27, 209n19,22
Union of Soviet Socialist Republics, 82, 116, 118–19, 121
United Kingdom, 77, 116, 118
United Nations, 151; Asian participation in, 125–26; size of, 125
United Nations Charter, 116–17, 132
United Nations Convention on the Rights of the Child, 165
United Nations General Assembly, 119; Resolution 32/130, 127
United Nations Human Rights Commission, 77, 91–93, 117, 129–30; human rights covenants, 119–20; International Covenant on Civil and Political Rights, 92, 120; International Covenant on Economic, Social, and Cultural Rights, 92, 101, 120; membership, 126; "no action motion," 92
United Nations Human Rights Committee, 120
United States: apparel industry, 102; Assistant Secretary of State for Human Rights, 123; Beijing embassy, 86; Carter administration, 122–23; Comprehensive Anti-Apartheid Act, 110; consumers, 23–24; Department of Justice, 37; Department of State, 85–86, 180, 214n21, 216n13, 224n2,4, 225n11; economic self-interest, 171; fear of wage erosion and job losses in, 171–72; foreign policy, 2, 34–35, 72–94, 122; Generalized System of Preferences, 125; human rights agreements, 120; human rights policy, 122–25; Jiang Zemin visit (1997), 107; manufacturing employment, 172; markets, 25; military aid, 122–25; policy of comprehensive engagement with China, 2–3, 34, 65–67, 72, 74; policy of containment, 122; preconceptions about China, 8; profound interests, 85, 88–89, 94; Reagan administration, 122–24; SA8000 audits, 165; Trade and Tariff Act of 1974, 174; trade policy, 122–25; and U.N. Charter, 116. See also Clinton Administration
United States Council for International Business, 175
United States–China Business Council, 13,

14f, 109, 208n2
United States–Sino relations, 73, 82; siege of U.S. embassy in Beijing, 86; strategic partnership, 86, 89–90; and Tiananmen Square massacre, 77
Universal Declaration of Human Rights, 80, 115–19, 139–40, 150; Article 19, 179; Article 20, 179; Article 21, 179; drafting of, 118, 125–26; Muslims and, 127–28; SA8000 and, 165
University of International Business and Economics, 52
University of Michigan, 8
University of Minnesota Human Rights Library, 149, 221n12
University of North Carolina, 25
urban employment, 54–55, 55f–56f
urban unemployment, 66
urbanization, 54–55, 54f
Uruguay, 47, 123
Uruguay Round treaty, 169, 178
U.S. Business Principles for Human Rights of Workers in China (May 1999), 166; text, 204–5

value(s): global, 6; high-tech, 4–7; human rights as, 84; of individual merit, 43
Van Der Werf, Martin, 224n18
Vanik, Charles, 124
Velasquez, Manuel, 221n2
Vietnam, 165, 219n34
Vincent, R. J., 147, 221n8
virtue, 185
Voice of America, 91
Volkswagen, 27
voluntary codes of conduct, 102
"Volunteers in Asia" program (Stanford University), 7–8

wages: annual household income, 26; annual salaries for local managers, 27; average compensation packages for expatriates, 27; average daily, 17; average monthly, 45; average per capita income, 47; "Business Partner Terms of Engagement" (Levi Strauss & Co.), 202; for Chinese factory workers, 100–101; fear of erosion of, 171–72; living, 22; minimum, 17; paid by multinational corporations, 45
Wah, Louisa, 222n2
Walder, Andrew G., 211n21